NOTES *from a* BIG COUNTRY

Also by Bill Bryson

THE LOST CONTINENT
MOTHER TONGUE
NEITHER HERE NOR THERE
MADE IN AMERICA
NOTES FROM A SMALL ISLAND
A WALK IN THE WOODS

NOTES *from a* BIG COUNTRY

BILL BRYSON

Doubleday

LONDON · NEW YORK · TORONTO · SYDNEY · AUCKLAND

TRANSWORLD PUBLISHERS LTD
61–63 Uxbridge Road, London W5 5SA

TRANSWORLD PUBLISHERS (AUSTRALIA) PTY LTD
15–25 Helles Avenue, Moorebank, NSW 2170

TRANSWORLD PUBLISHERS (NZ) LTD
3 William Pickering Drive, Albany, Auckland

Published 1998 by Doubleday
a division of Transworld Publishers Ltd
Copyright © 1998 by Bill Bryson
Illustrations by Alan Baker

The articles in this book first appeared in the
Mail on Sunday's *Night & Day* magazine
between 6 October 1996 and 17 May 1998.

A catalogue record for this book is available
from the British Library.
ISBN 0385 410190

Typeset in Garamond by Falcon Oast Graphic Art
Printed in Great Britain
by Mackays of Chatham plc, Kent.

CONTENTS

ACKNOWLEDGEMENTS

I AM DEEPLY INDEBTED TO THE FOLLOWING PEOPLE FOR VARIOUS expressions of kindness, patience, generosity and drink: Simon Kelner and all his dear, wonderful colleagues on *Night & Day*, including Tristan Davies, Kate Carr, Ian Johns, Rebecca Carswell and Nick Donaldson; Alan Baker for his ever-droll and inventive illustrations to the column; Patrick Janson-Smith, Marianne Velmans, Alison Tulett, Larry Finlay, Katrina Whone and Emma Dowson, among many, many others, at Transworld Publishers; my agent Carol Heaton; my old pal David Cook for yet another brilliant jacket; Allan Sherwin and Brian King for letting me write columns when I should have been doing work for them; and above all – way above all – my wife, Cynthia, and children, David, Felicity, Catherine and Sam, for so graciously letting me drag them into all this.

And a special thanks to little Jimmy, whoever he may be.

INTRODUCTION

IN THE LATE SUMMER OF 1996 SIMON KELNER, WHO IS BOTH AN OLD friend and an exceptionally nice fellow, rang me up in New Hampshire and asked me if I would write a weekly column about America for the *Mail on Sunday*'s *Night & Day* magazine, to which he had recently been appointed editor.

At various times over the years Simon had persuaded me to do all kinds of work that I didn't have time to do, but this was way out of the question.

'No,' I said. 'I can't. I'm sorry. It's just not possible.'

'So can you start next week?'

'Simon, you don't seem to understand. I can't do it.'

'We thought we'd call it "Notes from a Big Country." '

'Simon, you'll have to call it "Blank Space at the Start of the Magazine" because I cannot do it.'

'Great,' he said, but a trifle absently. I had the impression that he was doing something else at the time – reviewing models for a swimsuit issue would be my guess. In any case, he kept covering up the phone and issuing important editor-type instructions to other people in the vicinity.

'So we'll send you a contract,' he went on when he came back to me.

'No, Simon, don't do that. I can't write a weekly column for you. It's as simple as that. Are you taking this in? Simon, tell me you are taking this in.'

'Wonderful. I'm so pleased. Well, must run.'

'Simon, please listen to me. I can't do a weekly column. Just not possible. Simon, are you listening? Simon? Hello? Simon, are you there? Hello? Bugger.'

So here are seventy-eight columns from the first eighteen months of 'Notes from a Big Country'. And the thing is, I really *didn't* have time for this.

NOTES *from* *a* BIG COUNTRY

COMING HOME

I ONCE JOKED IN A BOOK THAT THERE ARE THREE THINGS YOU CAN'T do in life. You can't beat the phone company, you can't make a waiter see you until he's ready to see you, and you can't go home again. For the last seventeen months I have been quietly, even gamely, reassessing point number three.

A year ago last May, after nearly two decades in England, I moved back to the States with my wife and children. Returning home after such an absence is a surprisingly unsettling business, a little like waking from a long coma. You quickly discover that time has wrought changes that leave you feeling mildly foolish and out of touch. You proffer hopelessly inadequate sums when making small purchases. You puzzle over vending machines and payphones, and are quite astounded to discover, by means of a stern grip on your elbow, that gas station road maps are no longer free.

In my case, the problem was intensified by the fact that I had left as a youth and was returning in middle age. All those things one does as an adult – take out mortgages, have children, accumulate pension plans, develop an interest in household wiring – I had only ever done in England. Things like furnaces and screened windows were, in an American context, the preserve of my father.

So finding myself suddenly in charge of an old New England home, with its mysterious pipes and thermostats, its temperamental garbage disposal and life-threatening automatic garage door, was both unnerving and rather exhilarating.

Moving home after many years away is like that in most respects – an odd blend of the comfortingly familiar and oddly unknown. It is disconcerting to find yourself so simultaneously in your element and out of it. I can enumerate all manner of minutiae that mark me out as an American – which of the fifty states has a unicameral legislature, what a squeeze play is in baseball, who played Captain Kangaroo on TV. I even know about two-thirds of the words to The Star-Spangled Banner, which is more than some people who have sung it publicly.

But send me to the hardware store and even now I am totally lost. For months I had conversations with the sales clerk at our local True-Value that went something like this:

'Hi. I need some of that stuff you fill holes in walls with. My wife's people call it Polyfilla.'

'Oh, you mean spackle.'

'Very possibly. And I need some of those little plastic things that you use to hold screws in the wall when you put shelves up. I know them as Rawlplugs.'

'Well, we call them *anchors*.'

'I shall make a mental note of it.'

Really, I could hardly have felt more foreign if I had stood there dressed in Lederhosen. All this was a shock to me. Although I was always very happy in Britain, I never stopped thinking of America as home, in the fundamental sense of the term. It was where I came from, what I really understood, the base against which all else was measured.

In a funny way nothing makes you feel *more* like a native of your own country than to live where nearly everyone is not. For twenty years being an American was my defining quality. It was how I was identified, differentiated. I even got a job on the strength of it once when, in a moment of youthful audacity, I asserted to a senior editor of *The Times* that I would be the only person on the staff who could reliably spell Cincinnati. (And it was so.)

Happily, there is a flipside to this. The many good things about America also took on a bewitching air of novelty. I was as dazzled as any foreigner by the famous ease and convenience of daily life, the giddying abundance of absolutely everything, the wondrous unfillable vastness of an American basement, the delight of encountering waitresses who seemed to be enjoying themselves, the curiously astounding notion that ice is not a luxury item.

As well, there has been the constant, unexpected joy of re-encountering those things I grew up with but had largely forgotten: baseball on the radio, the deeply satisfying *whoing-bang* slam of a screen door in summer, sudden run-for-your-life thunderstorms, really big snow-falls, Thanksgiving and the Fourth of July, insects that glow, air-conditioning on really hot days, Jell-o jelly with chunks of fruit in it (which nobody actually eats, but it's nice just to have it there wobbling on your plate), the pleasingly comical sight of oneself in shorts. All that counts for a lot, in a strange way.

So, on balance, I was wrong. You *can* go home again. Just bring extra money for road maps and remember to ask for spackle.

6 October 1996

HELP!

THE OTHER DAY I CALLED MY COMPUTER HELPLINE, BECAUSE I NEEDED to be made to feel ignorant by someone much younger than me, and the boyish-sounding person who answered told me he required the serial number on my computer before he could deal with me.

'And where do I find that?' I asked warily.

'It's on the bottom of the CPU functional dysequilibrium unit,' he said, or words of a similarly confounding nature.

This, you see, is why I don't call my computer helpline very often. We haven't been talking four seconds and already I can feel a riptide of ignorance and shame pulling me out into the icy depths of Humiliation Bay. Any minute now, I know with a sense of doom, he's going to ask me how much RAM I have.

'Is that anywhere near the TV-screen thingy?' I ask helplessly.

'Depends. Is your model the Z-40LX Multimedia HPii or the ZX46/2Y Chromium B-BOP?'

And so it goes. The upshot is that the serial number for my computer is engraved on a little metal plate on the bottom of the main control box – the one with the CD drawer that is kind of fun to open and shut. Now call me an idealistic fool, but if I were going to put an identifying number on every computer I sold and then require people to regurgitate that number each time they wanted to communicate with me, I don't believe I would put it in a place that required the user to move furniture and get the help of a neighbour each time he wished to consult it. However, that is not my point.

My model number was something like CQ124765900-03312-DiP/22/4. So here is my point: *Why?* Why does my computer need a number of such breathtaking complexity? If every neutrino in the universe, every particle of matter between here and the furthest wisp of receding Big Bang gas, somehow acquired a computer from this company there would still be plenty of spare numbers under such a system.

Intrigued, I began to look at all the numbers in my life, and nearly every one of them was absurdly excessive. My Barclaycard number, for instance, has thirteen digits. That's enough for almost two *trillion* potential customers. Who are they trying to kid? My Budget Rent-a-Car card has no fewer than seventeen digits. Even my local video shop appears to have 1.999 billion customers on its rolls (which may explain why *L.A. Confidential* is always out).

The most impressive by far is my Blue Cross/Blue Shield medical card – that is the card every American must carry if he doesn't want to be left at an accident site – which not only identifies me as No. YGH475907018 00, but also as a member of Group 02368. Presumably, then, each group has a person in it with the same number as mine. You can almost imagine us having reunions.

Now all this is a long way of getting round to the main point of this discussion, which is that one of the great improvements in American life in the last twenty years is the advent of phone numbers that any fool can remember. Let me explain.

For complicated historical reasons, on American telephones all the punch buttons except 1 and 0 also come with three of the letters of the alphabet on them. Button 2 has ABC on it, button 3 has DEF, and so on.

A long time ago people realized that you could remember numbers more easily if you relied on the letters rather than the numbers. In my hometown of Des Moines, for instance, if you wanted to call time – or the talking clock as you people so charmingly term it – the official number was 244-5646, which of course no one could recall. But if you dialled BIG JOHN you got the same number, and everybody could remember that (except, curiously, my mother, who was a bit hazy on the Christian name part, and so generally ended up asking the time of strangers whom she had just woken, but that's another story).

Then at some point in the last twenty years big businesses discovered that they could make everyone's life easier, and generate lots of lucrative calls for themselves, if they based their numbers on catchy letter combinations. So now any time you make almost any call to a commercial enterprise you dial 1-800-FLY TWA, or 244-GET PIZZA, or whatever. Not many changes in the last twenty years have made life immeasurably better for simple folk like me, but this unquestionably has.

So while you, poor thing, are listening to a schoolmarmish voice telling you that the code for Chippenham is now 01724750, except with a four-figure number, when it is 9, I am eating pizza, booking airline tickets and feeling considerably less churlish about modern telecommunications.

Now here is my big idea. I think we should all have one number for everything. Mine, of course, would be 1-800-BILL. This number would do for everything – it would make my phone ring, it would appear on my cheques, it would adorn my passport, it would get me a video.

Of course, it would mean rewriting a lot of computer programs, but I'm sure it could be done. I intend to take it up with my own computer company, just as soon as I can get at that serial number again.

13 October 1996

WELL, DOCTOR, I WAS JUST TRYING TO LIE DOWN . . .

HERE'S A FACT FOR YOU. ACCORDING TO THE LATEST *STATISTICAL Abstract of the United States*, every year more than 400,000 Americans suffer injuries involving beds, mattresses or pillows. Think about that for a minute. That is more people than live in greater Coventry. That is almost 2,000 bed, mattress or pillow injuries a day. In the time it takes you to read this article, four Americans will somehow manage to be wounded by their bedding.

My point in raising this is not to suggest that Americans are somehow more inept than the rest of the world when it comes to lying down for the night (though clearly there are thousands who could do with additional training), but rather to observe that there is scarcely a statistic to do with this vast and scattered nation that doesn't in some way give one pause.

I had this brought home to me the other day when I was in our local library looking up something else altogether in the aforesaid *Abstract* and happened across 'Table No. 206: Injuries Associated with Consumer Products'. I have seldom passed a more diverting half-hour.

Consider this intriguing fact: almost 50,000 Americans are injured each year by pencils, pens and other desk accessories. How do they do it? I have spent many long hours sat at desks when I would have greeted almost any kind of injury as a welcome diversion, but never once have I come close to achieving actual bodily harm.

So I ask again: how do they do it? These are, bear in mind, injuries severe enough to warrant a trip to an emergency room. Putting a staple in the tip of your index finger (which I *have* done quite a lot, sometimes only semi-accidentally) doesn't count. I am looking around my desk now and unless I put my head in the laser printer or stab myself with the scissors I cannot see a single source of potential harm within 10 feet.

But then that's the thing about household injuries, if Table No. 206 is any guide – they can come at you from almost anywhere. Consider this one. In 1992 (the latest year for which figures are available) more than 400,000 people in the United States were injured by chairs, sofas and sofabeds. What are we to make of this? Does it tell us something trenchant about the design of modern furniture or merely that Americans are exceptionally careless sitters? What is certain is that the problem is worsening. The number of chair, sofa and sofa-bed injuries showed an increase of 30,000 over the previous year, which is quite a worrying trend even for those of us who are frankly fearless with regard to soft furnishings. (That may, of course, be the nub of the problem – overconfidence.)

Predictably, 'stairs, ramps and landings' was the most lively category, with almost two million startled victims, but in other respects dangerous objects were far more benign than their reputations might lead you to predict. More people were injured by sound-recording equipment (46,022) than by skateboards (44,068), trampolines (43,655), or even razors and razorblades (43,365). A mere 16,670 over-exuberant choppers ended up injured by hatchets and axes, and even saws and chainsaws claimed a relatively modest 38,692 victims.

Paper money and coins (30,274) claimed nearly as many victims as scissors (34,062). I can just about conceive how you might swallow a dime and then wish you hadn't ('You guys want to see a neat trick?'), but I cannot for the life of me construct hypothetical circumstances involving folding money and a subsequent trip to the ER. It would be interesting to meet some of these people.

I would also welcome a chat with almost any of the 263,000 people injured by ceilings, walls and inside panels. I can't imagine being hurt by a ceiling and not having a story worth hearing. Likewise, I could find time for any of the 31,000 people injured by their 'grooming devices'.

But the people I would really like to meet are the 142,000 hapless souls who received emergency-room treatment for injuries inflicted by their clothing. What *can* they be suffering from? Compound pyjama fracture? Sweatpants haematoma? I am powerless to speculate.

I have a friend who is an orthopaedic surgeon and he told me the other day that one of the occupational hazards of his job is that you get nervous about doing almost anything since you are constantly mending people who have come a cropper in unlikely and un-predictable ways. (Only that day he had treated a man who had a moose come through the windscreen of his car, to the consternation of both.) Suddenly, thanks to Table 206, I began to see what he meant.

Interestingly, what had brought me to the *Statistical Abstract* in the first place was the wish to look up crime figures for the state of New Hampshire, where I now live. I had heard that it is one of the safest places in America – and indeed the *Abstract* bore this out. There were just four murders in the state in the latest reporting year – compared with over 23,000 for the country as a whole – and very little serious crime.

All that this means, of course, is that statistically in New Hampshire I am far more likely to be hurt by my ceiling or under-pants – to cite just two potentially lethal examples – than by a stranger, and frankly I don't find that comforting at all.

20 October 1996

TAKE ME OUT TO THE BALL PARK

PEOPLE SOMETIMES ASK ME, 'WHAT IS THE DIFFERENCE BETWEEN baseball and cricket?'

The answer is simple. Both are games of great skill involving balls and bats, but with this crucial difference: baseball is exciting and when you go home at the end of the day you know who won.

I'm joking, of course. Cricket is a wonderful game, full of deliciously scattered micro-moments of real action. If a doctor ever instructs me to take a complete rest and not get over-excited, I shall become a fan at once. In the meantime, however, I hope you will understand when I tell you that my heart belongs to baseball.

It's what I grew up with, what I played as a boy, and that of course is vital to any meaningful appreciation of a sport. I had this brought home to me many years ago in England when I went out onto a football pitch with a couple of guys to knock a ball around.

I had watched football on TV and thought I had a fair idea of what was required, so when one of them lofted a ball in my direction, I decided to flick it casually into the net with my head, the way I had seen Kevin Keegan do it. I thought that it would be like heading a beachball – that there would be a gentle 'ponk' sound and that the ball would lightly leave my brow and drift in a pleasing arc into the net. But of course it was like heading a bowling ball. I have never felt anything so startlingly not like I expected it to feel. I walked around for four hours on wobbly legs with a big red circle and the word MITRE imprinted on my forehead, and vowed never again to do anything so foolish and painful.

I bring this up here because the World Series has just started and I want you to know why I am very excited about it. The World Series, I should perhaps explain, is the annual baseball contest between the champion of the American League and the champion of the National League.

Actually, that's not quite true because they changed the system some years ago. The trouble with the old way of doing things was that it only involved two teams. Now you don't have to be a brain surgeon to work out that if you could somehow contrive to include more teams there would be a lot more money in the thing.

So each league divided itself into three divisions of four or five teams. Now, the World Series is not a contest between the two best teams in baseball – at least not necessarily – but rather between the winners of a series of playoff games involving the Western, Eastern and Central divisional champions of each league, plus (and this was particularly inspired, I think) a pair of 'wild card' teams that didn't win anything at all.

It is all immensely complicated, but essentially it means that practically every team in baseball except the Chicago Cubs gets a chance to go to the World Series.

The Chicago Cubs don't get to go because they never manage to qualify even under a system as magnificently accommodating as this. Often they *almost* qualify, and sometimes they are in such a commanding position that you cannot believe they won't qualify, but always in the end they doggedly manage to come up short. Whatever it takes – losing seventeen games in a row, letting easy balls go through their legs, crashing comically into each other in the outfield – you can be certain the Cubs will manage it.

They have been doing this, reliably and efficiently, for over half a century. They haven't been in a World Series since, I believe, 1938. Mussolini had good years more recently than that. This heart-warming annual failure by the Cubs is almost the only thing in baseball that hasn't changed in my lifetime, and I appreciate that very much.

It's not easy being a baseball fan because baseball fans are a hope-lessly sentimental bunch, and there is no room for sentiment in something as wildly lucrative as an American sport. I haven't space here to elucidate all the misguided things they have done to my beloved game in the past forty years, so I'll just tell you the worst: they've torn down nearly all the great old stadiums and replaced them with big characterless, multi-purpose arenas.

It used to be that every big American city had a venerable ball park. Generally these were dank and creaky, but they had character. You would get splinters from the seats, the soles of your shoes would congeal to the floor from all the years of sticky stuff that had been spilled during exciting moments, and your view would inevitably be obscured by a cast-iron column supporting the roof, but that was all part of the glory.

There are only four of these old parks left. One is Fenway Park in Boston, home of the Red Sox. I won't say that Fenway's proximity was the absolute decisive consideration in our settling in New England, but it was a factor. Now the owners want to tear it down and build a new stadium. I keep saying that when they raze Fenway I won't go to the new stadium, but I know I'm lying because I am hopelessly addicted to the game.

All of which increases my respect and admiration for the hapless Chicago Cubs. To their eternal credit, the Cubs have never threat-ened to leave Chicago and continue to play at Wrigley Field. They even still play mostly day games – the way God intended baseball to be played. A day game at Wrigley Field is, believe me, one of the great American experiences.

And here's the problem. Nobody deserves to go to the World

Series more than the Chicago Cubs. But they can't go because that would spoil their tradition of never going. It is an irreconcilable conflict. You see what I mean when I say that it is not easy being a baseball fan.

27 October 1996

DUMB AND DUMBER

A FEW YEARS AGO AN ORGANIZATION CALLED THE NATIONAL ENDOWMENT
for the Humanities tested 8,000 American high school seniors and
found that a very large number of them didn't know, well, anything.

Two-thirds had no idea when the US Civil War took place or which
president penned the Gettysburg Address. Roughly the same proportion could not identify Joseph Stalin, Winston Churchill or
Charles de Gaulle. A third thought that Franklin Roosevelt was
president during the Vietnam War and that Columbus sailed to
America after 1750. Forty-two per cent – this is my favourite –
couldn't name a single country in Asia.

I am always a little dubious about these surveys because I know how easy it would be to catch me out. ('The study found that Bryson couldn't understand simple instructions for assembling a household barbecue and nearly always inadvertently washed both the front and back windscreens when driving round corners.') Still, there is a kind of emptiness of thought at large these days that is hard to overlook. The phenomenon is now widely known as the Dumbing Down of America.

I first noticed it myself a few months ago when I was watching something called the Weather Channel on TV and the meteorologist said, 'And in Albany today they had 12 inches of snow,' then brightly added, 'That's about a foot.'

No, actually that *is* a foot, you poor sad imbecile.

On the same night I was watching a documentary on the Discovery Channel (little realizing that I would be able to watch this same documentary on the Discovery Channel up to six times a month for the rest of eternity) when the narrator intoned: 'Owing to wind and rain, the Sphinx eroded by three feet in just three hundred years,' then paused and solemnly added: 'That's a rate of one foot a century.'

See what I mean? It sometimes feels as if nearly the whole nation has taken Nytol and that the effects haven't quite worn off. This isn't just some curious, occasional aberration. It happens all the time.

I was recently on a cross-country flight with Continental Airlines (suggested slogan: 'Not Quite the Worst') and, goodness knows why, I was reading that 'Letter from the President' that you get at the front of every airline magazine – the one that explains how they are constantly striving to improve services, evidently by making everyone change planes at Newark. Well, this one was about how they had just conducted a survey of their customers to find out their needs.

What the customers wanted, according to the incisive prose of Mr Gordon Bethune, President and CEO, was 'a clean, safe and reliable airline that took them where they wanted to go, on time and with their luggage'.

Gosh! Let me get a pen and a notebook! Did you say '*with* their luggage'? Wow!

Now don't get me wrong. I don't for a moment think that Americans are inherently more stupid or brain-dead than anyone else. It's just that they are routinely provided with conditions that spare them the need to think, and so they have got out of the habit.

Partly you can attribute it to what I call the 'London, England' syndrome, after the American newspaper practice of specifying the country as well as the city in datelines. If, say, the *New York Times* were to report on a British general election, it would dateline the story 'London, England', so that no reader anywhere would have to think: 'London? Now let's see, is that in Nebraska?'

American life is full of these little crutches, sometimes to a quite astonishing degree. A few months ago a columnist in the *Boston Globe* wrote a piece about unwittingly ridiculous advertisements and announcements – things like a notice in an optometrist's shop saying 'Eyes Examined While You Wait' – then carefully explained what was wrong with each one. ('Of course, it would be difficult to have your eyes examined *without* being there.')

It was excruciating, but hardly unusual. Just a couple of weeks ago a writer in the *New York Times* magazine did almost precisely the same thing, writing an essay on amusing linguistic misunderstandings and then explaining each in turn. For example, he noted that a friend of his had always thought the Beatles' lyric was 'the girl with colitis goes by', then chucklingly explained that in fact the lyric was— But *you* don't need me to tell you that, do you?

The idea is to spare the audience having to think. At all. Ever. I was recently asked by an American publication to remove a reference to David Niven 'because he's dead and we don't think he'll be familiar to some of our younger readers'.

Oh, but of course.

On another occasion when I made reference to someone in Britain attending a state school, an American researcher said to me: 'But I didn't think they had states in Britain.'

'I meant state in the rather broader sense of nation-state.'

'So you mean public schools?'

'Well, no, because public schools in Britain are private schools.'

Long pause. 'You're kidding.'

'It's a well-known fact.'

'So let me get this straight. They call private schools public schools in Britain?'

'Correct.'

'Then what do they call public schools?'

'State schools.'

Another long pause. 'But I didn't think they had states in Britain.'

But let us finish with my favourite inanity of the moment. It is the reply given by Bob Dole when he was asked to define the essence of his campaign.

'It's about the future,' he replied gravely, 'because that's where we're going.'

The scary thing is, he's right.

3 November 1996

DRUG CULTURE

DO YOU KNOW WHAT I REALLY MISS NOW THAT I LIVE IN AMERICA? I miss coming in from the pub about midnight in a blurry frame of mind and watching Open University on TV. Honestly.

If I were to come in about midnight now all I would find on the TV is a series of nubile actresses disporting in the altogether, plus the Weather Channel, which is diverting in its way, I grant you, but it doesn't begin to compare with the hypnotic fascination of the Open University after six pints of beer. I'm quite serious about this.

I'm not at all sure why, but I always found it strangely compelling to turn on the TV late at night and find a guy who looked as if he had bought all the clothes he would ever need during one shopping trip to C&A in 1977 (so that he would be free to spend the rest of his waking hours around oscilloscopes) saying in an oddly characterless voice, 'And so we can see, adding two fixed-end solutions gives us another fixed-end solution.'

Most of the time I had no idea what he was talking about – that was a big part of what made it so compelling somehow – but very occasionally (well, once) the topic was something I could actually follow and enjoy. I'm thinking of an unexpectedly diverting documentary I chanced upon three or four years ago comparing the marketing of proprietary healthcare products in Britain and the United States.

The gist of the programme was that the same product had to be sold in entirely different ways in the two markets. An advertisement in Britain for a cold relief capsule, for instance, would promise no more than that it might make you feel a bit better. You would still have a red nose and be in your dressing gown, but you would be smiling again, if wanly.

A commercial for the same product in America would guarantee total, instantaneous relief. An American who took this miracle compound would not only throw off his dressing gown and get back to work at once, he would feel better than he had for years and finish the day having the time of his life at a bowling alley.

The drift of all this was that the British don't expect over-the-counter drugs to change their lives, whereas Americans will settle for nothing less. The passing of the years has not, I can assure you, dulled the nation's touching faith in the notion.

You have only to watch any television channel for 10 minutes, flip through a magazine or stroll along the groaning shelves of any drugstore to realize that Americans expect to feel more or less perfect all the time. Even our household shampoo, I notice, promises to 'change the way you feel'.

It is an odd thing about Americans. They expend huge efforts exhorting themselves to 'Say No to Drugs', then go to the drugstore and buy them by the armloads. Americans spend almost $75 billion a year on medicines of all types, and pharmaceutical products are marketed with a vehemence and forthrightness that can take a little getting used to.

In one commercial running on television at the moment, a pleasant-looking middle-aged lady turns to the camera and says in a candid tone: 'You know, when I get diarrhoea I like a little comfort.' (To which I always say: 'Why wait for diarrhoea?')

In another a man at a bowling alley (men are pretty generally at bowling alleys in these things) grimaces after a poor shot and mutters to his partner, 'It's these haemorrhoids again.' And here's the thing. The buddy has some haemorrhoid cream in his pocket! Not in his gym bag, you understand, not in the glovebox of his car, but in his shirt pocket, where he can whip it out at a moment's notice and call the gang round. Extraordinary.

But the really amazing change in the last twenty years is that now even prescription drugs are advertised. I have before me a popular magazine called *Health* that is just chock-full of ads with bold headlines saying things like 'Why take two tablets when you can take one? Prempro is the only prescription tablet that combines Premarin and a progestin in one tablet,' or, 'Introducing Allegra, the new prescription seasonal allergy medicine that lets you get out there.'

Another more rakishly asks, 'Have you ever treated a vaginal yeast infection in the middle of nowhere?' (Not knowingly!) A fourth goes to the economic heart of the matter and declares, 'The doctor told me I'd probably be taking blood pressure pills for the rest of my life. The good news is how much I might save since he switched me to Adalat CC (nifedipine) from Procardia XL (nifedipine).'

The idea is that you read the advert, then badger your doctor (or 'healthcare professional') to prescribe it for you. It seems a curious concept to me, the idea of magazine readers deciding what medications are best for them, but then Americans appear to know a great deal about drugs. Nearly all the adverts assume an impressively high level of biochemical familiarity. The vaginal yeast ad confidently assures the reader that Diflucan is 'comparable to seven days of Monistat 7, Gyne-Lotrimin, or Mycelex-7', while the ad for Prempro promises that it is 'as effective as taking Premarin and a progestin separately'.

When you realize that these are meaningful statements for thousands and thousands of Americans, the idea of your bowling buddy carrying a tube of haemorrhoid unguent in his shirt pocket perhaps doesn't seem quite so ridiculous.

I don't know whether this national obsession with health is actually worth it. What I do know is that there is a much more agreeable way to achieve perfect inner harmony. Drink six pints of beer and watch Open University for 90 minutes before retiring. It has never failed for me.

10 November 1996

MAIL CALL

ONE OF THE PLEASURES OF LIVING IN A SMALL, OLD-FASHIONED NEW
England town is that you usually get a small, old-fashioned post
office. Ours is particularly agreeable. It's in an attractive federal-style
brick building, grand but not flashy, that looks like a post office
ought to. It even smells nice – a combination of gum adhesive and old
central heating turned up a little too high.

The counter staff are always briskly efficient and pleased to give
you an extra piece of sticky tape if it looks as if your envelope flap
might peel open. Moreover, American post offices deal only with
postal matters – they don't concern themselves with pensions, car
tax, family allowances, TV licences, passports, lottery tickets or any
of the hundred other things that make a visit to any British post office

such a popular, all-day event and provide a fulfilling and reliable diversion for chatty people who enjoy nothing so much as a good long hunt in their purses and handbags for exact change. Here there are never any queues and you are in and out in minutes.

Best of all, once a year every American post office has a Customer Appreciation Day. Ours was yesterday. I had never heard of this wonderful custom, but I was taken with it immediately. The employees had hung up banners, put out a long table with a nice checkered cloth and laid on a generous spread of doughnuts, pastries and hot coffee – all of it free.

It seemed a wonderfully improbable notion, the idea of a faceless government bureaucracy thanking me and my fellow townspeople for our patronage, but I was impressed and grateful – and, I must say, it was good to be reminded that postal employees are not just mindless automatons who spend their days mangling letters and whimsically sending my royalty cheques to a guy in Vermont named Bill Bubba, but rather are dedicated, highly trained individuals who spend their days mangling letters and sending my royalty cheques to a guy in Vermont named Bill Bubba.

Anyway, I was won over utterly. Now I would hate for you to think that my loyalty with respect to postal delivery systems can be cheaply bought with a chocolate twirl doughnut and a styrofoam cup of coffee, but in fact it can. Much as I admire the Royal Mail, it has never once offered me a morning snack, so I have to tell you that as I strolled home from my errand, wiping crumbs from my face, my thoughts towards American life in general and the US Postal Service in particular were pretty incomparably favourable.

But, as nearly always with government services, it couldn't last. When I got home, the day's mail was on the mat. There among the usual copious invitations to acquire new credit cards, save a rainforest, become a life member of the National Incontinence Foundation, add my name (for a small fee) to the *Who's Who of People Named Bill in New England*, examine without obligation Volume One of *Great Explosions*, help the National Rifle Association with its Arm-a-Toddler campaign and the scores of other unsought inducements, special offers and solicitations involving naff little adhesive rectangles with my name and address already printed on them which arrive each day at every American home – and you really cannot believe the volume of junk mail that you receive in this country nowadays – well, among all this clutter and detritus was a forlorn and mangled letter that I had sent forty-one days earlier to a friend in California, care of his place of employment, and that was now being returned to me marked 'Insufficient Address – Get Real and Try Again' or words to that effect.

At the sight of this I issued a small despairing sigh, and not merely because I had just sold the US Postal Service my soul for a doughnut. It happens that I had recently read an article on wordplay in the *Smithsonian* magazine in which the author asserted that some puckish soul had once sent a letter addressed, with playful ambiguity, to

HILL
JOHN
MASS

and it had got there after the American postal authorities worked out that it was to be read as 'John Underhill, Andover, Mass.' (Get it?)

It's a nice story, and I would truly like to believe it, but the fate of my letter to California, freshly returned after a forty-one-day adventure trip to the west, seemed to suggest a need for caution with regard to the postal service and its sleuthing abilities.

The problem with my letter was that I had addressed it to my friend merely 'c/o Black Oak Books, Berkeley, California', without a street name or number because I didn't know either. I appreciate that that is not a complete address, but it is a lot more explicit than 'Hill John Mass' and anyway Black Oak Books is a Berkeley institution. Anyone who knows the city – and I had assumed in my quaintly naive way that that would include the local postal authorities – would know Black Oak Books. But oh no. (Goodness knows, incidentally, what my letter had been *doing* in California for nearly six weeks, though it came back with a nice tan and an urge to get in touch with its inner feelings.)

Now just to give this plaintive tale a little heartwarming perspective, let me tell you that not long before I departed from England, the Royal Mail had brought me, within 48 hours of its posting in London, a letter addressed to 'Bill Bryson, Writer, Yorkshire Dales', which is a pretty impressive bit of sleuthing. (And never mind that the correspondent was a trifle off his head.)

So here I am, my affections torn between a postal service that never feeds me but can tackle a challenge, and one that gives me free sticky tape and prompt service but won't help me out when I can't remember a street name. The lesson to draw from this, of course, is that when you move from one country to another you have to accept that there are some things that are better and some things that are worse, and there's nothing you can do about it. That may not be the profoundest of insights, but I did get a free doughnut as well, so on balance I guess I'm happy.

Now if you will excuse me I have to drive to Vermont and collect some mail from a Mr Bubba.

17 November 1996

HOW TO HAVE FUN AT HOME

MY WIFE THINKS NEARLY EVERYTHING ABOUT AMERICAN LIFE IS wonderful. She loves having her groceries bagged for her. She adores free iced water and bookmatches. She thinks home-delivered pizza is a central hallmark of civilization. I haven't the heart to tell her that waitresses in the States urge everyone to have a nice day.

Personally, while I am fond of America and grateful for its many conveniences, I am not quite so slavishly uncritical. Take the matter of having your groceries bagged for you. I appreciate the gesture, but when you come down to it what does it actually achieve except give you an opportunity to stand there and watch your groceries being bagged? It's not as if it buys you some quality time. I don't want to get heavy here, but given the choice between free iced water at restaurants and, let us say, a national health service, I have to say my instinct is to go with the latter.

However, there are certain things that are so wonderful in American life that I can hardly stand it myself. Chief among these, without any doubt, is the garbage disposal. A garbage disposal is everything a labour-saving device should be and so seldom is – noisy, fun, extremely hazardous, and so dazzlingly good at what it does that you cannot imagine how you ever managed without one. If you had asked me eighteen months ago what the prospects were that shortly my chief hobby would be placing assorted objects down a hole in the kitchen sink, I believe I would have laughed in your face, but in fact it is so.

I have never had a garbage disposal before, so I have been learning its tolerances through a process of trial and error. Chopsticks give perhaps the liveliest response (this is not recommended, of course, but there comes a time with every piece of machinery when you just have to see what it can do), but cantaloupe rinds make the richest, throatiest sound and result in less 'down time'. Coffee grounds in quantity are the most likely to provide a satisfying 'Vesuvius effect', though for obvious reasons it is best not to attempt this difficult feat until your wife has gone out for the day, and to have a mop and stepladder standing by.

The most exciting event with a garbage disposal, of course, is when it jams and you have to reach in and unclog it, knowing that at any moment it might spring to life and abruptly convert your arm from a useful grasping tool into a dibber. Don't try to tell me about living life on the edge.

Equally satisfying in its way, and certainly no less ingenious, is the little-known fireplace ashpit. This is simply a metal plate – a kind of trapdoor – built into the floor of the living room fireplace above a deep, brick-lined pit. When you clean the fireplace, instead of sweeping the ash into a bucket and then trailing the dribblings through the house, you manoeuvre it into this hole and it disappears for ever. Brilliant.

In theory the ashpit must eventually fill up, but ours seems to be bottomless. Down in the basement there's a small metal door in the wall that allows you to see how the pit is doing, and occasionally I go down to have a look. It isn't really necessary, but it gives me an excuse to go down in the basement, and I always welcome that because basements are the third great feature of American life. They are wonderful chiefly because they are so amazingly, so spaciously, useless.

Now basements I know because I grew up with one. Every American basement is the same. They all have a clothesline that is rarely used, a trickle of water from an indeterminable source running diagonally across the floor, and a funny smell – a combination of old magazines, camping gear that should have been aired and wasn't, and something to do with a guinea pig named Mr Fluffy that escaped down a central heating grate six months ago and has not been seen since (and presumably would now be better called Mr Bones).

Basements are so monumentally useless, in fact, that you seldom go down there, so it always comes as a surprise to remember that you have one. Every dad who ever goes down in a basement pauses at some point and thinks: 'Gee, we really ought to do something with all this space. We could have a cocktail cabinet and a pool table and maybe a jukebox and a jacuzzi and a couple of pinball machines . . .' But of course it's just one of those things that you intend to do one day, like learn Spanish or take up home barbering, and never do.

Oh, occasionally, especially in starter homes, you will find that some young gung-ho dad has converted the basement into a playroom for the children, but this is always a mistake as no child will play in a basement. This is because no matter how loving your parents, no matter how much you would like to trust them, there is always the thought that they will quietly lock the door at the top of the stairs and move to Florida. No, basements are deeply and inescapably scary – that's why they always feature in spooky movies, usually with a shadow of Joan Crawford carrying an axe thrown on the far wall. That may be why even dads don't go down there very often.

I could go on and on cataloguing other small, unsung glories of American household life – refrigerators that dispense iced water and make their own icecubes, walk-in closets, electrical sockets in bathrooms – but I won't. I'm out of space and anyway Mrs B has just gone out to do some shopping and it has occurred to me that I have not yet seen what the disposal can do with a juice carton. I'll get back to you on this one.

24 November 1996

DESIGN FLAWS

I HAVE A TEENAGED SON WHO IS A RUNNER. HE HAS, AT A CONSERVATIVE estimate, 6,100 pairs of running shoes, and every one of them represents a greater investment of cumulative design effort than, say, Milton Keynes.

These shoes are amazing. I was just reading a review in one of his running magazines of the latest in 'sport utility sneakers', as they are called here, and it was full of passages like this: 'A dual-density EVA midsole with air units fore and aft provides stability while a gel heel-insert absorbs shock, but the shoe makes a narrow footprint, a characteristic that typically suits only the biomechanically efficient runner.' Alan Shepard went into space with less science at his disposal than that.

So here is my question. If my son can have his choice of a seemingly limitless range of scrupulously engineered, biomechanically efficient footwear, why does my computer keyboard suck? This is a serious enquiry.

My computer keyboard has 102 keys – almost double what my old manual typewriter had – which on the face of it seems awfully generous. Among other typographical luxuries, I can choose between three styles of bracket and two kinds of colon. I can dress my text with carets (^) and cedillas (~). I can have slashes that fall to the left or to the right, and goodness knows what else.

I have so many keys, in fact, that over on the right-hand side of the keyboard there are whole communities of buttons of whose function I haven't the tiniest inkling. Occasionally I hit one by accident and subsequently discover that several paragraphs of my w9rk n+w look l*ke th?s, or that I have written the last page and a half in an interesting but unfortunately non-alphabetic font called Wingdings, but otherwise I haven't the faintest idea what those buttons are there for.

Never mind that many of these keys duplicate the functions of other keys, while others apparently do nothing at all (my favourite in this respect is one marked 'Pause', which when pressed does absolutely nothing, raising the interesting metaphysical question of whether it is therefore doing its job), or that several keys are arrayed in slightly imbecilic places. The delete key, for instance, is right beside the overprint key, so that often I discover, with a trill of gay laughter, that my most recent thoughts have been devouring, Pacman-like, everything I had previously written. Quite often, I somehow hit a combination of keys that summons a box which says, in effect, 'This Is a Pointless Box. Do You Want It?' which is followed by another that says, 'Are Your *Sure* You Don't Want the Pointless Box?' Never mind all that. I have known for a long time that the computer is not my friend.

But here is what gets me. Out of all the 102 keys at my disposal, there is no key for the fraction ½. Typewriter keyboards always used to have a key for ½. Now, however, if I wish to write ½, I have to bring down the font menu and call up a directory called 'WP Characters', then hunt through a number of sub-directories until I remember or more often blunder on the particular one, 'Typographic Symbols', in which hides the furtive ½ sign. This is irksome and pointless and it doesn't seem right to me.

But then most things in the world don't seem right to me. On the dashboard of our family car is a shallow indentation about the size of a paperback book. If you are looking for somewhere to put your sunglasses or spare change, it is the obvious place, and it works extremely well, I must say, so long as the car is not actually moving. As soon as you put the car in motion, however, and particularly when you touch the brakes, turn a corner, or go up a gentle slope, everything slides off. There is, you see, no lip round this dashboard tray. It is just a flat space, with a dimpled bottom. It can hold nothing that has not been nailed to it.

So I ask you: what, then, is it *for*? Somebody had to design it. It didn't just appear spontaneously. Some person – perhaps, for all I know, a whole committee of people in the Dashboard Stowage Division – had to invest time and thought in incorporating into the design of this vehicle (it's a Dodge Excreta, if you're wondering) a storage tray that will actually hold nothing. That is really quite an achievement.

But it is nothing, of course, compared with the manifold design achievements of those responsible for the modern video recorder. Now I am not going to go on about how impossible it is to programme the typical video recorder because you know that already. Nor will I observe how irritating it is that you must cross the room and get down on your belly to confirm that it is actually recording. But I will just make one small passing observation. I recently bought a video recorder and one of the selling points – one of the things the manufacturer boasted about – was that it was capable of recording programmes up to twelve months in advance. Now think about this for a moment and tell me any circumstance – and I mean any circumstance at all – in which you can envision wanting to set a video machine to record a programme one year from now.

I don't want to sound like some old guy who is always moaning. I freely acknowledge that there are many excellent, well-engineered products that didn't exist when I was a boy – the pocket calculator and kettles that switch off automatically are two that fill me yet with gratitude and wonder – but it does seem to me that an awful lot of things out there have been designed by people who cannot possibly have stopped to think how they will be used.

Just think for a moment of all the everyday items you have to puzzle over – fax machines, photocopiers, central heating thermostats, airline tickets, television remote control units, hotel showers and alarm clocks, microwave ovens, almost any electrical product owned by someone other than you – because they are ill thought out.

And why are they so ill thought out? Because all the best designers are making running shoes. Either that, or they are just idiots. In either case, it really isn't fair.

1 December 1996

WIDE-OPEN SPACES

HERE ARE A COUPLE OF THINGS TO BEAR IN MIND AS YOU GO THROUGH life: Daniel Boone was an idiot, and it's not worth trying to go to Maine for the day from Hanover, New Hampshire. Allow me to explain.

I was fooling around with a globe the other night (one of the benefits of the awfulness of American television is that you find yourself fooling around with a lot of new things) and I was mildly astounded to realize that here in Hanover I am much closer to our old house in Yorkshire than to many other parts of the United States. Indeed, from where I sit to Attu, the westernmost of Alaska's Aleutian Islands, is almost 4,000 miles. Put another way, you are closer to Johannesburg than I am to the outermost tip of my own country.

Of course, you could argue that Alaska is not a fair comparison because there is so much non-American territory between here and there, but even if you confine yourself to the mainland US, the distances are impressive. From my house to Los Angeles is about the same as from your house to Lagos. We are, in a word, talking big scale here.

Here is another arresting fact to do with scale. In the past twenty years (a period in which, let the record show, I was doing my breeding elsewhere), the population of the United States increased by almost exactly the equivalent of a Great Britain. I find that quite amazing, too, not least because I don't know where all these new people are.

A remarkable thing about America, if you have been living for a long time in a snug little place like the UK, is how very big and very empty so much of it is. Consider this: Montana, Wyoming and North and South Dakota have an area twice the size of France but a population less than that of south London. Alaska is bigger still and has even fewer people. Even my own adopted state of New Hampshire, in the relatively crowded Northeast, is 85 per cent forest, and most of the rest is lakes. You can drive for very long periods in New Hampshire and never see anything but trees and mountains – not a house or a hamlet or even, quite often, another car.

I am constantly caught out by this. Not long ago, I had a couple of friends over from England and we decided to take a drive over to the lakes of western Maine. It had the makings of a nice day out. All we had to do was cross New Hampshire – which is after all the fourth tiniest state in America – and go a little way over the state line into our lovely, moose-strewn neighbour to the east. I figured it would take about two to two and a half hours.

Well, of course you have anticipated the punchline. Seven hours later we pulled up exhausted at the shore of Rangeley Lake, took two pictures, looked at each other, and wordlessly got back in the car and drove home. This sort of thing happens all the time.

The curious thing is that nearly all Americans, as far as I can tell, don't see it this way. They think the country is way too crowded. Moves are constantly afoot to restrict access to national parks and wilderness areas on the grounds that they are dangerously overrun. Parts of them *are* unquestionably crowded, but that is only because 98 per cent of visitors arrive by car, and 98 per cent of those venture no more than 400 yards from their metallic wombs. Elsewhere, however, you can have whole mountains to yourself even in the most crowded parks on the busiest days. Yet I may soon find myself barred from hiking in many wilderness areas, unless I had the foresight to book a visit weeks beforehand, because of perceived overcrowding.

Even more ominously, there is a growing belief that the best way of dealing with this supposed crisis is by expelling most of those not born here. There is an organization whose name escapes me (it may be Dangerously Small-Minded Reactionaries for a Better America) that periodically runs earnest, carefully reasoned ads in the *New York Times* and other important publications calling for an end to immigration because, as one of its ads explains, it 'is devastating our environment and the quality of our lives'. Give me a break. Elsewhere it adds, 'Primarily because of immigration we are rushing at breakneck speed toward an environmental and economic disaster.'

You could, I suppose, make a case for cutting back on immigration, but not on the grounds that the country is running out of room. Anti-immigration arguments conveniently overlook the fact that America already expels a million immigrants a year, and that those who are here mostly do jobs that are too dirty, dangerous or low-paying for Americans to do. Getting rid of immigrants is not suddenly going to open employment opportunities for the locals; all it's going to do is leave a lot of dishes unwashed and a lot of fruit unpicked. Still less is it going to miraculously create a lot more breathing space for the rest of us.

America already has one of the lowest proportions of immigrants in the developed world. Just 6 per cent of people in the United States are foreign born compared with, for instance, 8 per cent in Britain and 11 per cent in France. America may or may not be heading for an environmental and economic disaster, but if so it certainly isn't because six people in every hundred were born somewhere else. But try telling that to most Americans.

The fact is America is already one of the least crowded countries on earth with an average of just sixty-eight people per square mile, compared with 256 in France and over 600 in Britain. Altogether, only 2 per cent of the United States is classified as 'built up'.

Of course, Americans have always tended to see these things in a different way. Daniel Boone famously is supposed to have looked out of his cabin window one day, seen a wisp of smoke rising from a homesteader's dwelling on a distant mountain, and announced his intention to move on, complaining bitterly that the neighbourhood was getting too crowded.

Which is why I say Daniel Boone was an idiot. I just hate to see the rest of my country going the same way.

8 December 1996

RULE NUMBER 1: FOLLOW ALL RULES

I DID A FOOLISH THING THE OTHER EVENING. I WENT INTO ONE OF OUR local bars and seated myself without permission. You just don't do this in America, but I had an important recurring thought that I wanted to scribble down before it left my head (namely, 'There is *always* a little more toothpaste in the tube. Think about it'), and anyway the place was practically empty, so I just took a table near the door.

After a couple of minutes the hostess – the Customer Seating Manager – came up to me and said in a level tone, 'I see you've seated yourself.'

'Yup,' I replied proudly. 'Dressed myself too.'

'Didn't you see the sign?' She tilted her head at a big sign that said 'Please Wait to Be Seated.'

I have been in this bar about 150 times. I have seen the sign from every angle but supine.

'Is there a sign?' I said innocently. 'Gosh, I didn't notice it.'

She sighed. 'Well, the server in this section is *very* busy, so you may have to wait some time for her to get to you.'

There was no other customer within 50 feet, but that wasn't the point. The point was that I had disregarded a posted notice and would have to serve a small sentence in purgatory in consequence.

It would be entirely wrong to say that Americans love rules, but they have a certain regard for them. They behave towards rules in much the way the British behave towards queues – as something that is fundamental to the maintenance of a civilized and orderly society. I had, in effect, queue-jumped the 'Wait to Be Seated' sign.

I expect it may be something to do with our Germanic stock. On the whole I have no quibble with that. There are times, I have to say, when a little Teutonic order wouldn't go amiss in England – like when people take two spaces in a car park (the one offence for which, if I may speak freely here, I would welcome back capital punishment).

Sometimes, however, the American devotion to order goes too far. Our local public swimming pool, for example, has twenty-seven posted rules – twenty-seven! – of which my favourite is 'Only One Bounce Per Dive on Diving Board'. And they're enforced.

What is frustrating – no, maddening – is that it almost never matters whether these rules make any sense or not. A year or so ago, as a way of dealing with the increased threat of terrorism, America's airlines begin requiring passengers to present photographic identification when checking in for a flight. The first I heard of this was when I showed up to catch a plane at an airport 120 miles from my home.

'I need to see some picture ID,' said the clerk, who had the charm and boundless motivation you would expect to find in someone whose primary employment perk is a nylon tie.

'Really? I don't think I have any,' I said and began patting my pockets, as if that would make a difference, and then pulling cards from my wallet. I had all kinds of identification – library card, credit cards, Social Security card, health insurance card, airline ticket – all with my name on them, but nothing with a picture. Eventually, at the back of the wallet I found an old Iowa driver's licence that I had forgotten I even had.

'This is expired,' he sniffed.

'Then I won't ask to drive the plane,' I replied.

'Anyway, it's fifteen years old. I need something more up to date.'

I sighed and rooted through my belongings. Finally it occurred to me that I had a copy of one of my own books with my picture on the jacket. I handed it to him proudly and with some relief.

He looked at the book and then hard at me and then at a printed list. 'That's not on our list of Permissible Visual Cognitive Imagings,' he said, or something similarly vacuous.

'I'm sure it isn't, but it's still me. It couldn't *be* more me.' I lowered my voice and leaned closer to him. 'Are you seriously suggesting that I had this book specially printed so I could sneak onto a flight to Buffalo?'

He stared hard at me for another minute, then called in another clerk for consultation. They conferred and summoned a third party. Eventually we ended up with a crowd scene involving three check-in clerks, their supervisor, the supervisor's supervisor, two baggage handlers, several nosy bystanders straining to get a better view and a guy selling jewellery out of an aluminium case.

My flight was due to take off in minutes and froth was starting to form at the corners of my mouth. 'What is the point of all this anyway?' I said to the head supervisor. 'Why do you need a picture ID?'

'FAA rule,' he said, staring unhappily at my book, my invalid driver's licence and the list of permissible photo options.

'But *why* is it the rule? Do you honestly believe that you are going to thwart a terrorist by requiring him to show you a laminated photograph of himself? Do you think a person who could plan and execute a sophisticated hijacking would be thrown off his quest by a demand to see his driver's licence? Has it occurred to you that it might be more productive, vis-à-vis terrorism, if you employed someone who was actually awake, and perhaps with an IQ above that of a small mollusc, to monitor the TV screens on your X-ray machines?' I may not have said all this in exactly those words, but that was the drift of my sentiment.

But you see the requirement is not simply to identify yourself, but to identify yourself in a way that *precisely matches a written instruction*.

Anyway, I changed tack and begged. I promised never again to turn up at an airport without adequate ID. I took on an attitude of complete contrition. I don't suppose anyone has ever shown such earnest, remorseful desire to be allowed to proceed to Buffalo.

Eventually, with misgivings, the supervisor nodded at the clerk and told him to check me in, but warned me not to try anything as slippery as this again, and then departed with his colleagues.

The check-in clerk issued me a boarding pass and I started towards the gate, then turned back, and in a low, confidential tone shared with him a helpful afterthought.

'There is always a little more toothpaste in the tube,' I said. 'Think about it.'

15 December 1996

THE MYSTERIES OF CHRISTMAS

ONE OF THE MANY SMALL MYSTERIES I HOPED TO RESOLVE WHEN I FIRST
moved to England was this: when British people sang 'A-Wassailing
We'll Go', where was it they went and what exactly did they do when
they got there?

Throughout an American upbringing I heard this song every
Christmas without ever finding anyone who had the faintest idea of
how to go about the obscure and enigmatic business of wassailing.
Given the perky lilt of the carol and the party spirit in which it was
always sung, it suggested to my youthful imagination rosy-cheeked

wenches bearing flagons of ale in a scene of general merriment and abandon before a blazing yule log in a hall decked with holly, and with this in mind I looked forward to my first English Christmas with a certain frank anticipation. In my house, the most exciting thing you could hope for in the way of seasonal recklessness was being offered a cookie shaped like a Christmas tree.

So you may conceive my disappointment when my first Christmas in England came and went and not only was there no wassailing to be seen but no one I quizzed was any the wiser as to its arcane and venerable secrets. In fact, in nearly twenty years in England I never did find anyone who had ever gone a-wassailing, at least not knowingly. Nor, while we are at it, did I encounter any mumming, still less any hodening (a kind of organized group begging for coins with a view to buying drinks at the nearest public house, which I think is an outstanding idea), or many of the other traditions of an English Christmas that were expressly promised in the lyrics of carols and the novels of authors like Jane Austen and Charles Dickens.

It wasn't until I happened on a copy of T.G. Crippen's scholarly and ageless *Christmas and Christmas Lore*, published in London in 1923, that I finally found that *wassail* was originally a salutation. From the Old Norse *ves heil*, it means 'in good health'. In Anglo-Saxon times, according to Crippen, it was customary for someone offering a drink to say 'Wassail!' and for the recipient to respond 'Drinkhail!' and for the participants to repeat the exercise until comfortably horizontal.

It is clear from Crippen's tome that in 1923 this and many other ancient and agreeable Christmas customs were still commonly encountered in Britain. Now, alas, they appear to be gone for good.

Even so, Christmas in Britain is wonderful, far better than Christmas in America, and for all kinds of reasons. To begin with, in Britain – or at least in England – you still pretty much pack all your festive excesses (eating, drinking, gift-giving, more eating and drinking) into Christmas, whereas we in America spread ours out over three separate holidays.

In America, the big eating holiday is Thanksgiving, at the end of November. Thanksgiving is a great holiday – probably the very best holiday in America, if you ask me. (In case you've always wondered, it commemorates the first harvest feast at which the pilgrims sat down with the Indians to thank them for all their help and tell them,

'Oh, and by the way, we've decided we want the *whole* country.') It is a great holiday because you don't have to give gifts or send cards or do anything but eat until you begin to look like a balloon that has been left on a helium machine too long.

The trouble is that it comes less than a month before Christmas. So when on 25 December Mom brings out another turkey, you don't go, 'Turkey! YIPPEEE!' but rather, 'Ah, turkey again is it, Mother?' Under such an arrangement Christmas dinner is bound to come as an anticlimax.

Also, Americans don't drink much at Christmas, as a rule. Indeed, I suspect most people in America would think it faintly unseemly to imbibe anything more than, say, a small sherry before lunch on Christmas Day. Americans save their large-scale drinking for New Year's Eve.

Nor, come to that, do we have many of the standard features of Christmas that you take for granted. There are no Christmas panto-mimes in America. No mince pies and hardly any Christmas puddings. There's no bellringing on Christmas Eve. No crackers. No big double issue of the *Radio Times*. No brandy butter. No little dishes full of nuts. No hearing 'Merry Xmas Everybody' by Slade at least once every twenty minutes. Above all, there is no Boxing Day.

On 26 December, everybody in the United States goes back to work. In fact, Christmas as a noticeable phenomenon pretty well ends about midday on 25 December. There's nothing special on TV, and most large stores and shopping malls now open for the afternoon (so that people can exchange all the things they got but didn't want). You can go to the movies on Christmas Day in America. You can go *bowling*. It doesn't seem right somehow.

As for Boxing Day, most people in America have never heard of it, or at best have only the vaguest idea of what it is. It may surprise you to hear, incidentally, that Boxing Day is actually quite a modern invention. The *Oxford English Dictionary* can trace the term back no further than 1849. Its roots go back at least to medieval times, when it was the custom to break open church alms boxes at Christmas and distribute the contents to the poor, but as a holiday Boxing Day only dates from the last century, which explains why you have it and we don't.

Personally, I much prefer Boxing Day to Christmas, largely because it has all the advantages of Christmas (lots of food and drink, general good will towards all, a chance to doze in an armchair during daylight hours) without any of the disadvantages like spending hours on the floor trying to assemble doll's houses and bicycles from instructions written in Taiwan or the uttering of false professions of gratitude to Aunt Gladys for a hand-knitted jumper that even Gyles Brandreth wouldn't wear. ('No honestly, Glad, I've been looking everywhere for a jumper with a unicorn motif.')

No, if there is one thing I miss from England it's Boxing Day. That and of course hearing 'Merry Xmas Everybody' by Slade over and over. Apart from anything else, it makes you appreciate the rest of the year so much more.

22 December 1996

THE NUMBERS GAME

THE UNITED STATES CONGRESS, WHICH NEVER CEASES TO BE AMAZING, recently voted to give the Pentagon $11 billion more than it had asked for.

Do you have any idea how much $11 billion is? Of course you don't. Nobody does. It is not possible to conceive of a sum that large.

No matter where you turn with regard to America and its economy you are going to bump into figures that are so large as to be essentially incomprehensible. Consider just a few figures that I pulled from this past Sunday's papers. The annual gross domestic product of the United States is $6.8 trillion. The federal budget is $1.6 trillion. The federal deficit is nearly $200 billion. California alone has an economy worth $850 billion.

It's easy to lose sight of just how enormous these figures really are. America's cumulative debt at last count, according to *Time* magazine, was 'a hair' under $4.7 trillion. The actual figure was $4.692 trillion, so that statement is hard to argue with, yet it represents a difference of $8 billion – a pretty large hair in anybody's book.

I worked long enough on the business news desk of a national newspaper to know that even the most experienced financial journalists often get confused when dealing with terms like *billion* and *trillion*, and for two good reasons. First, they've usually had quite a lot to drink at lunch, and, second, such numbers really are confusing.

And that is the whole problem. Big numbers are simply beyond what we are capable of grasping. On Sixth Avenue in New York there is an electronic hoarding, erected and paid for by some anonymous source, that announces itself as 'The National Debt Clock'. When I was last there, in November, it listed the national debt at $4,533,603,804,000 – that's $4.5 trillion – and the figure was growing by $10,000 every second, or so fast that the last three digits on the electronic meter were just a blur. But what does $4.5 trillion actually *mean*?

Well, let's just try for a trillion. Imagine that you were in a vault with the whole of America's national debt and you were told you could keep each dollar bill you initialled. Say, too, for the sake of argument that you could initial one dollar bill each second and that you worked straight through without stopping. How long do you think it would take to count a trillion dollars? Go on, humour me and take a guess. Twelve weeks? Five years?

If you initialled one dollar per second, you would make $1,000 every 17 minutes. After twelve days of non-stop effort you would acquire your first $1 million. Thus it would take you 120 days to accumulate $10 million and 1,200 days – something over three years – to reach $100 million. After 31.7 years, you would become a billionaire, and after almost a thousand years you would be as wealthy as Bill Gates, the founder of Microsoft. But not until after 31,709.8 years would you count your trillionth dollar (and then you would be less than one-fourth of the way through the pile of money representing America's national debt).

That is what $1 trillion is.

What is interesting is that it is becoming increasingly evident that most of these inconceivably vast sums that get bandied about by economists and policy makers are almost certainly miles out anyway. Take gross domestic product, the bedrock of modern economic policy. GDP was a concept originated in the 1930s by the economist Simon Kuznets. It is very good at measuring physical things – tonnes of steel, board feet of lumber, potatoes, tyres, and so on. That was all very well in a traditional industrial economy. But now the greater part of output for nearly all developed nations is in services and ideas – things like computer software, telecommunications, financial services – which produce wealth but don't necessarily, or even generally, result in a product that you can load on a pallet and ship out to the marketplace.

Because such activities are so difficult to measure and quantify, no one really knows what they amount to. Many economists now believe that America may have been underestimating its rate of GDP growth by as much as two to three percentage points a year for several years. That may not seem a great deal, but if that is correct then the American economy – which obviously is already staggeringly enormous – may be one third larger than anyone had thought. In other words, there may be several hundred *billions* of dollars floating around in the American economy that no one ever suspected was there. Incredible.

Here's another arresting thought. None of this really matters because GDP is in any case a perfectly useless measurement. All that it is, literally, is a crude measure of national income – 'the dollar value of finished goods and services', as the textbooks put it – over a given period.

Any kind of economic activity adds to the gross domestic product. It doesn't matter whether it's a good activity or a bad one. It has been estimated, for instance, that the O.J. Simpson trial added $200 million to America's GDP through lawyers' fees, court costs, hotel bills for the press, and so on, but I don't think many people would argue that the whole costly spectacle made America a noticeably greater, nobler place.

In fact, bad activities often generate more GDP than good activities. I was recently in Pennsylvania at the site of a zinc factory whose airborne wastes were formerly so laden with pollutants that they denuded an entire mountainside. From the factory fence to the top of the mountain there was not a single scrap of growing vegetation to be seen. From a GDP perspective, however, this was wonderful. First there was the gain to the economy from all the zinc the factory had refined and sold over the years. Then there was the gain from the tens of millions of dollars the government must spend to clean up the site and restore the mountain. Finally, there will be a continuing gain from medical treatments for workers and towns-people made chronically ill by living amid all those contaminants.

In terms of conventional economic measurement, all of this is gain, not loss. So too is overfishing of lakes and seas. So too is deforest-ation. In short, the more recklessly we use up natural resources, the more the GDP glows.

As the economist Herman Daly once put it: 'The current national accounting system treats the earth as a business in liquidation.' Or as three other leading economists dryly observed in an article in the *Atlantic Monthly* last year: 'By the curious standard of the GDP, the nation's economic hero is a terminal cancer patient who is going through a costly divorce.'

So why do we persist with this preposterous gauge of economic performance? Because it's the best thing that economists have come up with yet. Now you know why they call it the dismal science.

5 January 1997

ROOM SERVICE

SOMETHING I HAVE LONG WANTED TO DO – AND IF THIS COLUMN CAME with expenses I'd be doing it right now – is visit the Motel Inn in San Luis Obispo, California.

On the face of it, this might seem an odd quest since the Motel Inn is not, by all accounts, a particularly prepossessing establishment. Built in 1925 in the Spanish colonial style much beloved by Californians, Zorro and almost no one else, it sits in the shadow of a busy elevated freeway amid a cluster of gas stations, fast-food outlets and other more modern motor inns.

Once, however, it was a famous stopping place on the coastal highway between Los Angeles and San Francisco. A Pasadena architect named Arthur Heineman gave it its exuberant style, but his most inspired legacy lies in the name he chose for it. Playing around with the words *motor* and *hotel*, he dubbed it a *mo-tel*, hyphenating the word to emphasize its novelty.

America already had lots of motels by then, but they were all called something else – *auto court, cottage court, hotel court, tour-o-tel, auto hotel, bungalow court, cabin court, tourist camp, tourist court, trav-o-tel*. For a long time it looked like *tourist court* would become the standard designation. It wasn't until about 1950 that *motel* achieved generic status.

I know all this because I have just been reading a book on the history of the motel in America called, with dazzling originality, *The Motel in America*. Written by three academics, it is an awfully dull piece of work, full of sentences like 'The needs of both consumers and purveyors of lodging strongly influenced the development of organized systems of distribution,' but I bought it and devoured it anyway because I love everything about motels.

I can't help myself. I still get excited every time I slip a key into a motel room door and fling it open. It is just one of those things – airline food is another – that I get excited about and should know better.

The golden age of motels was also, as it happens, the golden age of me – the 1950s – and I suppose that's what accounts for my fascination. For anyone who didn't travel around America by car in the 1950s, it is almost impossible now to imagine how thrilling they were. For one thing, the national chains like Holiday Inn and Ramada barely existed. As late as 1962, 98 per cent of motels were individually owned, so each one had its own character.

Essentially they were of two types. The first type were the good ones. These nearly always had a homely, cottagey air. Typically, they were built around a generous lawn with shady trees and a flowerbed decorated with a wagon wheel painted white. (The owners, for some reason, generally liked to paint all their rocks white, too, and array them along the edge of the drive.) Often they had a swimming pool and a gift shop or coffee shop.

Indoors they offered measures of comfort and elegance that would have the whole family cooing – thick carpet, purring air-conditioner, a nightstand with a private phone and a built-in radio, a TV at the foot of the bed, a private bath, sometimes a dressing area, Vibromatic beds, which gave you a massage for a quarter.

The second kind of motels were the appalling ones. We always stayed at these. My father, who was one of history's great cheapskates, was of the view that there was no point in spending money on . . . well, on anything really, and certainly not on anything that you were mostly going to be asleep in.

In consequence, we normally camped in motel rooms where the beds sagged and the furnishings were battered, and where you could generally count on being awakened in the night by a piercing shriek, the sounds of splintering furniture and a female voice pleading, 'Put the gun down, Vinnie. I'll do anything you say.' I don't wish to suggest that these experiences left me scarred and embittered, but I can remember watching Janet Leigh being hacked up in the Bates Motel in *Psycho* and thinking, 'At least she got a shower curtain.'

All of this, even at its worst, gave highway travel a kind of exhilarating unpredictability. You never knew what quality of comfort you would find at the end of the day, what sort of small pleasures might be on offer. It gave road trips a piquancy that the homogenized refinements of the modern age cannot match.

That changed very quickly with the rise of motel chains. Holiday Inn, for instance, went from seventy-nine outlets in 1958 to almost 1,500 in less than twenty years. Today just five chains account for one-third of all the motel rooms in America. Travellers these days don't want uncertainty in their lives. They want to stay in the same place, eat the same food, watch the same TV wherever they go.

Recently, while driving from Washington, DC, to New England with my own family, I tried explaining this to my children, and got the idea that we should stop for the night at an old-fashioned family-run place. Everyone thought this was an immensely stupid idea, but I insisted that it would be a great experience.

Well, we looked everywhere. We passed scores of motels, but they were all part of national chains. Eventually, after perhaps 90 minutes of futile hunting, I pulled off the interstate for the seventh or eighth time and – lo! – there shining out of the darkness was the Sleepy Hollow Motel, a perfect 1950s sort of place.

'There's a Comfort Inn across the street,' one of my children pointed out.

'We don't want a Comfort Inn, Jimmy,' I explained, temporarily forgetting in my excitement that I don't have a child named Jimmy. 'We want a real motel.'

My wife, being English, insisted on having a look at the room. It was awful, of course. The furnishings were battered and threadbare. The room was so cold you could see your breath. There was a shower curtain, but it hung by just three rings.

'It's got character,' I insisted.

'It's got nits,' said my wife. 'We'll be across the road at the Comfort Inn.'

In disbelief, I watched them troop out. 'You'll stay, won't you, Jimmy?' I said, but even he left without a backward glance.

I stood there for about 15 seconds, then switched off the light, returned the key and went across to the Comfort Inn. It was very bland and just like every Comfort Inn I had ever stayed in. But it was clean, the TV worked and, it must be said, the shower curtain was very nice.

12 January 1997

OUR FRIEND THE MOOSE

MY WIFE HAS JUST CALLED UP THAT DINNER IS ON THE TABLE (I'D RATHER it was on plates, but there you are), so this week's column may be shorter than usual.

In our house, you see, if you don't get to the table within five minutes there's nothing left but gristle and that greyish piece of string they use to hold the joint together. But at least – and here's a nice thing about living in America these days, or indeed anywhere other than Britain – we can eat beef here without having to wonder if when we rise from the table we will walk sideways into the wall.

I was recently back in the UK and I noticed that a lot of you are eating beef again, which makes me conclude that you didn't watch the recent excellent *Horizon* two-parter on BSE or read John Lanchester's equally excellent account in the *New Yorker* on same. If you had, believe me, you'd never wish to eat beef again. (But not as much as you'd wish you hadn't eaten it at all between 1986 and 1988. I ate it then too and boy are *we* in for it!)

However, my purpose today is not to make you feel bad about your future prospects (though having said that, my advice is to get your affairs in order while you can still hold a pen), but rather to suggest an alternative use for all those poor cows that are being sent to slaughter.

My idea is that we should ship all those cows over here and set them loose in the Great North Woods which extend across northern New England from Vermont to Maine, and let America's hunters at them. My thinking is that this might distract the hunters from shooting moose.

Goodness knows why anyone would want to shoot an animal as harmless and retiring as the moose, but thousands do – so many, in fact, that states now hold lotteries to decide who gets a licence. Maine last year received 82,000 applications for 1,500 permits. Over 12,000 out-of-staters happily parted with a non-refundable $20 just to be allowed to take part in the draw.

Hunters will tell you that a moose is a wily and ferocious forest creature. In fact, a moose is a cow drawn by a three-year-old. That's all there is to it. Without doubt, the moose is the most improbable, endearingly hopeless creature ever to live in the wilds. It is huge – as big as a horse – but magnificently ungainly. A moose runs as if its legs have never been introduced to each other. Even its antlers are hopeless. Other creatures grow antlers with sharp points that look wonderful in profile and command the respect of adversaries. Moose grow antlers that look like oven gloves.

Above all what distinguishes the moose is its almost boundless lack of intelligence. If you are driving down a highway and a moose steps from the woods ahead of you, he will squint at you for a long minute, then abruptly hie off down the road away from you, legs flailing in eight directions at once. Never mind that there are perhaps 10,000 square miles of safe, dense forest on either side of the highway. Clueless as to where he is and what exactly is going on, the moose doggedly follows the highway halfway to New Brunswick before his peculiar gait inadvertently steers him back into the woods, where he immediately stops and takes on a perplexed expression that says, 'Hey – woods. Now how the heck did I get here?'

Moose are so monumentally muddle-headed, in fact, that when they hear a car or truck approaching they will often bolt *out* of the woods and on to the highway in the curious hope that this will bring them to safety. Every year in New England about 1,000 moose are fatally struck by cars or trucks. (Since a moose weighs 2,000 pounds and is exactly built so that a car bonnet will take its spindly legs out from under it while leaving the bulk of it to fall through the windscreen, collisions are often equally fatal to the motorist.) When you see how quiet and empty are the roads that run through the northern woods and realize how manifestly unlikely it is that any creature could emerge onto the highway just as a vehicle is passing, you will appreciate just how amazing those numbers are.

More amazing still, given the moose's lack of cunning and curiously blunted survival instincts, is that it is one of the longest-surviving creatures in North America. When mastodons walked the earth, moose were there with them. Woolly mammoths, sabre-toothed tigers, mountain lions, wolves, caribou, wild horses and even camels all once thrived in the eastern United States but gradually stumbled into extinction, while the moose just plodded on, untroubled by ice ages, meteor impacts, volcanic eruptions and shifting continents.

It hasn't always been so. At the turn of the century it was estimated that there were no more than a dozen moose in the whole of New Hampshire and probably none at all in Vermont. Today New Hampshire has an estimated 5,000 moose, Vermont 1,000 more and Maine anything up to 30,000.

It is because of these robust and growing numbers that hunting has been gradually re-introduced as a way of keeping the numbers from getting out of hand. However, there are two problems with this. First, the population numbers are really just guesses. Moose clearly don't line up for censuses. At least one leading naturalist thinks the population numbers may have been overstated by as much as 20 per cent, which would mean that moose aren't so much being selectively culled as carelessly slaughtered.

Even more pertinent, to my mind, is the thought that there is just something wrong about hunting and killing an animal as dopily unassuming as a moose. Shooting a moose is not an achievement. I have encountered moose in the wild and can tell you that you could just about go up and kill one with a folded newspaper. The fact that over

90 per cent of hunters manage to bag a moose in a season that lasts only a week is testament to the ease with which they can be hunted down.

Which is why I suggest that you send all your poor addled bovines to us. It would provide our hunters with the sort of manly challenge they evidently long for, and, as I say, might help save the odd moose.

So send those mad cows over. Address them to Bob Smith. He's one of our New Hampshire senators, and if his voting record is any guide he's already at ease with disorders of the mind.

Now if you will excuse me I have to go see if there is any meat left on that greyish piece of string.

19 January 1997

CONSUMING PLEASURES

I BELIEVE I HAVE JUST SECURED DEFINITIVE PROOF THAT AMERICA IS THE ultimate shopping paradise. It came in a video catalogue that arrived unsolicited with the morning mail. There, among the usual diverse offerings – *Fiddler on the Roof*, *T'ai Chi for Health and Fitness*, every movie ever made by John Wayne – was a self-help video called *Do the Macarena Totally Nude*, which promises to guide the naked home viewer through 'the hot moves of this Latin-influenced dance that is sweeping the nation'.

Among the catalogue's other intriguing offerings were a document- ary called *Antique Farm Tractors*, a boxed set representing the complete oeuvre of Don Knotts, and an interesting compilation entitled *Nude Housewives of America* (Vols 1&2), depicting ordinary housewives 'doing their daily chores in the buff!'

And to think I asked for a socket wrench for Christmas.

My point is that there is almost nothing you cannot buy in this remarkable country. Of course, shopping has been the national sport in America for decades, but three significant retailing developments in recent years have elevated the shopping experience to a higher, giddier plane. They are:

• **Telemarketing**. This is an all-new business in which platoons of salespeople phone up complete strangers, more or less at random, and doggedly read to them a prepared script promising a free set of steak knives or AM–FM radio if they buy a certain product or service. These people have become positively relentless.

The possibility that I would buy a time-share in Florida from a stranger over the telephone is about as likely as the possibility that I would change religion on the basis of a doorstep visit from a brace of Mormons, but evidently this feeling is not universal. According to the *New York Times*, telemarketing in America is now worth $35 *billion* a year. That figure is so amazing that I cannot think about it without getting a headache, so let us move on to retail development number two:

• **Outlet malls**. These are malls in which companies like Ralph Lauren and Calvin Klein sell their own lines at discounts. They are, in short, clusters of shops where everything is permanently on sale, and they have become huge.

In many cases, outlet malls are not malls at all, but rather whole communities that have been taken over by outlet stores. Easily the most remarkable of these is Freeport, Maine, home of L.L. Bean, a popular supplier of outdoor apparel and sporting equipment for yuppies.

We stopped there last summer on the way through Maine and I am still trembling from the experience. The procedure for a visit to Freeport is unvarying. You creep into town in a long line of traffic, spend forty minutes hunting for a parking space, then join a crowd of thousands shuffling along Main Street past a succession of shops selling every known brand name that ever was or will be.

At the centre of it all is the L.L. Bean store, which is enormous. It is open twenty-four hours a day, 365 days a year. You can buy a kayak there at 3 a.m. if you want. People apparently do. My brain is beginning to hurt again.

• **Finally, catalogues**. Shopping by post has been around for a long time, but it has proliferated to a degree that is just beyond astounding. Almost from the moment we arrived in America catalogues began plopping unbidden onto our mat with the daily mail. Now we get perhaps a dozen a week, sometimes more – catalogues for videos, gardening implements, lingerie, books, camping and fishing gear, things to make your bathroom a more stylish and convivial place, you name it.

For a long time I tossed these out with the rest of the unsolicited mail. What a fool I was. I now realize they not only provide hours of reading pleasure, but open up a world of possibilities I scarcely knew existed.

Just today, along with the aforementioned nude macarena brochure, we received a catalogue called *Tools for Serious Readers*. It was full of the usual assortment of blotters and desk tidies, but what particularly caught my eye was something called the Briefcase Valet – a small wheeled trolley that sits about four inches off the floor.

Available in dark or natural cherry and attractively priced at $139, it is designed to alleviate one of the most intractable office storage problems of our age. As the catalogue copy explains: 'Most of us are faced with the same nagging problem of what to do with our briefcase when we put it down at home or in the office. That's why we designed our Briefcase Valet. It holds your briefcase up off the floor, making it easier to insert and retrieve things as the day progresses.'

I especially like those last four words, 'as the day progresses'. How many times have I got to the end of a working day myself and thought: 'Oh, what I'd give for a small wheeled device in a choice of wood tones to save me reaching those last four inches.'

The scary thing is that often these descriptions are written so artfully that you are almost taken in by them. I was just reading in another catalogue about a fancy kitchen accessory from Italy called a *porto rotolo di carta*, which boasts 'a spring tension arm', 'stainless steel guide', 'crafted brass finial' and 'rubber gasket for exceptional stability' – all for just $49.95 – when I realized that it was a paper towel holder.

Obviously the catalogue couldn't say, 'No matter how you look at it, this is just a paper towel dispenser and you'd be a sap to buy it,' so they must try to dazzle you with its exotic pedigree and technical complexity.

In consequence, even the most mundane catalogue items boast more design features than a 1954 Buick. I have before me a glossy book from another company announcing with undisguised pride that their flannel shirts feature, among much else, gauntlet buttons, extra-long sleeve plackets, two-ply 40S yarn construction ('for a superior nap'), boxed back pleat, double stitching at stress points, handy locker loop and non-fused collar, whatever all that may be. Even socks come with lengthy, scientific-sounding descriptions extolling their seamless closures, one-to-one fibre loops and hand-linked yarns.

I confess I have sometimes been briefly tempted by these seductive blandishments to make a purchase, but in the end I realize that given a choice between paying $37.50 for a shirt with a superior nap and just having a nap, I will always go for the latter.

However, let me say right here that if anyone comes up with a Totally Nude Macarena Socket-Wrench Home Workout Video with handy locker loop in a choice of colours, I am ready to buy.

26 January 1997

JUNK FOOD HEAVEN

I DECIDED TO CLEAN OUT THE FRIDGE THE OTHER DAY. WE DON'T USUALLY clean out our fridge – we just box it up every four or five years and send it off to the Centers for Disease Control in Atlanta with a note to help themselves to anything that looks scientifically promising – but we hadn't seen one of the cats for a few days and I had a vague recollection of having glimpsed something furry on the bottom shelf towards the back. (Turned out to be a large piece of Gorgonzola.)

So there I was, down on my knees unwrapping pieces of foil and peering cautiously into Tupperware containers, when I came across an interesting product called a breakfast pizza and I examined it with a kind of rueful fondness, as you might regard an old photograph of yourself dressed in clothes that you cannot believe you ever thought

were stylish. The breakfast pizza, you see, represented the last sur-
viving relic of a bout of very serious retail foolishness on my part.

Some weeks ago I announced to my wife that I was going to the
supermarket with her next time she went because the stuff she
kept bringing home was – how can I put this? – not fully in the spirit
of American eating. Here we were living in a paradise of junk
food – the country that gave the world cheese in a spray can – and
she kept bringing home healthy stuff like fresh broccoli and packets
of Ryvita.

It was because she was English, of course. She didn't really understand the rich, unrivalled possibilities for greasiness and goo that the
American diet offers. I longed for artificial bacon bits, melted cheese
in a shade of yellow unknown to nature, and creamy chocolate fill-
ings, sometimes all in the same product. I wanted food that squirts
when you bite into it or plops onto your shirt front in such gross
quantities that you have to rise carefully from the table and limbo
over to the sink to clean yourself up. So I accompanied her to the
supermarket and while she was off squeezing melons and pricing
shiitake mushrooms I made for the junk food section – which was
essentially all the rest of the store. Well, it was heaven.

The breakfast cereals alone could have occupied me for most of
the afternoon. There must have been 200 types, and I am not
exaggerating. Every possible substance that could be dried, puffed
and coated with sugar was there. The most immediately arresting was
a cereal called Cookie Crisp, which tried to pretend it was a
nutritious breakfast but was really just chocolate chip cookies that
you put in a bowl and ate with milk. Brilliant.

Also of note were cereals called Peanut Butter Crunch, Cinnamon
Mini Buns, Count Chocula ('with Monster Marshmallows'), and a
particularly hardcore offering called Cookie Blast Oat Meal, which
contained *four* kinds of cookies. I grabbed one of each of the cereals
and two of the oatmeal – how often I've said that you shouldn't start
a day without a big steaming bowl of cookies – and sprinted with
them back to the trolley.

'What's that?' my wife asked in the special tone of voice with
which she often addresses me in retail establishments.

I didn't have time to explain. 'Breakfast for the next six months,' I
panted as I dashed past, 'and don't even *think* about putting any of
it back and getting muesli.'

I had no idea how the market for junk food had proliferated. Everywhere I turned I was confronted with foods guaranteed to make you waddle, most of which were entirely new to me – jelly creme pies, moon pies, pecan spinwheels, peach mellos, root beer buttons, chocolate fudge devil dogs and a whipped marshmallow sandwich spread called Fluff, which came in a tub large enough to bath a baby in.

You really cannot believe the bounteous variety of non-nutritious foods available to the American supermarket shopper these days or the quantities in which they are consumed. I recently read that the average American eats 17.8 *pounds* of pretzels every year.

Aisle seven ('Food for the Seriously Obese') was especially productive. It had a whole section devoted exclusively to a product called Toaster Pastries, which included, among much else, eight different types of toaster strudel. And what exactly is toaster strudel? Who cares? It was coated in sugar and looked drippy. I grabbed an armload.

I admit I got a little carried away – but there was so much and I had been away so long.

It was the breakfast pizza that finally made my wife snap. She looked at the box and said, 'No.'

'I beg your pardon, my sweet?'

'You are not bringing home something called breakfast pizza. I will let you have' – she reached into the trolley for some specimen samples – 'root beer buttons and toaster strudel and . . .' She lifted out a packet she hadn't noticed before. 'What's this?'

I looked over her shoulder. 'Microwave pancakes,' I said.

'Microwave pancakes,' she repeated, but with less enthusiasm.

'Isn't science wonderful?'

'You're going to eat it all,' she said. 'Every bit of everything that you don't put back on the shelves now. You do understand that?'

'Of course,' I said in my sincerest voice.

And do you know she actually made me eat it. I spent weeks working my way through a symphony of American junk food, and it was all awful. Every bit of it. I don't know whether American junk food has got worse or whether my taste buds have matured, but even the treats I'd grown up with now seemed discouragingly pallid or disgustingly sickly.

The most awful of all was the breakfast pizza. I tried it three or four times, baked it in the oven, zapped it with microwaves, and once in desperation served it with a side of marshmallow Fluff, but it never rose beyond a kind of limp, chewy listlessness. Eventually I gave up altogether and hid the box in the Tupperware graveyard on the bottom shelf of the fridge.

Which is why, when I came across it again the other day, I regarded it with mixed feelings. I started to chuck it out, then hesitated and opened the lid. It didn't smell bad – I expect it was pumped so full of chemicals that there wasn't any room for bacteria – and I thought about keeping it a while longer as a reminder of my folly, but in the end I discarded it. And then, feeling peckish, I went off to the larder to see if I couldn't find a nice plain piece of Ryvita and maybe a stick of celery.

2 February 1997

TALES OF THE NORTH WOODS

ABOUT A YEAR AGO, IN THE DEPTHS OF WINTER, A YOUNG COLLEGE student left a party in a village near the small town in New Hampshire in which I live to walk to his parents' house a couple of miles away. Foolishly – for it was dark and he had been drinking – he decided to take a shortcut through the woods. He never made it.

The next day when his disappearance became known hundreds of volunteers took to the woods to search for him. They searched for days, but without success. It wasn't until spring that someone walking in the woods stumbled on his body.

Five weeks ago, something broadly similar happened. A small private jet with two people aboard had to abort its approach as it came in to land at our local airport in poor weather. As the pilot swung round to the northeast to make a new approach, he radioed his intentions to the control tower.

A moment later the little green blip that was his plane disappeared from the airport radar screen. Somewhere out there, abruptly and for reasons unknown, the plane came down in the woods.

Again a large-scale search was mounted, this time with a dozen planes and eleven helicopters augmenting more than 200 volunteer searchers on the ground. Again they searched for days, and again without luck. The missing jet was an eighteen-seater, so it must have made quite an impact, yet there were no signs of strewn wreckage, no crash paths through the trees. The plane had simply vanished without trace.

I don't mean to imply that we live on the edge of some kind of Bermuda triangle of the deciduous world, merely that the woods of New Hampshire are a rather strange and sinister place.

To begin with they are full of trees – and I don't mean that as a joke. I spent some weeks last summer hiking in these woods and I can tell you that the one thing you see in numbers beyond imagining is trees. At times it's actually unsettling because it is essentially just one endlessly repeated scene. Every bend in the path presents a prospect indistinguishable from every other, and it remains like that no matter how far you go. If you somehow lost the path, you could easily find yourself – very probably would find yourself – helplessly bereft of bearings. You could walk to the point of exhaustion before realizing that your route described a large and sadly pointless circle.

Knowing this, it's much less surprising to learn that the woods sometimes swallow aircraft whole or keep for ever people unfortunate enough to get lost in their featureless embrace. New Hampshire is as big as Wales and is 85 per cent forest. There's a lot of forest out there to get lost in. Every year at least one or two people on foot go missing, sometimes never to be seen again.

Yet here's a remarkable thing. Until only about a century ago, and less than that in some areas, most of these woods didn't exist. Nearly the whole of rural New England – including all the area around our part of New Hampshire – was open, meadowy farmland.

I had this brought home to me with a certain potency the other week when our local council sent us, as a kind of New Year's present, a calendar containing old photographs of the town from the local archives. One of the pictures, a hilltop panorama taken in 1874, showed a scene that looked vaguely familiar, though I couldn't tell why. It showed a corner of the Dartmouth College campus and a dirt road, leading off into some distant hills. The rest was spacious farm fields.

It took me some minutes to work out that I was looking at the future site of my own neighbourhood. It was odd because our street looks like a traditional New England street, with clapboard houses shaded by tall and shapely trees, but in fact nearly all of it dates from the early 1920s, half a century after the photograph. The hill from which the picture was taken is now a 20-acre wood and nearly all the landscape from the back of our houses to the distant hills is swathed in dense, mature forest, but hardly a twig of it existed in 1874.

The farms disappeared because the farmers moved west, to richer lands in places like Illinois and Ohio, or moved to the burgeoning industrial cities, where earnings were more reliable and generous. The farms they left behind – and sometimes the villages that supported them – sank into the ground and gradually returned to wilderness. All over New England if you go for a walk in the woods you will come across the remains of old stone walls and the foundations of abandoned barns and farmhouses hidden in the ferns and bracken of the forest floor.

Near our house is a woodland path that follows the route of an eighteenth-century post road. For eighteen miles the path winds through dark, tangled, seemingly ancient woodland, yet there are people alive who remember when all that land was farmland. Just off the old post road, four miles or so from here, there once stood a village called Quinntown, which had a mill and a school and several houses. You can find it on old Geological Survey maps.

I've looked out for Quinntown a couple of times as I've passed, but even with a good map the site is deucedly hard to find because the woods are so lacking in distinguishing landmarks. I know a man who has looked for Quinntown off and on for years and still not found it.

Last weekend I decided to try again. There was a fresh fall of snow, which always makes the woods agreeable. Naturally the thought flitted through my mind that I might stumble on some sign of the missing jet. I didn't *really* expect to find anything – I was seven or eight miles from the presumed crash site – but on the other hand the plane has to be out there somewhere and it was altogether possible that no one had looked in this area.

So I went out in the woods and had a good tramp around. I got a lot of healthy fresh air and exercise, and the woods were stunning in their snowy softness. It was strange to think that in all that vast stillness there were the remains of a once-thriving village, and stranger still that somewhere out there with me was a crumpled, unfound plane with two bodies aboard.

I would love to be able to tell you that I found Quinntown or the missing plane or both, but alas I did not. Sometimes life has inconclusive endings.

Columns, too.

9 February 1997

HAIL TO THE CHIEF

IT'S PRESIDENTS DAY TOMORROW IN AMERICA. I KNOW. I CAN HARDLY
stand the excitement either.

Presidents Day is a new holiday to me. When I was growing up, we
had two presidential holidays in February – Lincoln's Birthday on 12
February and Washington's Birthday on 22 February. I may not be
exactly right on those dates, or indeed even very close, because
frankly it's been a long time since I was growing up and anyway they
weren't very interesting holidays. You didn't receive presents or get
to go on a picnic or anything.

The problem with birthdays, as I am sure you have noticed your-self, is that they can fall on any day of the week, whereas most people like to have their public holidays on Mondays so that they get a nice long weekend.

So for a while America celebrated Washington's Birthday and Lincoln's Birthday on the Mondays nearest the appropriate dates. However, this bothered some people of a particular nature, so it was decided to have a single holiday on the third Monday of February and call it Presidents Day.

The idea now is to honour all the presidents, whether they were good or bad, which I think is swell because it gives us an opportunity to commemorate the more obscure or peculiar presidents – people like Grover Cleveland, who, according to legend, had the interesting habit of relieving himself out of his office window, or Zachary Taylor, who never voted in an election and didn't even vote for himself.

All things considered, America has produced quite a few great presidents – Washington, Lincoln, Jefferson, Franklin and Teddy Roosevelt, Woodrow Wilson, John F. Kennedy. It has also produced several great men who incidentally became president, among them James Madison, Ulysses S. Grant and – you may be surprised to hear me say this – Herbert Hoover.

I have a certain regard for Hoover – fondness would be much too strong a word – because he was from Iowa, and so am I. Besides, you have to feel a little sorry for the poor man. He was the only person in American history for whom attaining the White House was a bad career move. Nowadays when people think of Hoover at all, it is as the man who gave the world the Great Depression. Hardly anyone remembers the half-century of remarkable, even heroic, achieve-ments that preceded it.

Consider his CV: orphaned at eight, he put himself through college (he was in the first graduating class from Stanford University) and became a successful mining engineer in the western United States. He then went off to Australia, where he more or less started the mining industry in Western Australia – still one of the most pro-ductive regions in the world – and eventually ended up in London, where he became a vastly wealthy and influential pillar of the business community.

Such was his stature that at the outbreak of the First World War he was invited to join the British Cabinet, but declined and instead took on the job of directing famine relief throughout Europe, which he managed with such distinction that he is estimated to have saved ten million lives. By the end of the war he was one of the most admired and respected men in the world, known everywhere as the Great Humanitarian.

Returning to America, he became a trusted adviser to Woodrow Wilson, then served as Secretary of Commerce under Harding and Coolidge, where he oversaw a 58 per cent rise in American exports in eight years. When he ran for president in 1928, he was elected in a record landslide.

In March 1929 he was inaugurated. Seven months later Wall Street crashed and the economy went into freefall. Contrary to common belief, Hoover responded at once. He spent more money on public works and unemployment relief than all his predecessors combined, provided $500 million in assistance to troubled banks, even donated his own salary to charity. But he lacked the common touch and alienated the electorate by insisting repeatedly that recovery was just around the corner. In 1932 he was defeated as resoundingly as he had been elected four years before, and has been remembered ever since as an abject failure.

Still, at least he is remembered for something, which is more than can be said for many of our Chief Executives. Of the forty-one men who have risen to the office of president, at least half served with such lack of eminence as to be almost totally forgotten now, which I think is deserving of the warmest approbation. To be President of the United States and not accomplish anything is, after all, a kind of accomplishment in itself.

By almost universal agreement, the most vague and ineffectual of all our leaders was Millard Fillmore, who succeeded to the office in 1850 upon the death of Zachary Taylor, and spent the next three years demonstrating how the country would have been run if they had just propped Taylor up in a chair with cushions. However, Fillmore has become so celebrated for his obscurity that he is no longer actually obscure, which rather disqualifies him from serious consideration.

Far more noteworthy to my mind is the great Chester A. Arthur, who was sworn in as President in 1881, posed for an official photograph and then, as far as I can make out, was never heard from again. If Arthur's goal in life was to grow rather splendid facial hair and leave plenty of room in the history books for the achievements of other men, then his presidency can be ranked a sterling success.

Also admirable in their way were Rutherford B. Hayes, who was President from 1877 to 1881 and whose principal devotions in life were the advocacy of 'hard money' and the repeal of the Bland–Allison Act, both of which were so pointless and abstruse that no one can remember now what they were, and Franklin Pierce, whose term of office from 1853 to 1857 was an interlude of indistinction between two longer periods of anonymity. He spent virtually the whole of his incumbency hopelessly intoxicated, prompting the affectionate slogan 'Franklin Pierce, the Hero of Many a Well-Fought Bottle'.

My favourites, however, are the two Presidents Harrison. The first was William Henry Harrison, who heroically refused to don an overcoat for his inaugural ceremony in 1841, contracted pneumonia and with engaging swiftness expired. He was president for just thirty days, nearly all of it spent unconscious. Forty years later his grandson, Benjamin Harrison, was elected president, and succeeded in the challenging ambition of achieving as little in four years as his grandfather had in a month.

As far as I am concerned, all these men deserve public holidays of their own. So you may imagine my dismay at news that moves are afoot in Congress to abolish Presidents Day and return to observing Lincoln's and Washington's birthdays separately, on the grounds that Lincoln and Washington were truly great men and, moreover, didn't pee out of the window. Can you believe that? Some people have no sense of history.

16 February 1997

LIFE IN A COLD CLIMATE

SOMETHING DARING THAT I LIKE TO DO AT THIS TIME OF YEAR IS TO GO out without putting on my coat or gloves or any other protection against the elements and walk the thirty or so yards to the bottom of our drive to bring in the morning paper from a little box on a post.

Now you might say that that doesn't sound very daring at all, and in a sense you would be right because it only takes about 20 seconds there and back, but here is the thing that makes it special: sometimes I hang around out there just to see how long I can stand the cold.

I don't want to sound boastful, but I have devoted much of my life to testing the tolerance to extremes of the human body, often with very little thought to the potential long-term peril to myself – for instance, allowing a leg to go fast asleep in a cinema and then seeing what happens if I try to go for popcorn, or wrapping an elastic band around my index finger to see if I can make it explode. It is through this work that I have made some important breakthroughs, notably the discovery that very hot surfaces don't necessarily look hot, and that temporary amnesia can be reliably induced by placing the head immediately beneath an open drawer.

I expect your instinct is to regard such behaviour as foolhardy, but let me remind you of all those occasions when you yourself have stuck a finger into a small flame just to see what would happen (and what exactly *did* happen, eh?) or stood first on one leg and then on the other in a scalding bath waiting for an inflow of cold water to moderate the temperature, or sat at a kitchen table quietly absorbed with letting melted candle wax drip onto your fingers, or a great deal else I could mention.

At least when I engage in these matters it is in a spirit of serious scientific enquiry. Which is why, as I say, I like to go for the morning paper in the least encumbering apparel that decency and Mrs Bryson will allow.

This morning when I set off it was minus 19°F (minus 28°C) out there – cold enough to reconfigure the anatomy of a brass monkey, as I believe the saying has it. Unless you have a particularly vivid imagination, or are reading this in a chest freezer, you may find such extreme chilliness difficult to conceive. So let me tell you just how cold it is: *very*.

When you step outside in such weather, for the first instant it is startlingly invigorating – not unlike the experience of diving into cold water, a sort of wakeup call to every corpuscle. But that phase passes quickly. Before you have trudged a few yards your face feels as it would after a sharp slap, your extremities are aching, and every breath you take hurts. By the time you return to the house your fingers and toes are throbbing with a gentle but insistent pain and you notice with interest that your cheeks yield no sensation at all. The little residual heat you brought from the house is long gone, and your clothes have ceased to have any insulating value. It is decidedly uncomfortable.

Nineteen degrees below zero is unusually cold even for northern New England, so I was interested to see how long I could bear such an exposure, and the answer was 39 seconds. I don't mean that that's how long it took for me to get bored with the idea, or to think, 'Gracious, it is rather chilly; I guess I'll go in now.' I mean that's how long it took me to be so cold that I would have climbed over my mother to get inside first.

New Hampshire is famous for its harsh winters, but in fact there are plenty of places much worse. The coldest temperature ever recorded here was minus 46°F, back in 1925, but twenty other states – nearly half – have had lower lows than that. The bleakest thermometer reading yet seen in the US was at Prospect Creek, Alaska, in 1971, when the temperature fell to minus 79.8°F.

Of course, almost any place can have a cold snap. The real test of a winter is in its duration. In International Falls, Minnesota, the winters are so long and ferocious that the mean annual temperature is just 36.5°F (2.5°C), which is very mean indeed. Nearby there is a town called (honestly) Frigid, where I suspect the situation is even worse but they are just too depressed to report.

However, the record for the most wretched inhabited place ever must surely go to Langdon, North Dakota, which in the winter of 1935–6 recorded 176 consecutive days of below freezing temperatures, including sixty-seven consecutive days in which the temperature fell below 0°F (i.e., into the shrieking brass monkey zone) for at least part of the day, and forty-one consecutive days when the temperature did not rise above 0°F.

Just to put that in perspective, 176 days is the span of time that lies between now and next August. Personally, I would find it very hard to spend 176 consecutive days in North Dakota at any time, but I guess that is another matter.

In any case, I have all I can handle right here in New Hampshire. I was dreading the long, cruel winters in New England, but to my surprise they delight me. Partly it is because they are so shocking. There really is something exhilarating about the sharpness of the cold, the cleanness of the air. And winters here are stunningly pretty. Every rooftop and mailbox wears a jaunty cap of snow for months on end. Nearly every day the sun shines, so there is none of the oppressive grey gloom that characterizes winter in so many other places. And when the snow begins to get trampled or dirty, there is generally a big new fall that fluffs it up again.

People here actually get excited about winter. There is skiing and ice skating and sledging on the local golf course. One of our neighbours floods his back garden and turns it into a skating pond for the kids on our street. The local college has a winter carnival, with ice sculptures on the college green. It is all very cheery.

Best of all, you know that winter is just one in an endless cycle of reliable, well-defined seasons. When the cold starts to get to you, there is the reassurance of knowing that a good hot summer is just around the corner. Apart from anything else, it means a whole new set of interesting experimental challenges involving sunburn, poison ivy, infectious deer tics, electric hedge clippers and – this goes without saying – barbecue lighter fluid. I can't wait.

23 February 1997

DROWNING IN RED TAPE

I'M NOT EVEN GOING TO BEGIN TO TELL YOU ABOUT THE FRUSTRATION OF trying to get a foreign-born spouse or other loved one registered as a legal resident in the United States because I haven't space and anyway it is much too boring. Also, I can't talk about it without weeping copiously. Also, you would think I was making most of it up.

You would scoff, I am quite sure, if I told you that an acquaintance of ours – an academic of high standing – sat open-mouthed while his daughter was asked such questions as 'Have you ever engaged in any unlawful commercial vice, including, but not limited to, illegal gambling?' and 'Have you ever been a member of, or in any way affiliated with, the Communist Party or any other totalitarian party?' and – my particular favourite – 'Do you plan to practise polygamy in the US?' His daughter, I should point out, was five years old.

You see, I am weeping already.

There is something seriously wrong with a country that asks such questions of any person, not simply because the questions are intrusive and irrelevant, and not because enquiries into one's political affinities fly in the face of the American Constitution, but because they are such a monumental waste of everyone's time. Who, after all, when asked if he intends to engage in genocide, espionage, hijacking, multiple marriages or any other of an extremely long and interestingly paranoid list of undesirable activities is going to say: 'I certainly do! Say, will this harm my chances of getting in?'

If all that was involved was answering a list of pointless questions under oath, then I would just sigh and let it be. But it is infinitely more than that. Acquiring legal status in America involves fingerprints, medical examinations, blood tests, letters of affidavit, birth and marriage certificates, employment records, proof of financial standing, and much else – and all of it must be assembled, validated, presented and paid for in very specific ways. My wife recently had to make a 250-mile round trip to give a blood sample at a clinic recognized by the US Immigration and Naturalization Service even though one of the finest teaching hospitals in America is here in the town in which we live.

There are endless forms to fill in, each with pages of instructions, which often contradict other instructions and almost always lead to the need for more forms. Here is a typical fragment of instructions regarding the presentation of fingerprints:

'Submit a complete set of fingerprints on Form FD-258 ... Complete the information on the top of the chart and write your A# (if any) in the space marked 'Your no. OCA' or 'Miscellaneous no. MNU'.

If you don't have form FD-258 (and you don't) or aren't sure which is your MNU number (and you aren't), you can spend days repeatedly dialling a phone number that is forever engaged, only to be told when you finally do get through that you must call another number, which the person tells you once in a mumble and you don't quite catch before you are cut off. It is like this with every encounter you have with every branch of the American government. After a while you begin to understand why flinty-eyed cowpokes in places like Montana turn their ranches into fortresses and threaten to shoot any government officer fool enough to walk into the cross-hairs.

And it's no good just filling in the forms to the best of your ability, because if anything is even a tiny bit out of order, it is all sent back.

My wife had her file returned once because the distance between her chin and hairline on a passport-sized photograph was out by one-eighth of an inch.

This has been going on for two years for us. Understand, my wife does not want to practise brain surgery, engage in espionage, assist or collude in the trafficking of drugs, participate in the overthrow of the American government (though frankly I would not stand in her way), or take part in any other proscribed activity. She just wants to do a little shopping and be legally resident with her family. Doesn't seem too much to ask.

Goodness knows what the hold-up is. Occasionally we get a request for some additional document. Every few months I write to ask what is happening, but I never get a response. Three weeks ago we received a letter from the INS office in London, which we thought must be the official approval at last. Good joke! It was a computer-generated letter saying that because her application had been inactive for twelve months it was being cancelled.

All this is a very roundabout way of getting to a story concerning some British friends of ours here in Hanover. The husband is a professor at the local university, and has been for some years. Eighteen months ago, he and his family went back to England for a year's sabbatical. When they arrived at Heathrow, excited to be home, the immigration officer asked them how long they were staying.

'A year,' my friend answered brightly.

'And what about the American child?' the officer asked with a cocked eyebrow.

Their youngest, you see, had been born in America, and they had never bothered to register him as British. He was only four, so it wasn't as if he would be looking for work or anything.

They explained the situation. The immigration man listened gravely, then went off to consult a supervisor.

It had been eight years since my friends had left Britain, and they weren't sure just how much more like America it might have grown in that period. So they waited uneasily. After a minute the immigration man returned, followed by his supervisor, and said to them in a low voice, 'My supervisor is going to ask you how long you intend to stay in Britain. Say, "Two weeks."'

So the supervisor asked them how long they intended to stay, and they said, 'Two weeks.'

'Good,' said the supervisor, then added as if by way of after-thought, 'It might be an idea to register your child as British within the next day or two, in case you should decide to extend your stay.'

'Of course,' said my friend.

And they were in. And that is why I love Britain. That and the pubs and Branston pickle and country churchyards and a great deal else, but mostly because you still have a public service that is capable of genuine humanity and doesn't act as if it loathes you.

And on that note, I am going to go off and stock up on ammo.

2 March 1997

THE WASTELAND

I HAVE BEEN WATCHING A MOVIE CALLED *MAGNIFICENT OBSESSION*
lately. Made in 1954 and starring Rock Hudson and Jane Wyman, it is
one of those stupefyingly mediocre movies they made in abundance
in the early 1950s when people would still watch almost anything (as
opposed to now when you have to put in lots of fiery explosions and
at least one scene involving the hero abseiling down a liftshaft).

Anyway, if I've got it right, *Magnificent Obsession* involves a handsome young racing-car driver played by Rock who carelessly causes
Ms Wyman to go blind in a car crash. Rock is so consumed with guilt
at this that he goes off and studies eye medicine at the 'University of
Oxford, England', or some place, then comes back to Perfectville
under an assumed name and dedicates his life to restoring Jane's
sight. Only of course she doesn't know it's him on account of she is

blind, as well as apparently a little slow with regard to recognizing the voices of people who have left her maimed.

Needless to say, they fall in love and she gets her sight back. The best scene is when Rock removes her bandages and she says, 'Why, it's . . . *you!*' and slumps into a comely faint, but unfortunately does not strike her head a sharp blow and lose her vision again, which would have improved the story considerably, if you ask me. Also, Jane has a ten-year-old daughter played by one of those syrupy, pig-tailed, revoltingly precocious child actors of the fifties that you just ache to push out of a high window. I expect also Lloyd Nolan is in there somewhere because Lloyd Nolan is always in 1950s movies with parts for doctors.

I may not have all the details right because I have not been watching this movie in order, or even on purpose. I have been watching it because one of our cable channels has shown it at least fifty-four times in the last two months, and I keep coming across it while trawling around looking for something I actually want to watch.

You cannot believe – you really cannot believe – the awfulness, the jaw-slackening direness, of American television. Oh, I know that British TV can be pretty appalling itself. I lived in England for twenty years, so I am well acquainted with the dismay that comes when you look at the television listings and discover that the featured highlights for the evening are *Carry On Ogling*, a nature special on ice maggots of Lake Baikal, and a new Jeremy Beadle series called *Ooh, I Think I May Be Sick*. But even at its grimmest – even when you find yourself choosing between *Prisoner: Cell Block H* and Peter Snow being genuinely interested in European farm subsidies – British TV cannot begin to touch American television for the capacity to make you want to go out and lie down on a motorway.

We get about fifty channels in our house – it is possible on some systems now to get up to 200, I believe – so you think at first that you are going to be spoiled for choice, but you gradually realize that the idea of TV here is simply to fill up the air with any old sludge.

Programmes that even Sky One would be embarrassed to put on (I know, it hardly seems possible, but it is so) here get lavish airtime. It is as if the programmers just pull down a cassette from the shelves and slap it into the machine. I have watched 'current affairs' investigations that were ten years old. I have seen Barbara Walters interviewing people who died a dozen years ago, and weren't that interesting to begin with. Seven nights a week you can watch Johnny Carson shows that were witless in 1976 and now are witless and dated.

There is almost no concept that TV might, just sometimes, be innovative and good. On this very evening, under the category of 'Drama', my cable channel magazine lists as its most sublime and compelling offerings *Matlock* and *Little House on the Prairie*. Tomorrow it recommends *The Waltons* and *Dallas*. The next day it is *Dallas* again and *Murder, She Wrote*.

You begin to wonder who watches it all. One of our channels is a 24-hour cartoon network. That there are people out there who wish to watch cartoons through the night is remarkable enough, but what is truly astounding to me is that the channel carries commercials. What could you possibly sell to people who voluntarily watch Deputy Dawg at 2.30 a.m.? Bibs?

But perhaps the most mind-numbing feature of American television is that the same programmes are shown over and over at the same times each night. Tonight at 9.30 p.m. on Channel 20 we can watch the *Munsters*. Last night at 9.30 p.m. on Channel 20 it was the *Munsters*. Tomorrow night at 9.30 p.m. on Channel 20 it will be – did you guess correctly? – the *Munsters*. Each *Munsters* showing is preceded by an episode of *Happy Days* and followed by an episode of the *Mary Tyler Moore Show*. It has been like this for years, as far as I can tell, and will stay like this for ever.

And it is like this on virtually every channel for every time slot. If you turn on the Discovery channel and find a programme on Hollywood stunts (and you will), you can be certain that the next time you turn to the Discovery channel at the same hour, it will be a programme on Hollywood stunts. Probably it will be the same episode.

With so many channels to choose from, and nearly all of it so hopelessly undiverting, you don't actually watch anything. And that is the scary part of all this. Although American television is totally imbecilic, although it makes you weep and rend your hair and throw soft foods at the screen, it is also strangely irresistible. As a friend once explained to me, you don't watch television here to see what is on, you watch it to see what else is on. And the one thing to be said for American TV is that there is always something else on. You can trawl infinitely. By the time you have reached the fiftieth channel you have forgotten what was on the first, so you start the cycle again in the pathetically optimistic hope that you might find something absorbing this time through.

I haven't begun to cover this topic. TV is my life, so we'll be coming back to this a lot in future months. But I must leave you now. I notice that *Magnificent Obsession* is about to start and I really would like to see Jane Wyman lose her sight. It's the best part. Besides, I keep thinking that if I watch long enough Lloyd Nolan will shove that little girl out of an upstairs window.

9 March 1997

COMMERCIALS, COMMERCIALS, COMMERCIALS

THERE IS AN ADVERT RUNNING ON TELEVISION AT THE MOMENT THAT says something like 'The new Dodge Backfire. Rated number one against the Chrysler Inert for handling. Rated number one against the Plymouth Repellent for mileage. Rated number one against the Ford Eczema for repair costs.'

As you will notice, because luckily for you your brain has not been dented and dimmed by years of over-exposure to rapid-fire American advertising, in each category the Dodge is rated against only one other competitor, which makes comparisons a trifle hollow, if not actually suspect. I mean to say, if the Dodge were rated top against ten or twelve or fifteen competitors in any of these categories, then presumably the ad would have said so. Because it doesn't say so, one must naturally conclude that the Dodge performed worse than all its competitors except the one cited. Ergo, it is effectively inviting you to think twice before buying a Dodge.

The flimsiness of commercial assertions here is something that often leaves me quietly boggled. Last year some other manufacturer proudly boasted that its vehicles had been rated 'tops for reliability among cars manufactured or assembled in the United States', which seemed to me positively to invite the audience to go out and buy a foreign car. But clearly audiences don't see it that way.

Being carefully selective with the truth is a venerable tradition in American advertising. I retain a special fondness for a series of ads run by an insurance company in which 'real people in real situations' discussed their personal finances. When a journalist asked the company who these 'real people' were, a spokesman replied that actually they were actors and 'in that sense they are not real people'. That tells you about as much as you need to know about the American approach to advertising.

To be fair, not all American commercials are vacuous or misleading. Quite a lot of them – well, two of them – are droll and original. I am particularly taken at the moment with a commercial for pizza by the foot in which a deliveryman with an overlong pizza destroys everything he comes in contact with. (My least favourite, for the record, is one in which a gorgeous-and-don't-I-know-it young woman turns to the camera and says, 'Don't hate me because I'm beautiful.' To which I always reply, 'Oh, I don't. I hate you because you make me gip.')

No, the problem with American commercials is that they are simply so constant. Most channels have a commercial break about every five or six minutes. CNN, as far as I can tell, has nothing but commercial breaks.

It occurred to me that this is rather a sweeping statement, so I have just taken a half-hour, at no extra cost to you, to monitor a typical CNN programme, and here are my findings. In a single 30-minute period, CNN interrupted its programme five times to show twenty commercials. Altogether it showed 10 minutes of commercials in a 30-minute slot. Apart from a 7-minute span at the start of the programme, the longest period without commercials was 4 minutes and 59 seconds. The shortest interval between commercials was 2 minutes. For the benefit of people who suffered a serious brain injury during the programme, three of the commercials were repeated.

This, I hasten to add, is completely typical. Last night, one of the networks showed the movie *The Fugitive*, and I did a similar exercise. In order to watch about 100 minutes of movie, it was necessary to sit through almost 50 minutes of commercials, spread over about twenty interruptions. (One every 7 minutes, on average.)

According to Neil Postman in his book *Amusing Ourselves to Death*, the average American is exposed to 1,000 television commercials a week. By the time he is eighteen, the typical American child has sat goggle-eyed through no fewer than 350,000 television adverts.

Increasingly nowadays even when you are not watching commercials you are watching commercials, so to speak. For example, the ABC network recently aired a special on the making of the Disney movie *The Hunchback of Notre Dame*. According to the *New York Times*, several ABC stations also devoted a portion of their evening news broadcasts to 'a gala celebration that Disney threw for the movie in New Orleans'. It just happens that ABC owns the Disney Company.

Meanwhile, the History Channel unveiled plans to run a series called *The Spirit of Enterprise* celebrating the history and achievements of corporations like Boeing, DuPont and General Motors. The programmes were to be made by – yup – the corporations themselves. The History Channel later cancelled the series when it was brought to its attention that the whole undertaking was just too, too tacky.

Less troubled by considerations of credibility and impartiality was CNBC, another cable network, which announced the launch of a weekly news magazine called *Scan*. This programme was to report on all the latest developments in technology – or, to be slightly more precise, on all the latest developments that met with the approval of its sponsor, IBM, to which it had handed editorial control. 'This is not hard news,' a CNBC spokesman explained. 'It is a feature programme.' Oh, well, that makes it all right, then.

In short, commercials are inescapable here – and not just at home. I am appalled to report that many thousands of schools across America now rely, at least in part, on educational materials provided by corporations, so that pupils are learning about nutrition from

McDonald's and conservation and the environment from Exxon, among others. Since 1989, a company called Channel One has been beaming educational programmes to schools via a closed-circuit system. The programmes are free but they are interspersed with commercials aimed specifically at young audiences. Now I would call that obviously, palpably unacceptable and exploitative, but this is evidently a minority view. Channel One has been a big hit; its sets are in 350,000 classrooms.

Even Sesame Street programmes – this is truly heartbreaking – have become, in the words of the *Boston Globe*, 'uninterrupted 30-minute commercials'. As the *Globe* points out, Sesame Street products generate over $800 million in retail sales every year, and its executives enjoy salaries of up to $200,000 a year. Yet because the programme is aired on public television here, it receives an annual government subsidy of $7 million.

I was about to say think what would happen if that $7 million were spent instead on inner-city schools, but then it occurred to me that what would happen is that they would go out and buy more TVs to hook more classrooms into Channel One.

Inevitably, this has made my brain throb, so I'm off to take a Tylenol. I understand that in a survey it was preferred over other brands by two to one. Or maybe I'm thinking of Pepsi.

16 March 1997

FRIENDLY PEOPLE

I WAS INTENDING THIS WEEK TO WRITE ABOUT SOME EXASPERATION OR other of modern American life when Mrs Bryson (who is, may I say, a dear woman) brought me a cup of coffee, read the first few lines off the computer screen, and muttered, 'Bitch, bitch, bitch,' and shuffled off.

'Pardon, my dewy English rose?' I called.

'You're always complaining in that column.'

'But the world needs righting, my luscious, cherry-cheeked daughter of Boadicea,' I rejoined tranquilly. 'Besides, complaining is what I do.'

'Complaining is all you do.'

Well, excuse me, but not quite. I believe on these very pages I once said a few words of praise for American garbage disposal units and I clearly recall commending our local post office for providing me with a free doughnut on Customer Appreciation Day. But perhaps she had a point.

There are many wonderful things about the United States of America that deserve praise – the Bill of Rights, the Freedom of Information Act and free bookmatches are three that leap to mind – but none is more outstanding than the friendliness of the people.

When we moved to this little town in New Hampshire, people received us as if the one thing that had kept them from total happiness to this point was the absence of us in their lives. They brought us cakes and pies and bottles of wine. Not one of them said, 'So you're the people who paid a fortune for the Smith place,' which I believe is the traditional greeting in England. Our next-door neighbours, upon learning that we were intending to go out to eat, protested that it was too dreary to dine in a strange restaurant on one's first night in a new town and insisted we come to them for dinner there and then, as if feeding six extra mouths was the most trifling of burdens.

When word got round that our furniture was on a container ship making its way from Liverpool to Boston, evidently by way of Port Said, Mombasa and the Galápagos Islands, and that we were temporarily without anything to sleep on, sit on, or eat from, a stream of friendly strangers (many of whom I have not seen since) began traipsing up the walk with chairs, lamps, tables, even a microwave oven.

It was dazzling, and it has remained so. At Christmas this year we went to England for ten days and returned home late at night and hungry to find that a neighbour had stocked the fridge with both essentials and goodies, and filled vases with fresh flowers. This sort of thing happens all the time.

Recently I went with one of my children to a local college basketball game. We arrived just before game time and joined a queue at one of the ticket windows. After a minute a man came up to me and said, 'Are you waiting to buy tickets?'

No, I wanted to reply, I'm standing here to make the line more impressive, but of course all I said was, 'Yes, I am.'

'Because you can have these,' he said and thrust two tickets at me.

My immediate thought, born of years of stupidly misreading situations, was that he was a tout and that there must be some catch. 'How much?' I said warily.

'No, no, you can have them. For free. We can't go to the game, you see.' He indicated a car outside with the motor running and a woman in the passenger seat.

'Really?' I said. 'Well, thank you very much.' And then I was struck by a thought. 'Did you make a special trip here to give away two tickets?'

'They were going to go to waste otherwise,' he said apologetically. 'Enjoy the game.'

I could go on and on about this sort of thing – about the young man who returned my son's lost wallet with nearly all his summer's wages in it and wouldn't take a reward, about the employees of the cinema who go out if it starts to rain and roll up all the windows of cars parked along nearby streets on the assumption that at least some of them will belong to cinema customers who don't know it is raining, how after the wife of the local police chief lost her hair during chemotherapy treatment every member of the force had his head shaved to raise money for a cancer charity and to make the chief's wife feel less conspicuous.

That people leave their cars unlocked and the windows open tells you something more about the town, of course. The fact is, there is no crime here. None. People will casually leave a $500 bicycle propped against a tree and go off to do their shopping. If someone did steal it, I am almost certain the victim would run after the thief shouting, 'Could you please return it to 32 Wilson Avenue when you've finished? And watch out for the third gear – it sticks.'

No one locks anything. I remember being astounded by this on my first visit when an estate agent took me out to look at houses (and there's another thing – estate agents in America know how to stand up and move around) and she kept leaving her car unlocked, even when we went into a restaurant for lunch and even though there was a portable phone on the seat and some shopping in the back.

At one of the houses she discovered she had brought the wrong key. 'Back door'll be unlocked,' she announced confidently, and it was. I subsequently realized that there was nothing unusual in this. We know people who go away on holiday without locking their doors, don't know where their house key is, aren't even sure if they still have one.

Now you might reasonably wonder why, then, this is not a thief's paradise. There are two reasons, I believe. First, there is no market for stolen goods here. If you sidled up to anyone in New Hampshire and said, 'Wanna buy a car stereo?' the person would look at you as if you were off your head and say, 'No, I already have a car stereo.' Then they would report you to the police and – here is the second thing – the police would come and shoot you.

But of course the police don't shoot people here because they don't need to because there is no crime. It is a rare and heartwarming example of a virtuous circle. We have grown used to this now, but when we were still new in town and I expressed wonder about it all to a woman who grew up in New York City but has lived here for twenty years, she laid a hand on my arm and said, as if imparting a great secret, 'Honey, you're not in the real world any longer. You're in New Hampshire.'

23 March 1997

ON THE HOTLINE

I CAME ACROSS SOMETHING IN OUR BATHROOM THE OTHER DAY WHICH has occupied my thoughts off and on since. It was a little dispenser of dental floss.

It isn't the floss itself that is of interest to me, but that the container has a freephone number printed on it. You can call the company's Floss Hotline 24 hours a day. But here is the question: Why would you need to? I keep imagining some guy calling up and saying in an anxious voice, 'OK, I've got the floss. Now what?'

As a rule of thumb, I would submit that if you need to call your floss provider, for any reason, you are probably not ready for this level of oral hygiene.

My curiosity aroused, I had a look through all our cupboards and discovered with interest that nearly all household products in America carry a hotline number. You can, it appears, ring up for guidance on how to use soap and shampoo, gain helpful tips on where to store ice cream so that it doesn't turn to soup and run out of the bottom of the container, and receive professional advice on which parts of your body you can most successfully and stylishly apply nail polish. ('So let me get this straight. You're saying *not* on my forehead?')

For those who do not have access to a telephone, or who perhaps have a telephone but have not yet mastered its use, most products also carry helpful printed tips such as 'Remove Shells Before Eating' (on peanuts) and 'Caution: Do Not Re-Use as Beverage Container' (on a bleach bottle). We recently bought an electric iron which admonished us, among other things, not to use it in conjunction with explosive materials. In a broadly similar vein, I read a couple of weeks ago that computer software companies are considering re-writing the instruction 'Strike Any Key When Ready' because so many people have been calling in to say they cannot find the 'Any' key.

Until a few days ago my instinct would have been to chortle richly at people who need this sort of elemental guidance, but then three things happened that made me modify my views.

First, I read in the paper how John Smoltz, a pitcher for the Atlanta Braves baseball team, showed up at a training session one day with a painful-looking red welt across his chest and, when pressed for an explanation, sheepishly admitted that he had tried to iron a shirt while he was wearing it.

Second, it occurred to me that although I have never done any-thing quite so foolish as that, it was only because I had not thought of it.

Third, and perhaps most conclusively, two nights ago I went out to run two small errands – specifically, to buy some pipe tobacco and post some letters. I bought the tobacco, carried it straight across the street to a Post Office letter box, opened the lid, and deposited it. I won't tell you how far I walked before it dawned on me that this was not a 100 per cent correct execution of my original plans.

You see my problem. People who need labels on pillarboxes say-ing 'Not for Deposit of Tobacco or Other Personal Items' can't very well smirk at others, even those who iron their chests or have to seek lathering guidance from a shampoo hotline.

I mentioned all this at dinner the other night and was appalled to see the enthusiasm and alacrity with which all the members of the family began suggesting labels that would be particularly apt for me, like 'Caution: When Door Says "Pull" It's Absolutely No Use Pushing' and 'Warning: Do Not Attempt to Remove Sweater Over Head While Walking Among Chairs and Tables'. A particular favourite was 'Caution: Ensure That Shirt Buttons Are in Correct Holes Before Leaving House'. This went on for some hours.

I concede that I am somewhat inept with regard to memory, personal grooming, walking through low doorways, and much else, but the thing is it's my genes. Allow me to explain.

I recently tore out of the newspaper an article concerning a study at the University of Michigan, or perhaps it was the University of Minnesota (at any rate it was somewhere cold with 'University' in the title), which found that absent-mindedness is a genetically inherited trait. I put it in a file marked 'Absent-Mindedness' and, of course, immediately mislaid the file.

However, in searching for it this morning I found another file intriguingly marked 'Genes and So On', which is just as interesting and – here was the lucky part – not altogether irrelevant. In it I found a copy of a report from the 29 November 1996 issue of the journal *Science* entitled 'Association of Anxiety-Related Traits with a Polymorphism in the Serotonin Transporter Gene Regulatory Region'.

Now to be perfectly frank, I don't follow polymorphism in serotonin transporters as closely as I ought, at least not during basketball season, but when I saw the sentence 'By regulating the magnitude and duration of serotonergic responses, the 5-HT transporter (5-HTT) is central to the fine-tuning of brain serotonergic neurotransmission,' I thought, *Hey, these fellows could be onto something.*

The upshot of the study is that scientists have located a gene (specifically gene number SLC6A4 on chromosome 17q12, in case you want to experiment at home) which determines whether you are a born worrier or not. To be absolutely precise, if you have a long version of the SLC6A4 gene, you are very probably easy-going and serene, whereas if you have the short version you can't leave home without saying at some point, 'Stop the car. I think I left the bath-water running.'

What this means in practice is that if you are not a born worrier then you have nothing to worry about (though of course you wouldn't be worrying anyway), whereas if you *are* a worrier by nature there is absolutely nothing you can do about it, so you may as well stop worrying, except of course you can't. Now put this together with the aforementioned findings about absent-mindedness at the University of Somewhere Cold, and I think you can see that our genes have a great deal to answer for.

Here's another interesting fact from my 'Genes and So On' file. According to Richard Dawkins in *The Blind Watchmaker*, each one of the 10 trillion cells in the human body contains more genetic information than the entire *Encyclopedia Britannica* (and without sending a salesman to your door), yet it appears that 90 per cent of all our genetic material doesn't do anything at all. It just sits there, like Uncle Fred and Aunt Muriel when they drop by on a Sunday.

From this I believe we can draw four important conclusions, namely: (1) Even though your genes don't do much they can let you down in a lot of embarrassing ways, (2) always post your letters first, then buy the tobacco, (3) never promise a list of four things if you can't remember the fourth one, and (4).

30 March 1997

THOSE BORING FOREIGNERS

JULIAN BARNES, IN A LINE I INTEND TO MAKE MY OWN WHEN THE moment is right, once observed that any foreigner visiting the United States can perform an easy magic trick: 'Buy a newspaper and see your own country disappear.'

Actually, you don't need to read a newspaper. You can read a magazine or watch TV or just talk to people. My son recently reported to me that in a current affairs quiz in one of his high school classes only one person was able to name the British prime minister, and he was that person. I am quite certain that not one American in 500 has any idea that a general election is looming in the UK.

Of course, let's be fair, most people in most places don't know much about the rest of the world. I mean to say, could you name the leaders of Denmark or The Netherlands or even Ireland? Of course you couldn't – and you are immensely intelligent and attentive. I can see that from here. No reason why you should. There is a lot of world out there to follow, and you have your hands full just keeping up with *EastEnders*. I understand.

But there is a difference. You are at least vaguely aware from reading the papers and watching or listening to the news that there is a world beyond the English Channel, and that people are doing things in that world (mostly blockading ports and making life jolly difficult for law-abiding lorry drivers from more civil nations, if memory serves).

It used to be like that here. *Time* magazine would be full of stories about tottering coalition governments in Italy and corruption scandals in South America, and the evening news would have at least a sprinkling of reports each showing a serious-looking correspondent in a Burberry standing with a microphone in front of a bourse or sampan or Congress of the People's Revolution – something in any case that was patently not in Nebraska. Even if you paid no attention to these dispatches, they at least reminded you that you existed in a wider world.

No longer. In the first three months of this year the US edition of *Time* did not have a single report from France, Italy, Spain or Japan, to name just a few of the countries that seem to have escaped its notice. Britain made it into the pages only because of Dolly the cloned sheep. Germany got in because of the government's row there with Scientologists. Otherwise all has been darkness in Western Europe. The 'International' section of *Time* these days generally consists of a single story, almost never more than two. The amazing thing is that if you look at the masthead, *Time* has correspondents all over – in Paris, London, Rome, Vienna, you name it. Give me one of those jobs, please!

Television news is no better. Just to make sure I wasn't talking through my hat here (or indeed anything else round and inappropriate), I monitored the NBC evening news last night. This is one of the main national news programmes, the equivalent of the BBC's *Six o'Clock News*, but with the addition of several minutes of advertising for denture fixatives, haemorrhoid creams and laxatives. (People who watch the evening news in America are evidently in a bad way.)

The NBC bulletin consisted of eleven items, of which ten were exclusively about the United States. Only one, concerning a visit by Vice-President Gore to China, acknowledged life beyond American shores, though in fact the report was really about American trade prospects and anyway lasted just 22 seconds. Still, it did include a two-second shot of flocks of people riding bicycles in front of a pagoda-like structure, so I guess it counts.

Later, I undertook a similar exercise with CNN's main evening bulletin. It lasted an hour, so it offered even more adverts for painkillers, salves and mentholated unguents (somebody really should get these viewers to a hospital), but also managed to squeeze in twenty-two snippets of news, of which all twenty-two were about the United States. This on a programme that calls itself *The World Today*.

Because there is so little exposure to non-American things, people here often get quite severely out of patience with anything that is not immediately recognizable to them. I have before me a review from the *New York Times* of a book by the British journalist Stephen Fay on Nick Leeson and the collapse of Barings, in which the reviewer complains, with really quite profound irritation, that the book is 'littered with needlessly confusing Britspeak'. Among the confounding expressions she cites are 'cock-up', 'just not on' and a reference to a trading floor being 'the size of a football pitch'. Well, imagine that – a book by a British writer about a British employee of a British bank containing some British expressions. That is, like, *so* inconsiderate. The next thing, they'll be expecting us to know who the prime minister is.

I find that sad. One of the things I liked about reading British books or watching British films when I was growing up was *not* knowing precisely what was going on – wondering what the characters meant when they said, 'I say, we jolly well knocked Jerry out of touch for six into a sticky wicket with those bouncing buzz bombs the boffins in G-section came up with at high tea yesterday fortnight, what?' and trying to deduce what Marmite could possibly be (never for a moment guessing that it's an edible lubricant). Americans don't want to do that now, I'm afraid.

I recently sat through a showing of *The English Patient* at our local cinema in which a woman behind me followed every line spoken by Juliette Binoche by turning to her partner and saying in a loud, pained, nasal voice, 'What's she *saying*?' It became so irksome that I finally had to smother the woman with my jacket.

In the same week, I read a newspaper review of a Jackie Chan movie in which the reviewer complained, again with deep exasperation, that Chan's dialogue was incomprehensible to him. (Hint to reviewer: the appeal of Jackie Chan movies does not lie in the quality of the discourse.) I have heard or read similar complaints about all or parts of *Secrets and Lies*, *My Left Foot*, *The Commitments*, *Shine*, *Shallow Grave* – indeed, almost any film to emerge from the non-American-speaking world.

I could go on and on, but alas I am out of space and I sense that you can't wait to get to the wireless to hear the outcome of those Belgian by-elections. Meanwhile, I shall be monitoring British affairs as closely as I can from here. But I would ask just one thing. If Mrs Thatcher is turned out of office, let me know at once. And please stop calling it a wireless.

6 April 1997

THE CUPHOLDER REVOLUTION

I AM ASSURED THAT THIS IS A TRUE STORY.

A man calls up his computer helpline complaining that the cupholder on his personal computer has snapped off, and he wants to know how to get it fixed.

'Cupholder?' says the computer helpline person, puzzled. 'I'm sorry, sir, but I'm confused. Did you buy this cupholder at a computer show or receive it as a special promotion?'

'No, it came as part of the standard equipment on my computer.'

'But our computers don't come with cupholders.'

'Well, pardon me, friend, but they do,' says the man a little hotly. 'I'm looking at mine right now. You push a button on the base of the machine and it slides right out.'

The man, it transpired, had been using the CD drawer in his computer to hold his coffee cup.

I bring this up here by way of introducing our topic this week: cupholders. I don't know if cupholders exist in Britain yet, but if not, trust me, they are on their way. Cupholders are taking over the world.

If you are not familiar with them, cupholders are little trays, lids or other receptacles with holes for holding cups and other drinks containers, which are found in multiple locations throughout every modern American automobile. Often they are mounted on the backs of seats or built into armrests, but just as often they are ingeniously tucked away in places you would never think to look for a beverage stowage device. Generally, in my experience, if you push an unfamiliar button anywhere in an American car, either it will activate the back windscreen wiper, which will rub with a heavy dragging noise across the glass once every six seconds for the rest of eternity no matter what you do to try to stop it, or it will make a cupholder slide out, rise up, drop down or otherwise magically enter your life.

It would be almost impossible to exaggerate the importance of cupholders in American automotive circles these days. The *New York Times* recently ran a long article in which it tested a dozen family cars. It rated each of them for ten features, such as engine size, boot space, handling, quality of suspension, and, yes, number of cupholders. A car dealer acquaintance of ours tells us that they are one of the first things people remark on, ask about or play with when they come to look at a car. People buy cars on the basis of cupholders. Nearly all car advertisements note them prominently in the text.

Some cars, like the newest model of the Dodge Caravan, come with as many as seventeen cupholders. Seventeen! The largest Caravan holds seven passengers. You don't have to be a nuclear physicist, or even wide awake, to work out that that is 2.43 cupholders per passenger. Why, you may reasonably wonder, would each passenger in a vehicle need 2.43 cupholders? Good question.

Americans, it is true, consume positively staggering volumes of fluids. One of our local petrol stations, I am told, sells a flavoured confection called a Slurpee in containers up to 60 ounces in size. That is three English pints of sickly stuff that turns your tongue blue. But even if every member of the family had a Slurpee *and* a personal bottle of Milk of Magnesia for dealing with the after-effects, that would still leave three cupholders spare.

There is a long tradition of endowing the interiors of American cars with lots of gadgets and comforts, and I suppose a superfluity of cupholders is just an outgrowth of that tradition.

The reason Americans want a lot of comfort in their cars is because they live in them. Almost 94 per cent of all American trips from home involve the use of a car. (The figure in Britain is about 60 per cent, which is bad enough.) People in America don't just use their cars to get to the shops, but to get between shops. Most businesses in America have their own car parks, so someone running six errands will generally move the car six times on a single outing, even to get between two places on opposite sides of the same street.

There are 200 million cars in the United States – 40 per cent of the world's total, for about 5 per cent of its population – and an additional two million new ones hit the roads each month (though obviously many are also retired). Even so, there are about twice as many cars in America as there were twenty years ago, driving on twice as many roads, racking up about twice as many miles.

So, because Americans have a lot of cars and spend a lot of time in them, they like a lot of comforts. However, there is a limit to how many different features you can fit into a car interior. What better, then, than to festoon it with nifty cupholders, particularly when people seem to go for them in a big way? That's my theory.

What is certainly true is that not putting cupholders in a car is a serious mistake. I read a couple of years ago that Volvo had to redesign all its cars for the American market for this very reason. Volvo's engineers had foolishly thought that what buyers were looking for was a reliable engine, side-impact bars and heated seats, when in fact what they craved was little trays into which to insert their Slurpees. So a bunch of guys named Nils Nilsson and Lars Larsson were put to work designing cupholders into the system, and Volvo was thus saved from beverage ignominy, if not actual financial ruin.

Now from all the foregoing we can draw one important conclusion – that no matter how hard you try, it is not quite possible to fill a column space with a discussion just of cupholders.

So let me tell you how I happen to know that those fellows at Volvo were called Nils Nilsson and Lars Larsson.

Some years ago when I was in Stockholm and had nothing better to do one evening (it was after 7 p.m., you see, so the city had long since turned in for the night), I passed the hours before bedtime thumbing idly through the local phone directory and tallying various names. I had heard that there were only a handful of surnames in Sweden, and this was essentially so. I counted over 2,000 each for Eriksson, Svensson, Nilsson and Larsson. There were so few names (or, it has to be said, the Swedes were so cosmically dull) that many people used the same name twice. There were 212 people in Stockholm named Erik Eriksson, 117 named Sven Svensson, 126 named Nils Nilsson and 259 named Lars Larsson. I wrote these names and numbers down on a piece of paper, and have been wondering all these years when I would ever find a use for it.

From this, I believe, we can draw two further conclusions. Save all scraps of paper bearing useless information, for one day you may be glad you did, and if you go to Stockholm, take drink.

13 April 1997

YOUR TAX FORM EXPLAINED

ENCLOSED IS YOUR 1997 UNITED STATES INTERNAL REVENUE SERVICE TAX
Form 1040-ES OCR: 'Estimated Tax for Self-Employed Individuals'.
You may use this form to estimate your 1997 fiscal year tax *if*:

1. You are the head of a household *and* the sum of the ages of
your spouse and dependents, minus the ages of qualifying pets
(see Schedule 12G), is divisible by a whole number. (Use
Supplementary Schedule 142C if pets are deceased but buried on
your property.)

2. Your Gross Adjusted Income does not exceed your Adjusted
Gross Income (except where applicable) *and* you did not pay taxable
interest on dividend income prior to 1903.

3. You are not claiming a foreign tax credit, except as a 'foreign' tax credit. (Warning: claiming a foreign tax credit for a foreign 'tax' credit, except where a foreign 'tax credit' is involved, may result in a fine of $125,000 and 25 years' imprisonment.)

4. You are one of the following: married and filing jointly; married and not filing jointly; not married and not filing jointly; jointed but not filing; other.

INSTRUCTIONS

Type all answers in ink with a number two lead pencil. Do not cross anything out. Do not use abbreviations or ditto marks. Do not misspell 'miscellaneous'. Write your name, address and social security number, and the name, address and social security numbers of your spouse and dependents, in full on each page twice. Do not put a tick in a box marked 'cross' or a cross in a box marked 'tick' unless it is your wish to do the whole thing again. Do not write 'Search me' in any blank spaces. Do not make anything up.

Complete sections 47 to 52 first, then proceed to even-numbered sections and complete in reverse order. Do *not* use this form if your total pensions and annuities disbursements were greater than your advanced earned income credits *or* vice versa.

Under 'Income', list all wages, salaries, net foreign source taxable income, royalties, tips, gratuities, taxable interest, capital gains, air miles, pints paid on, and money found down the back of the sofa. If your earnings are derived wholly, or partially but not primarily, or wholly *and* partially but not primarily, from countries other than the United States (if uncertain, see USIA Leaflet 212W, 'Countries That Are Not the United States') *or* your rotated gross income from Schedule H was greater than your earned income credit on non-taxable net disbursements, you *must* include a Grantor/Transferror Waiver Voucher. Failure to do so may result in a fine of $1,500,000 and seizure of a child.

Under Section 890f, list total farm income (if none, give details). If you were born after 1 January 1897, and are *not* a widow(er), include excess casualty losses and provide carryover figures for depreciation on line 27iii. You must list number of turkeys slaughtered for export. Subtract, but do not deduct, net gross dividends from pro rata interest payments, multiply by the total number of steps in your home, and enter on line 356d.

On Schedule F1001, line c, list the contents of your garage. Include all electrical and non-electrical items on Schedule 295D, but do not include electrical or non-electrical items not listed on Supplementary Form 243d.

Under 'Personal Expenditures', itemize all cash expenditures of more than $1, and include verification. If you have had dental work *and* you are not claiming a refund on the federal oil spill allowance, enter your shoe sizes since birth and enclose specimen shoes. (Right foot only.) Multiply by 1.5 or 1,319, whichever is larger, and divide line 3f by 3d. Under Section 912g, enter federal income support grants for the production of alfalfa, barley (but not sorghum, unless for home consumption) and okra *whether or not* you received any. Failure to do so may result in a fine of $3,750,000 and death by lethal injection.

If your children are dependent but not living at home, or living at home but not dependent, or dependent and living at home but hardly ever there *and* you are not claiming exemption for leases of maritime vessels in excess of 12,000 tonnes deadweight (15,000 tonnes if you were born in Guam), you *must* complete and include a Maritime Vessel Exemption Form. Failure to do so may result in a fine of $111,000,000 and a nuclear attack on a small, neutral country.

On pages 924–926, Schedule D, enter the names of people you know personally who are Communist or use drugs. (Use extra pages if necessary.)

If you have interest earnings from savings accounts, securities, bearer bonds, certificates of deposit or other fiduciary instruments but *do not* know your hat size, complete Supplementary Schedules 112d and 112f and enclose with all relevant tables. (Do not send chairs at this time.) Include, but do not collate, ongoing losses from mining investments, commodities transactions and organ transplants, divide by the total number of motel visits you made in 1996, and enter in any remaining spaces. If you have unreimbursed employee expenses, tough.

To compute your estimated tax, add lines 27 through 964, deduct lines 45a and 699f from Schedule 2F (if greater or less than 2.2% of average alternative minimum estimated tax for last five years), multiply by the number of RPMs your car registers when stuck on ice, and add 2. If line 997 is smaller than line 998, start again. In the space marked 'Tax Due', write a very large figure.

Make your cheque payable to 'Internal Revenue Service of the

United States of America and to the Republic for Which It Stands',
and mark for the attention of Patty. On the back of your cheque write
your social security number, Taxpayer Identification Number, IRS
Tax Code Audit Number(s), IRS Regional Office Sub-Unit Zone
Number (*unless* you are filing a T/45 Sub-Unit Zone Exclusion
Notice), sexual orientation and smoking preference, and send to:

Internal Revenue Service of the United States of America
Tax Reception and Orientation Center
Building D/Annexe G78
Suite 900
Subduction Zone 12
Box 132677-02
Drawer 2, About Halfway Back
Federal City
Maryland 10001

If you have any questions about filing, or require assistance with
your return, phone 1-800-BUSY SIGNAL. Thank you and have a
prosperous 1998. Failure to do so may result in a fine of $125,000
and a long walk to the cooler.

20 April 1997

WARNING: ANYONE HAVING FUN
WILL BE REPORTED

ONE OF OUR BARS HERE IN THE SWEET AND ORDERLY LITTLE TOWN IN NEW
Hampshire in which I live recently placed small printed notices in
plastic holders on each of the tables – the sort of notices that normally
invite you to order a jug of pina coladas at a special price or perhaps
join mine hosts Chip and Tiffany for their convivial daily happy hour.

However, far from inviting anyone to engage in anything as
hedonistic as that, what these notices said was this: 'We take our
responsibility to the community seriously. Therefore we are introducing a policy of limiting each customer to a maximum of three
drinks. We thank you for your understanding and cooperation.'

When a bar (and in a college town at that) starts telling you that you must leave after as little as three bottles of beer – that's about one and a half English pints – you know something is going on. The problem isn't that townsfolk here in Hanover have been disgracing themselves, you understand. The problem is that they might enjoy themselves more than the modest amount that is deemed socially acceptable in this challenging age in which we live.

H.L. Mencken once defined puritanism as 'the haunting fear that someone, somewhere, may be happy'. It was seventy years ago that he said it, but it is as true today as it was then. Everywhere you turn in America these days you encounter a strange and insistent kind of nannying, as in these preposterous new notices in our local bar.

The thing is, the notices are in any case completely unnecessary. I have discovered to my dismay that when an American friend invites you out for a beer that is exactly what he means – a beer. You sip it delicately for about 45 minutes until it is gone and then your companion says, 'Hey, that was fun. Let's do it again next year.' I don't know anybody – anybody – who would be so rakish as to consume three drinks at a sitting. All the people I know barely drink at all, never touch tobacco, watch their cholesterol as if it were HIV-positive, jog up to Canada and back about twice a day, and go to bed early. Now that is all very sensible and I know they will outlive me by decades, but it isn't much fun.

And Americans these days find the most extraordinary things to worry about. Newspaper reviews of movies, for instance, nearly always end with a paragraph noting what qualities the film contains that viewers may find disturbing – violence, sexual content, strong language, and so on. That seems unobjectionable enough in principle, but what is remarkable is the things the papers believe worthy of inclusion. The *New York Times* recently concluded a review of a new Chevy Chase movie with this sombre warning: '*Vegas Vacation* is rated PG (Parental Guidance suggested). Besides sexual suggestiveness, it shows rattlesnakes and gambling.'

Oh well, that's out, then.

The *Los Angeles Times*, meanwhile, warns its readers that *As Good as It Gets* contains 'strong language and thematic elements' (whatever they are), while *Mouse Hunt* has 'mayhem, comic sensuality and language'. Not strong language or suggestive language, but just 'language'. My God, think of it. Language in a movie! Not to mention mayhem. And to think I nearly took the children.

There is, in short, a huge and preposterous disquiet in the land about almost everything. The bookshops and bestseller lists are full of books like Robert Bork's *Slouching to Gomorrah*, suggesting that America is on the brink of some catastrophic moral collapse. Among the literally hundreds of things Bork is worried about are 'the angry activists of feminism, homosexuality, environmentalism [and] animal rights'. Oh, please.

Things that would raise barely a flicker in other countries are here looked upon as almost dangerously licentious. A woman in Hartford, Connecticut, recently was threatened with arrest when a security guard saw her breastfeeding her baby – discreetly, mind you, with a baby blanket over her shoulder and her back turned to the world – in her car in a remote corner of a restaurant car park. She had left the restaurant and gone to her car to feed the baby because it was more private – but not private enough. Someone with binoculars might have glimpsed what she was doing, and, well, you can imagine the consequences for a stable and orderly society.

Meanwhile, in Boulder, Colorado, which has one of the strictest anti-smoking ordinances in America (i.e., they shoot you), an actor in an amateur stage production was threatened with arrest, if you can believe it, for smoking a cigarette onstage during a performance, as his part required. Smoking is of course the great forbidden activity these days. Light up a cigarette almost anywhere in America now and you are looked upon as a pariah. Light up indoors in a public place and you will almost certainly be swept upon by a phalanx of security people.

Many states – Vermont and California to name two – have laws making it illegal to smoke virtually anywhere indoors, apart from private residences, and often even outdoors. Now I'm all for discouraging smoking, but increasingly this is getting carried to neurotic and even sinister extremes. A company here in New Hampshire recently instituted a policy that any employee who is suspected of having smoked a cigarette within 45 minutes of coming to work faces dismissal, even if he was smoking within the privacy of his own home, on his own time, with government-approved smoking materials.

But the most amazing thing of all is that even young people are voluntarily relinquishing fun. One of the most astounding stories I have encountered lately was a report in the *Boston Globe* last month that two college fraternity organizations – live-in clubs for university students – are banning intoxicating beverages of all kinds from their chapters.

If any student is found on the premises with a single can of beer – no matter that he may be legally entitled by age to own it and drink it – he will be instantly dismissed, and if the fraternity house itself dares to organize a function involving so much as a thimble of sherry, it will be summarily shut down without appeal.

When I was young the whole apparent purpose of fraternities was to keep America's breweries humming. You could judge the quality of a fraternity by the number of bodies on the lawn on a Saturday night. Now I am not arguing for unbridled alcoholic consumption at universities (actually I am, but we'll pretend I'm not). But to suggest that a bunch of students can't knock back a few beers on graduation day or after a big football victory or upon the conclusion of final exams, or, what the hell, whenever they want seems to me ludicrously puritanical.

Astonishingly, all but one of the several students quoted in the article favoured the new proposal.

'It's about time we had a policy like this,' said one priggish young scholar from the Massachusetts Institute of Technology, who, in my view, wants a good sound slapping.

Call me heartless, but I hope the next movie he sees has scenes involving rattlesnakes, gambling, thematic elements and language, and that it disturbs the dickens out of him. Wouldn't that just serve him right?

27 April 1997

THE STATES EXPLAINED

MY FATHER, WHO LIKE ALL DADS SOMETIMES SEEMED TO BE PRACTISING
for a world's most boring man competition, used to have the habit,
when I was a boy, of identifying and reporting the state of origin of
all the other cars on any highway we happened to be travelling along.

In America, as I expect you know, each state issues its own
numberplates, so you can tell at a glance where another car is from,
which enabled my father to make trenchant observations like, 'Hey,
another car from Wyoming. That's three this morning.' Or:
'Mississippi. Wonder what he's doing way up here?' Then he would
look around hopefully to see if anyone wanted to elaborate or offer
speculation, but no one ever did. He could go on like that all day, and
often did.

I once wrote a book making good-natured fun of the old man for
his many interesting and unusual talents when behind the wheel – the
unerring ability to get lost in any city, to drive the wrong way down a

one-way street so many times that people would eventually come and watch from their doorways, or spend an entire afternoon driving around within sight of an amusement park or other eagerly sought attraction without actually finding the entrance. One of my teenaged children recently read that book for the first time and came with it into the kitchen where my wife was cooking and said in a tone of amazed discovery, 'But this is *Dad*,' meaning of course me.

I have to admit it. I have become my father. I even read number-plates, though my particular interest is the slogans. Many states, you see, include a friendly message or nugget of information on their plates, like 'Land of Lincoln' for Illinois, 'Vacationland' for Maine, 'Sunshine State' for Florida, and the zippily inane 'Shore Thing' for New Jersey.

I like to make quips and comments on these so when, for instance, we see Pennsylvania's 'You've Got a Friend in Pennsylvania', I turn to the passengers and say in an injured tone, 'Then why doesn't he call?' However, I am the only one who finds this an amusing way to pass a long journey.

It's interesting – well, perhaps not interesting exactly, but certainly a fact – that many states append slogans that are pretty well meaningless. I have never understood what Ohio was thinking when it called itself the 'Buckeye State' and I haven't the remotest idea what New York means by dubbing itself the 'Empire State'. As far as I am aware, New York's many undoubted glories do not include overseas possessions.

Indiana, meanwhile, calls itself the 'Hoosier State' and has done for 150 years. No one has ever satisfactorily deduced (possibly because who after all cares?) where the term comes from, though I can tell you from experience that if you mention this in a book 250 people from Indiana will write to you with 250 different explanations and the unanimous view that you are a dunce.

All this is by way of introducing our important lesson of the day, namely that the United States isn't so much a country as a collection of fifty small independent nations, and you forget this at your peril. It all goes back to the setting up of a federal government after the War of Independence when the former colonies didn't trust each other. In order to keep them happy, the states were given an extra-ordinary range of powers. Even now each state controls all kinds of matters to do with your personal life – where, when and at what age you can legally drink; whether you may carry a concealed weapon, own fireworks, or legally gamble; how old you have to be to drive; whether you will be killed in the electric chair, by lethal injection or not at all, and how bad you have to be to get yourself in such a fix; and so on.

If I leave our town of Hanover, and drive over the Connecticut River to Vermont, I will find myself suddenly subject to perhaps 500 completely different laws. I must, among much else, buckle my seat belt, acquire a licence if I wish to practise dentistry, and give up all hope of erecting roadside hoardings, since Vermont is one of just two states to outlaw highway advertising. On the other hand, I may carry a gun on my person with impunity and if I am arrested for drunken driving I may legally decline to give a blood sample.

Since I always buckle up anyway, don't own a gun, and haven't the faintest desire to stick my fingers in other people's mouths, even for very good money, these matters don't impinge on me. Elsewhere, however, differences between state laws can be dramatic, even alarming.

States decide what may or may not be taught in their schools, and in many places, particularly in the Deep South, curricula must accord with very narrow religious views. In Alabama, for instance, it is illegal to teach evolution as anything other than an 'unproven belief'. All biology textbooks must carry a disclaimer stating 'This textbook discusses evolution, a controversial theory some scientists present as a scientific explanation for the origin of living things.' By law, teachers must give equal weight to the notion that Earth was created in seven days and everything on it – fossils, coal deposits, dinosaur bones – is no more than 7,500 years old. I don't know what slogan Alabama puts on its numberplates, but 'Proud to Be Backward' sounds apt to me.

I shouldn't talk because New Hampshire has some pretty retrograde laws of its own. It is the only state that declines to observe Martin Luther King Day (he associated with communists, you see) and one of only a couple not to guarantee at least a few basic rights to gay people. Worse, it has the most demented numberplate slogan, the strange and pugnacious 'Live Free or Die'. Perhaps I take these things too literally, but I really don't like driving around with an explicit vow to expire if things don't go right. I would much prefer something a bit more equivocal and less terminal – 'Live Free or Pout' perhaps, or 'Live Free If It's All the Same to You Thanks Very Much'.

On the other hand, New Hampshire is the only state to guarantee in its constitution the right of the people to rise up and overthrow the government. I have no intention of exercising this option, you understand, but there is a certain comfort in having it in reserve, especially if they start messing with our schoolbooks.

4 May 1997

THE WAR ON DRUGS

1 cortaderia. **2** life imprisonment. **3** lachenalia aloides.

I RECENTLY LEARNED FROM AN OLD FRIEND IN IOWA THAT IF YOU ARE CAUGHT in possession of a single dose of LSD in my native state you face a mandatory sentence of seven years in prison without possibility of parole.

Never mind that you are, say, eighteen years old and of previous good character, that this will ruin your life, that it will cost the state $25,000 a year to keep you incarcerated. Never mind that perhaps you didn't even know you had the LSD – that a friend put it in the glovebox of your car without your knowledge or maybe saw police coming through the door at a party and shoved it into your hand before you could react. Never mind any extenuating circumstances whatever. This is America in the 1990s and there are no exceptions where drugs are concerned. Sorry, but that's the way it is. Next.

It would be nearly impossible to exaggerate the ferocity with which the United States now prosecutes drug offenders. In fifteen states you can be sentenced to life in prison for owning a single marijuana plant. Newt Gingrich, the House Speaker, recently proposed that anyone caught bringing as little as two ounces of marijuana into the United States should be imprisoned for life without possibility of parole. Anyone caught bringing more than two ounces would be executed. A law to this effect is currently working its way through Congress.

According to a 1990 study, 90 per cent of all first-time drug offenders in federal courts were sentenced to an average of five years in prison. Violent first-time offenders, by contrast, were imprisoned less often and received on average just four years in prison. You are, in short, less likely to go to prison for kicking an old lady down the stairs than you are for being caught in possession of a single dose of any illicit drug. Call me soft, but that seems to me a trifle disproportionate.

Please understand it is not remotely my intention here to speak in favour of drugs. I appreciate that drugs can mess you up in a big way. I have an old schoolmate who made one LSD voyage too many in about 1977 and since that time has sat on a rocker on his parents' porch examining the backs of his hands and grinning to himself. So I know what drugs can do. I just haven't reached the point where it seems to me appropriate to put to death someone for being foolish.

Not many of my fellow countrymen would agree with me. It is the clear and fervent wish of most Americans to put drug users behind bars, and they are prepared to pay almost any price to achieve this. The people of Texas recently voted down a $750 million bond proposal to build new schools, but overwhelmingly endorsed a $1 billion bond for new prisons, mostly to house people convicted of drug offences.

America's prison population has more than doubled since 1982. There are now 1,630,000 people in prison in the United States. That is more than the populations of all but the three largest cities in the country. Sixty per cent of federal prisoners are serving time for non-violent offences, mostly to do with drugs. America's prisons are crammed with non-violent petty criminals whose problem is a weakness for illegal substances.

Because most drug offences carry mandatory sentences and

exclude the possibility of parole, other prisoners are having to be released early to make room for all the new drug offenders pouring into the system. In consequence, the average convicted murderer in the United States now serves less than six years, the average rapist just five. Moreover, once he is out, the murderer or rapist is immediately eligible for welfare, food stamps and other federal assistance. A convicted drug user, no matter how desperate his circumstances may become, is denied these benefits for the rest of his life.

The persecution doesn't end there. My friend in Iowa once spent four months in a state prison for a drug offence. That was almost twenty years ago. He did his time and since then has been completely clean. Recently, he applied for a temporary job with the Postal Service as a holiday relief mail sorter – part of an army of casual workers taken on each year to deal with Christmas post. Not only did he not get the job, but a week or so later he received by recorded delivery an affidavit threatening him with prosecution for failing to declare on his application that he had a felony conviction involving drugs.

The Postal Service had taken the trouble to run a background check for drug convictions on someone applying for a temporary job sorting mail. Apparently it does this as a matter of routine – but only with respect to drugs. Had he killed his grandmother and raped his sister twenty-five years ago, he would in all likelihood have got the job.

It gets more amazing. The government can seize your property if it was used in connection with a drug offence, even if you did not know it. In Connecticut, according to a recent article in the *Atlantic Monthly* magazine, a federal prosecutor named Leslie C. Ohta made a name for herself by seizing the property of almost anyone even tangentially connected with a drug offence – including a couple in their eighties whose grandson was found to be selling marijuana out of his bedroom. The couple had no idea that their grandson had marijuana in the house (let me repeat: they were in their eighties) and of course had nothing to do with it themselves. They lost the house anyway.

(Soon after, Ohta's own eighteen-year-old son was arrested for selling LSD out of his mother's car and was alleged also to have sold drugs from her house. And did the adorable Ms Ohta lose her house and car? Did she hell. She was merely transferred to another assignment.)

The saddest part of this zealous vindictiveness is that it simply does not work. America spends $50 billion a year fighting drugs, and yet drug use goes on and on. Confounded and frustrated, the government enacts increasingly draconian laws until we find ourselves at the ludicrous point where the Speaker of the House can seriously propose to execute people – strap them to a gurney and snuff out their lives – for possessing the botanical equivalent of two bottles of vodka, and no one anywhere seems to question it.

My solution to the problem would be twofold. First, I would make it a criminal offence to be Newt Gingrich. This wouldn't do anything to reduce the drug problem, but it would make me feel much better. Then I would take most of that $50 billion and spend it on rehabilitation and prevention. Some of it could be used to take coachloads of youngsters to look at that schoolmate of mine on his Iowa porch. I am sure it would persuade most of them not to try drugs in the first place. It would certainly be less brutal and pointless than trying to lock them all up for the rest of their lives.

11 May 1997

WHY NO ONE WALKS

I'LL TELL YOU THIS, BUT YOU HAVE TO PROMISE THAT IT WILL GET NO further. Not long after we moved here we had the people next door round for dinner and – I swear this is true – they drove.

I was astounded (I recall asking them jokingly if they used a light aircraft to get to the supermarket, which simply drew blank looks and the mental scratching of my name from all future invitation lists), but I have since come to realize that there was nothing especially odd in their driving less than a couple of hundred feet to visit us. Nobody walks anywhere in America nowadays.

A researcher at the University of California at Berkeley recently made a study of the nation's walking habits and concluded that

85 per cent of people in the United States are 'essentially' sedentary and 35 per cent are 'totally' sedentary. The average American walks less than 75 miles a year – about 1.4 miles a week, barely 350 yards a day. I'm no stranger to sloth myself, but that's appallingly little. I rack up more mileage than that just looking for the channel changer.

One of the things we wanted when we moved to America was to live in a town within walking distance of shops. Hanover, where we settled, is a small, typical New England college town, pleasant, sedate and compact. It has a broad green, an old-fashioned Main Street, nice college buildings with big lawns, and leafy residential streets. It is, in short, an agreeable, easy place to stroll. Nearly everyone in town is within a level five-minute walk of the shops, and yet as far as I can tell virtually no one does.

I walk to town nearly every day when I am at home. I go to the post office or library or the local bookshop, and sometimes, if I am feeling particularly debonair, I stop at Rosey Jekes Café for a cappuccino. Every few weeks or so I call in at the barbershop and let one of the guys there do something rash and lively with my hair. All this is a big part of my life and I wouldn't dream of doing it other than on foot. People have got used to this curious and eccentric behaviour now, but several times in the early days passing neighbours would slow by the kerb and ask if I wanted a lift.

'But I'm going your way,' they would insist when I politely declined. 'Really, it's no bother.'

'Honestly, I enjoy walking.'

'Well, if you're absolutely sure,' they would say and depart reluctantly, even guiltily, as if they felt they were leaving the scene of an accident.

People have become so habituated to using the car for everything that it would never occur to them to unfurl their legs and see what they can do. Sometimes it's almost ludicrous. The other day I was in a little nearby town called Etna waiting to bring home one of my children from a piano lesson when a car stopped outside the local post office and a man about my age popped out and dashed inside (and left the motor running – something else that exercises me inordinately). He was inside for about three or four minutes, then came out, got in the car and drove exactly 16 feet (I had nothing better to do so I paced it off) to the general store next door, and popped in again, engine still running.

And the thing is this man looked really fit. I'm sure he jogs extravagant distances and plays squash and does all kinds of exuberantly healthful things, but I am just as sure that he drives to each of these undertakings. It's crazy. An acquaintance of ours was complaining the other day about the difficulty of finding a place to park outside the local gymnasium. She goes there several times a week to walk on a treadmill. The gymnasium is, at most, a six-minute walk from her front door. I asked her why she didn't walk to the gym and do six minutes less on the treadmill.

She looked at me as if I were tragically simple-minded and said, 'But I have a programme for the treadmill. It records my distance and speed, and I can adjust it for degree of difficulty.' It had not occurred to me how thoughtlessly deficient nature is in this regard.

According to a concerned and faintly horrified recent editorial in the *Boston Globe*, the United States spends less than 1 per cent of its $25 billion-a-year roads budget on facilities for pedestrians. Actually, I'm surprised it's that much. Go to almost any suburb developed in the last thirty years – and there are thousands to choose from – and you will not find a pavement anywhere. Often you won't find a single pedestrian-crossing. I am not exaggerating.

I had this brought home to me last summer when we were driving across Maine and stopped for coffee in one of those endless zones of shopping malls, motels, petrol stations and fast-food places that sprout everywhere in America these days. I noticed there was a bookshop across the street, so I decided to skip coffee and pop over. I needed a particular book and anyway I figured this would give my wife a chance to spend some important private quality time with four restive, overheated children.

Although the bookshop was no more than 50 or 60 feet away, I discovered that there was no way to get there on foot. There was a traffic crossing for cars, but no provision for pedestrians and no way to cross without dodging through three lanes of swiftly turning traffic. I had to get in the car and drive across. At the time it seemed ridiculous and exasperating, but afterwards I realized that I was probably the only person ever even to have entertained the notion of negotiating that intersection on foot.

The fact is, Americans not only don't walk anywhere, they *won't* walk anywhere, and woe to anyone who tries to make them, as a town here in New Hampshire called Laconia discovered to its cost. A few years ago Laconia spent $5 million pedestrianizing its town centre, to make it a pleasant shopping environment. Aesthetically it was a triumph – urban planners came from all over to coo and take photos – but commercially it was a disaster. Forced to walk one whole block from a car park, shoppers abandoned downtown Laconia for suburban malls.

In 1994 Laconia dug up its pretty brick paving, took away the benches and tubs of geraniums and decorative trees, and put the street back to the way it had been in the first place. Now people can park right in front of the shops again and downtown Laconia thrives anew. And if that isn't sad, I don't know what is.

18 May 1997

GARDENING WITH MY WIFE

I'M GOING TO HAVE TO BE QUICK BECAUSE IT'S A SUNDAY AND THE weather is glorious and Mrs Bryson has outlined a big, ambitious programme of gardening. Worse, she's wearing what I nervously call her Nike expression – the one that says 'Just do it.'

Now don't get me wrong. Mrs Bryson is a rare and delightful creature and goodness knows my life needs structure and super-vision, but when she gets out a pad and pen and writes the dread words 'Things To Do' (vigorously underscored several times) you know it's going to be a long time till Monday.

I love to garden – there is something about the combination of mindless activity and the constant unearthing of worms that suits me somehow – but frankly I am not crazy about gardening with my wife. The trouble, you see, is that she is English and thus can intimidate me. She can say things like, 'Have you heeled in the nodes on the *Dianthus chinensis?*' and 'Did you remember to check the sequestrene levels on the *Phlox subulata?*'

All British people can do this, I find, and it's awful – terrifying. Even now I remember the astonishment of listening to *Gardeners' Question Time* for the first time many years ago and realizing with quiet horror that I was in a nation of people who not only knew and understood things like powdery mildew, peach leaf curl, optimum pH levels, and the difference between *Coreopsis verticillata* and *Coreopsis grandiflora*, but cared about them – indeed, found it gratifying to engage in long and lively discussions on such matters.

I come from a background where you are considered to have a green thumb if you can grow a cactus on a windowsill, so my own approach to gardening has always been rather less scientific. My method, which actually works pretty well, is to treat as a weed anything that hasn't flowered by August and to sprinkle everything else with bone meal, slug pellets, and whatever else I find lying around the potting shed. Once or twice a summer I tip everything with a skull and crossbones on the label into a spray canister and give everything a jolly good dousing. It's an unorthodox approach and occasionally, I admit, I have to leap out of the way of an abruptly falling tree that has failed to respond to ministrations, but generally it has been a success and I have achieved some interesting and novel mutational effects. I once got a fence post to fruit, for instance.

For years, especially when the children were small and capable of almost anything, my wife left me to the garden. Occasionally she would step out to ask what I was doing, and I would have to confess that I was dusting some weedy-looking things with an unknown powdery substance which I had found in the garage and which I was pretty confident was either nitrogen or cement mix. Usually at that moment one of the children would come out to announce that little Jimmy's hair was on fire, or something else similarly but usefully distracting, and she would fly off, leaving me to get on with my experiments in peace. It was a good arrangement and our marriage prospered.

Then the children grew large enough to attend to their own cranial blazes and we moved to America, and now I find Mrs B out there with me. Or rather I am there with her, for I seem to have acquired a subsidiary role which principally involves bringing or taking away the wheelbarrow at a trot. I used to be a keen gardener; now I'm a kind of rickshaw boy.

Anyway, gardening just isn't the same here. People don't even have gardens in America. They have yards. And they don't garden in those yards. They work in them. They actually call it 'yardwork'. Takes all the fun out of it somehow.

In Britain, nature is fecund and kindly. The whole country is a kind of garden, really. I mean to say, look at how wildflowers pop up along every roadside and dance across meadows. Farmers actually have to go out and exterminate them (well, they don't have to, but they sure like to). In America, the instinct of nature is to be a wilderness. What you get here are triffid-like weeds that come creeping in from every margin and must be continually hacked back with sabres and machetes. I am quite sure that if we left the property for a month we would come back to find that the weeds had captured the house and dragged it off to the woods to be slowly devoured.

American gardens are mostly lawn, and American lawns are mostly big. This means that you spend your life raking. In the autumn the leaves fall together with a single great *whoomp* – a sort of vegetative mass suicide – and you spend about two months dragging them into piles, while the wind does its best to put them all back where you found them. You rake and rake, and cart the leaves off to the woods, then hang up your rake and go inside for the next seven months.

But as soon as you turn your back, the leaves begin creeping back. I don't know how they do it, but when you come out in spring, there they all are again, spread ankle deep across your lawn, choking thorny shrubs, clogging drains. So you spend weeks and weeks raking them up and carting them back to the woods. Finally, just when you get the lawn pristine, there is a great *whoomp* sound and you realize it's autumn again. It's really quite dispiriting.

And now on top of all that my dear missus has suddenly taken a commanding interest in the whole business of domestic horticulture. It's my own fault, I have to admit. Last year I filled the lawn spreader with a mixture of my own devising – essentially fertilizer, moss killer, rabbit food (initially by mistake, but then I thought, 'What the heck?' and tossed in the rest) and a dash of something lively called buprimate and triforine. Two days later the front lawn erupted in vivid orange stripes of a sufficiently arresting and persistent nature to attract sightseers from as far as northern Massachusetts. So now I find myself on a kind of permanent probation.

Speaking of which, I've got to go. I've just heard the hard, clinical snap of gardening gloves going on and the ominous sound of metal tools being taken down from their perches. It's only a matter of time before I hear the cry of 'Boy! Bring the barrow – and look sharp!' But you know the part I really hate? It's having to wear this stupid coolie hat.

25 May 1997

WHY EVERYONE IS WORRIED

HERE'S A FACT FOR YOU. IN 1995, ACCORDING TO THE *WASHINGTON POST*, computer hackers successfully breached the Pentagon's security systems 161,000 times. That works out at eighteen illicit entries every hour around the clock, one every 3.2 minutes.

Oh, I know what you are going to say. This sort of thing could happen to any monolithic defence establishment with the fate of the earth in its hands. After all, if you stockpile a massive nuclear arsenal, it's only natural that people are going to want to go in and have a look around, maybe see what all those buttons marked 'Detonate' and 'Code Red' mean. It's only human nature.

Besides, the Pentagon has got quite enough on its plate, thank you, with trying to find its missing logs from the Gulf War. I don't know if you've read about this, but the Pentagon has mislaid – irretrievably lost, actually – all but thirty-six of the 200 pages of official records of its brief but exciting desert adventure. Half of the missing files, it appears, were wiped out when an officer at Gulf War headquarters – I wish I was making this up, but I'm not – incorrectly downloaded some games into a military computer. The other missing files are, well, missing. All that is known is that two sets were dispatched to Central Command in Florida, but now nobody can find them (probably those cleaning ladies again), and a third set was somehow 'lost from a safe' at a base in Maryland, which sounds eminently plausible in the circumstances.

Now to be fair to the Pentagon, its mind has no doubt been distracted by the unsettling news that it has not been getting very good reports from the CIA. It has recently emerged, according to other news reports, that despite spending a decidedly whopping $2 billion a year monitoring developments in the Soviet Union, the CIA failed to foresee the break-up of the USSR – indeed, I understand, is still trying to confirm the rumour through its contacts at the McDonald's in Moscow – and understandably this has unnerved the Pentagon. I mean to say, you can't expect people to keep track of their wars if they're not getting reliable reports from the field, now can you?

The CIA, in its turn, was almost certainly distracted from its missions by the news – and again let me stress that I am not making any of this up – that the FBI had spent years filming one of its agents, Aldrich Ames, going into the Soviet embassy in Washington with bulging files and coming out empty-handed, but had not yet quite figured out what he was up to. The FBI knew Ames was a CIA employee, knew that he made regular visits to the Soviet embassy, and knew the CIA was looking for a mole in its midst, but had never managed to make the leap of thought necessary to pull these tantalizing strands together.

Ames was eventually caught and sentenced to a zillion years in prison for passing information, but no thanks to the FBI. But then, to be fair, the FBI has been absolutely snowed under with screwing up everything it comes in contact with.

First, there was its wrongful arrest of Richard Jewell, the security guard it suspected of last year's bombing in Atlanta's Olympic Park. Jewell, according to the FBI, planted the bomb and made a phone call alerting authorities, then raced a couple of miles in a minute or so in order to be back at the scene in time to be a hero. Even though there was not a shred of evidence to connect him with the bomb and it was conclusively demonstrated that he could not have made the call and returned to the park in the time alleged, it took the FBI months to realize it had the wrong man.

Then in April came news that FBI forensic labs had for years been botching, losing, spilling, contaminating, stepping in and tracking out to the car park most of the vital evidence that came its way. Occasionally they just made things up. In one incident, a lab scientist wrote an incriminating report based on microscopic findings without actually bothering to look through a microscope. Thanks to the labs' dogged and inventive work, at least 1,000 convictions, and perhaps many thousands more, have been placed at risk.

Among its continuing achievements, the FBI has still not found the perpetrator of the Atlanta bombing or a series of church bombings across the South, hasn't arrested anyone in a mysterious fatal derailment of a passenger train in Arizona in 1995, failed to catch the Unabomber (he was turned in by his brother), and still isn't able to say whether the crash of TWA flight 800 last year was a crime or an accident or what.

A lot of people conclude from this that the FBI and its agents are dangerously inept. Although this is indubitably so, there are extenuating circumstances for the bureau's low morale and poor performance – namely the discovery last year that there is a group of people even more astoundingly incompetent. I refer to America's sheriff's departments.

Space does not permit a comprehensive survey of the singular accomplishments of America's sheriff's departments, so I will cite just two. First, there was the news that the Los Angeles County Sheriff's Department set a record last year by incorrectly releasing twenty-three prisoners, some of them quite dangerous and cranky. After the release of prisoner number twenty-three, a supervisor explained to journalists that a clerk had received papers ordering that the prisoner be sent to Oregon to serve out a long sentence for burglary and rape, but had taken this to mean giving him back all his possessions, escorting him to the door and recommending a good pizza place around the corner.

Even better, in my view, were the sheriff's deputies in Milwaukee who were sent to the airport with a team of sniffer dogs to practise hunting out explosives. The deputies hid a five-pound packet of live explosives somewhere in the airport and then – I just love this – forgot where. Needless to say, the dogs couldn't find it. That was in February and they're still looking. It was the second time that the Milwaukee sheriff's department has managed to mislay explosives at the airport.

I could go on and on, but I'm going to break off here because I want to see if I can get into the Pentagon's computer. Call me a devil, but I've always had a hankering to blow up a minor country. It will be the perfect crime. The CIA won't notice it, the Pentagon will notice it but will lose the records, the FBI will spend eighteen months investigating and then arrest Mr Ed the Talking Horse, and the Los Angeles County Sheriff's Department will let him go. If nothing else, it will take people's minds off all these other things they have to worry about.

1 June 1997

A FAILURE TO COMMUNICATE

OF ALL THE THINGS THAT HAVE BEEN PLACED ON EARTH TO TRY MY patience – and gosh aren't there a lot? – none has been more successful over the years than AT&T, the American telephone company.

Given a choice between, say, spilling a beaker of hydrochloric acid on my lap and dealing with AT&T, I would always choose the hydrochloric acid as less painful. AT&T has the world's most indestructible payphones. I know this for a fact because I have never had an experience with AT&T from a payphone that did not result in my giving their equipment a thorough workout.

As you are probably gathering, I don't much like AT&T. But that's OK because it doesn't like me. It doesn't like any of its customers, as far as I can tell. It dislikes them so much, in fact, that it won't even talk to them. It uses synthesized voices for everything now, which means that no matter how wrong things go – and you can be certain they will – you can never get through to a real person. All you get is a strange, metallic, curiously snotty robotic voice saying things like: 'The number you have dialled is not within a recognized dialling parameter.' It is immensely frustrating.

I was reminded of this the other day when I found myself stranded at Logan Airport in Boston because the mini-coach company that was supposed to pick me up and take me home forgot to. I knew that it had forgotten me, and not broken down or had an accident, because as I stood at the designated pick-up point the familiar Dartmouth Mini-Coach van approached and, as I bent to pick up my bags, sailed past and continued on to the airport exit road and disappeared into the distance, on a general heading for New Hampshire.

So I went off to find a payphone to ring the mini-coach company – just to say hello, you know, and let them know that I was there and ready to go if they would only throw open a door and slow down enough to let me jump on – and this meant calling AT&T. I gave a ruptured sigh at the prospect. I had just had a long flight. I was tired and hungry and stranded at a charmless airport. I knew it would be at least three hours before the next mini-coach was due. And now I had to deal with AT&T. I approached a bank of payphones outside the airport terminal with deep foreboding.

I didn't have the number for the mini-coach company on me, so I read the instructions for directory inquiries and rang the number. After a minute a synthetic voice came on and brusquely instructed me to deposit $1.05 in change. I was taken aback by this. Directory inquiries always used to be free. I searched through my pockets, but I only had 67 cents. So I conducted a brief resiliency test with the receiver – yes, still indestructible – grabbed my bags and stalked off to the terminal to acquire change.

Of course none of the businesses would give change without a purchase, so I had to buy a copy of the *New York Times*, *Boston Globe* and *Washington Post* – each purchased separately, with a different note, as no other approach appeared to be allowable – until I had accumulated $1.05 in assorted silver coins.

Then I returned to the phone and repeated the process, but it was one of those phones that are very choosy about what coins they take, and it seemed to have a particular dislike for Roosevelt dimes. It's not easy to feed coins into a slot when you have a receiver pressed to your ear with a shoulder and three newspapers under your arm, and especially not when the phone is spitting back every third coin you feed it. After about 15 seconds a robotic voice came on and started scolding me – I swear it, scolding me, in an irksome synthetic quaver – and telling me in effect that if I didn't get myself organized pronto it would cut me off. And then it cut me off. A moment later it re-gurgitated the coins I had deposited. But here's the thing. It didn't return all of them. Between what it had given back and what it wouldn't take, I now had just 90 cents.

So I conducted another, slightly more protracted resiliency test and trudged back into the terminal. I bought a *Providence Journal* and a *Philadelphia Inquirer* and returned to the phone. This time I got through to directory inquiries, announced the number I wanted and hastily pulled out a pen and notepad. I knew from experience that directory inquiries gives a number just once and then hangs up, so you have to get it down carefully. I listened intently and started to write. The pen was dry. I immediately forgot the number.

I returned to the terminal, bought a *Bangor Daily-News*, a *Poughkeepsie Journal* and a plastic biro, and returned. This time I got the number, carefully recorded it and dialled. Success at last.

A moment later a voice on the other end said brightly, 'Good morning! Dartmouth College!'

'Dartmouth College?' I stammered, aghast. 'I wanted the Dartmouth Mini-Coach Company.' I had used up all my remaining coins on this call and couldn't believe that I would have to go back into the terminal yet again to accumulate more. I suddenly wondered how many of those people in America who come up to you on corners and ask for spare change were once just people like me – respectable cit-izens who had led normal lives and ended up destitute, homeless and in need of constant small change for a payphone somewhere.

'I can give you the number if you'd like,' the lady offered.

'Really? Oh, yes please.'

She rattled off a number, clearly from memory. It was nothing like the number – not even remotely like the number – I had been given by AT&T. I thanked her profusely.

'No problem,' she said. 'It happens all the time.'

'What, they give your number when people ask for Dartmouth Mini-Coach?'

'All the time. Was it AT&T you used?'

'Yes.'

'Thought so,' she said simply. I thanked her again. 'It's been my pleasure. And hey – don't forget to give that phone a really good pounding before you leave.'

She didn't say that, of course. She didn't need to.

I had to wait four hours for the next mini-coach. But it could have been worse. At least I had plenty to read.

8 June 1997

LOST AT THE MOVIES

EVERY YEAR ABOUT THIS TIME I DO A MILDLY FOOLISH THING. I GATHER up some of the smaller children and take them to one of the summer movies.

Summer movies are big business in America. This year between Memorial Day and Labor Day – our equivalents of the British May and August bank holidays – Americans will spend $2 billion on cinema tickets, plus half as much again on chewy things to stuff into their mouths while staring saucer-eyed at images of extremely costly mayhem.

Summer movies are nearly always bad, of course, but I believe this may be the worst summer ever. I base this entirely, but confidently, on a quotation I saw in the *New York Times* from Jan de Bont, director of *Speed 2: Cruise Control*, who boasted that the movie's biggest dramatic event – in which an out-of-control cruise ship carrying Sandra Bullock ploughs into a Caribbean village – came to him in a dream. 'The entire screenplay was written backward from that image,' he revealed proudly. There, I think, you have all you need to know about the intellectual quality of the average summer movie.

I always tell myself not to set my expectations too high, that summer movies are the cinematic equivalent of amusement park rides, and no one ever expected a rollercoaster to provide a satisfying plot line. But the thing is, summer movies have become so dumb – so very, very dumb – that it is hard to abide them. No matter how much money has been spent on them – and it is worth noting that at least eight of this year's crop have budgets over $100 million – there is always such a large measure of preposterous implausibility as to make you wonder whether the script was concocted over canapés the night before filming began.

This year we went to the new Jurassic Park movie, *Lost World*. Now never mind that it is largely identical to the last Jurassic Park movie – same booming footfalls and trembling puddles whenever T-rex comes into the vicinity, same mortified people backing away from a door against which velociraptors are hurling themselves (only to find another toothy creature looming over their shoulders), same scenes of vehicles dangling precariously from a jungly bluff while the heroes hold on for dear life. No matter. The dinosaurs are terrific and a dozen or so people get squashed or eaten in the first hour. This is what we've come for!

And then it all falls apart. In a culminating scene a Tyrannosaurus escapes, in an improbable manner, from a ship, runs rampant through downtown San Diego, crushing buses and destroying petrol stations, and then – suddenly, inexplicably – is in the middle of a heavily slumbering suburban neighbourhood, alone and unobserved. Now does it strike you as remotely likely that a prehistoric, 20-foot-high creature not seen on earth for 65 million years could cause mayhem in a city centre and then slip off into a residential zone without anyone's noticing? Does it not seem a trifle nagging and unsatisfactory that while downtown San Diego is full of people doing lively, mid-evening sorts of things – queueing up at cinemas, strolling round hand in hand – out in the residential area the streets are silent and every last soul is fast asleep?

And so it goes on from there. While police cars are dashing around bumping helplessly into each other, the hero and heroine manage to find the T-rex unaided and – undetected by anyone in this curiously unobservant city – lure him some miles back to the boat, so that he can be returned to his tropical island home, thus setting up the happy, inevitable and commercially gratifying possibility of a *Jurassic Park 3*. *Lost World* is slack and obvious and, for all its $100 million-plus budget, contains about $2.35 worth of actual thought, and so of course it is on its way to setting all kinds of records at the box office. In its first weekend alone it took in $92.7 million.

However, my problem is not really with *Lost World* or any of the other summer fare. I'm way past expecting Hollywood to provide me with a cerebral experience during the warmer months. My problem is with the Sony 6 Theatres of West Lebanon, New Hampshire, and the thousands of other suburban cinema complexes like it, which are doing to the American movie-going experience essentially what Steven Spielberg's Tyrannosaurus rex did to San Diego.

Anyone who grew up in America in the 1960s or before will remember the days when going to the pictures meant visiting a single-screen institution, usually vast, usually downtown. In my hometown, Des Moines, the main cinema (imaginatively called The Des Moines) was a palatial extravaganza with spooky lighting and a decor that brought to mind an Egyptian crypt. By my era, it was something of a dump – I am sure from the smell that there was a dead horse in there somewhere, and certainly it hadn't been cleaned since Theda Bara was in her prime – but just being there, facing a vast screen in a cubic acre of darkness, was an entrancing experience.

Except in a few major cities, nearly all those great downtown cinemas are gone now. (The Des Moines went in about 1965.) Instead what you get nowadays are suburban multiplexes with an abundance of tiny screening rooms. Although *Lost World* is the hottest movie around, we saw it in a chamber of almost laughable minuteness, barely large enough to accommodate nine rows of seats, which were grudgingly padded and crammed so tight together that my knees ended up more or less hooked around my ears. The screen had the dimensions of a large beach towel and was so ill-placed that everyone in the first three rows had to look almost straight up, as if in a planetarium. The sound was bad and the picture frequently jerky. Before it started, we had to sit through 30 minutes of commercials. The popcorn and confections were outrageously expensive, and the salespeople had been programmed to try to sell you things you didn't want and hadn't asked for. In short, every feature of this cinema seemed carefully designed to make a visit a deeply regretted experience.

I'm not cataloguing all this to make you feel sorry for me, though sympathy is always welcome, but to point out that this is increasingly the standard experience for cinema goers in America. I can handle a little audio-visual imbecility, but I can't bear to see the magic taken away.

I was talking about this to one of my older children the other day. She listened attentively, even sympathetically, then said a sad thing. 'Dad,' she told me, 'you need to understand that people don't want the smell of a dead horse when they go to the movies.'

She's right, of course. But if you ask me they don't know what they are missing.

15 June 1997

THE RISK FACTOR

NOW HERE IS SOMETHING THAT SEEMS AWFULLY UNFAIR TO ME. BECAUSE I am an American and you, bless your heart, are not, it appears that I am twice as likely as you to suffer an untimely and accidental death.

I know this because I have just been reading something called *The Book of Risks: Fascinating Facts About the Chances We Take Every Day* by a statistical wonk (to use the engaging new American slang term for a boffin-type person) named Larry Laudan.

It is full of interesting and useful statistics, mostly to do with coming irremediably a cropper in the United States. Thus I know that if I happen to take up farm work this year I am three times more likely to lose a limb, and twice as likely to be fatally poisoned, than if I just sit here quietly. I now know that my chances of being murdered some time in the next twelve months are one in 11,000, of choking to death one in 150,000, of being killed by a dam failure one in 10 million, and of being fatally conked on the head by something falling from the sky about one in 250 million. Even if I stay indoors, away from the windows, it appears that there is a one in 450,000 chance that something will kill me before the day is out. I find that rather alarming.

However, nothing is more galling than the discovery that just by being an American, by standing to attention for the 'Star-Spangled Banner' and having a baseball cap as a central component of my wardrobe, I am twice as likely to die in a mangled heap as you are. This is not a just way to decide mortality, if you ask me.

Mr Laudan does not explain why Americans are twice as dangerous to themselves as Britons (too upset, I daresay), but I have been thinking about it a good deal, as you can imagine, and the answer – very obvious when you reflect for even a moment – is that America is an outstandingly dangerous place.

Consider this: every year in New Hampshire a dozen or more people are killed crashing their cars into moose. Now correct me if I am wrong, but this is not something that is likely to happen to you on the way home from Sainsbury's. Nor are you likely to be eaten by a grizzly bear or mountain lion, butted senseless by buffalo, or seized about the ankle by a seriously perturbed rattlesnake – all occurrences that knock off a few dozen hapless Americans every year. Then there are all the violent acts of nature – tornadoes, rockslides, avalanches, flash floods, paralyzing blizzards, the odd earthquake – that scarcely exist in your tranquil little island, but kill hundreds and hundreds of Americans every year.

Finally, and above all, there is the matter of guns. There are 200 million guns in the United States and we do rather like to pop them off. Each year, 40,000 Americans die from gunshot wounds, the great majority of them by accident. Just to put that in perspective for you, that's a rate of 6.8 gunshot deaths per 100,000 people in America, compared with a meagre 0.4 per 100,000 in the UK.

America is in short a pretty risky place. And yet, oddly, we get alarmed by all the wrong things in this country. Eavesdrop on almost any conversation at Lou's Diner here in Hanover and the talk will all be of cholesterol and sodium levels, mammograms and resting heart rates. Show most Americans an egg yolk and they will recoil in terror, but the most palpable and avoidable risks scarcely faze them.

Forty per cent of Americans still don't use a seatbelt, which I find simply amazing because it costs nothing to buckle up and clearly has the potential to save you from exiting through the windscreen like Superman. Even more remarkably, since a spate of recent newspaper reports about young children being killed by airbags in minor crashes, people have been rushing to get their airbags disconnected. Never mind that in every instance the children were killed because they were sitting on the front seat, where they should not have been in the first place, and in nearly all cases weren't wearing seatbelts. Airbags save thousands of lives, yet many people are having them disabled on the bizarre assumption that they present a danger.

Much the same sort of statistical illogic applies to guns. Forty per cent of Americans keep guns in their homes, typically in a drawer beside the bed. The odds that one of those guns will ever be used to shoot a criminal are comfortably under one in a million. The odds that it will be used to shoot a member of the household – generally a child fooling around – are at least twenty times that figure. Yet over one hundred million people resolutely ignore this fact, even sometimes threaten to pop you one themselves if you make too much noise about it.

Nothing, however, better captures the manifest irrationality of people towards risks as one of the liveliest issues of recent years: passive smoking. Four years ago, the Environmental Protection Agency released a report concluding that people who are over thirty-five and don't smoke but are regularly exposed to the smoke of others stand a one in 30,000 risk of contracting lung cancer in a given year. The response was immediate and electrifying. All over the country smoking was banned at work and in restaurants, shopping malls and other public places.

What was overlooked in all this was how microscopically small the risk from passive smoking actually is. A rate of one in 30,000 sounds reasonably severe, but it doesn't actually amount to much. Eating one pork chop a week is statistically more likely to give you cancer than sitting routinely in a roomful of smokers. So, too, is consuming a carrot every seven days, a glass of orange juice once a fortnight, or a head of lettuce every two years. You are five times more likely to contract lung cancer from your pet budgie than you are from secondary smoke.

Now I am all for banning smoking on the grounds that it is dirty and offensive, unhealthy for the user and leaves unsightly burns in the carpet. All I am saying is that it seems a trifle odd to ban it on grounds of public safety when you are happy to let any old fool own a gun or drive around unbuckled.

But then logic seldom comes into these things. I remember some years ago watching my brother buy a lottery ticket (odds of winning: about one in 12 million), then get in his car and fail to buckle up (odds of having a serious accident in any year: one in forty). When I pointed out the inconsistency of this, he looked at me for a moment and said: 'And what are the odds, do you suppose, that I will drop you four miles short of home?'

Since then, I have kept these thoughts pretty much to myself. Much less risky, you see.

22 June 1997

AH, SUMMER!

IN NEW ENGLAND, A FRIEND HERE RECENTLY EXPLAINED TO ME, THERE are three times of year. Either winter has just been, or winter is coming, or it's winter.

I know what he meant. Summers here are short – they start on the first of June and end on the last day of August, and the rest of the time you had better know where your mittens are – but for the whole of those three months the weather is agreeably warm and nearly always sunny. Best of all, the weather stays at a generally agreeable level, unlike Iowa, where I grew up and where the temperature and humidity climb steadily with every passing day of summer until by mid-August it is so hot and airless that even the flies lie down on their backs and just quietly gasp.

It's the mugginess that gets you. Step outside in Iowa in August and within 20 seconds you will experience a condition that might be called perspiration incontinence. It gets so hot that you will see department store mannequins with sweat circles under their arms. I have particularly vivid memories of Iowa summers because my father was the last person in the Midwest to buy an air-conditioner. He thought they were unnatural. (He thought anything that cost more than $30 was unnatural.)

The one place you could get a little relief was the screened porch. Up until the 1950s nearly every American home had one of these. A screened porch is a kind of summer room on the side of the house, with walls made of a fine but sturdy mesh to keep out insects. They give you all the advantages of being outdoors and indoors at the same time. They are wonderful and will always be associated in my mind with summer things – corn on the cob, watermelon, the nighttime chirr of crickets, the sound of my parents' neighbour Mr Piper arriving home late from one of his lodge meetings, parking his car with the aid of his dustbins, then serenading Mrs Piper with two choruses of 'Rose of Seville' before settling down for a nap on the lawn.

So when we came to the States, the one thing I asked for in a house was a screened porch, and we found one. I live out there in the summer. I am writing this on the screened porch now, staring out on a sunny garden, listening to twittering birds and the hum of a neighbour's lawnmower, caressed by a light breeze and feeling pretty darned chipper. We will have our dinner out here tonight (if Mrs B doesn't trip over a rucked carpet with the tray again, bless her) and then I will lounge around reading until bedtime, listening to the crickets and watching the cheery blink of fireflies. Summer wouldn't be summer without all this.

Soon after we moved into our house, I noticed that a corner of the mesh had come loose near the floor and that our cat was using it as a kind of cat flap to come in and sleep on an old sofa we kept out there, so I just left it. One night after we had been here about a month, I was reading unusually late when out of the corner of my eye I noticed the cat come in. Only here's the thing. The cat was with me already.

I looked again. It was a skunk. Moreover, it was between me and the only means of exit. It headed for the table and I realized it probably came in every night about this time to hoover up any dinner bits that had fallen on the floor. (And there very often are, on account of a little game the children and I play called 'Vegetable Olympics' when Mrs Bryson goes off to answer the phone or get more gravy.)

Being sprayed by a skunk is absolutely the worst thing that can happen to you that doesn't make you bleed or put you in the hospital.

If you smell skunk odour from a distance, it doesn't smell too bad at all. It's rather strangely sweet and arresting – not attractive exactly, but not revolting. Everybody who has ever smelled a skunk from a distance for the first time thinks, 'Well, that's not so bad. I don't know what all the fuss is about.'

But get close – or, worse still, get sprayed – and believe me it will be a long, long time before anyone asks you to dance slow and close. The odour is not just strong and disagreeable, but virtually ineradicable. The most effective treatment, apparently, is to scrub yourself with tomato juice, but even with gallons of the stuff the best you can hope is to subdue the odour fractionally.

A schoolmate of my son's had a skunk get into her family's basement one night. It sprayed and the family lost virtually everything in their home. All their curtains, bedding, clothes, soft furnishings – everything, in short, that could absorb an odour – had to be thrown on a bonfire, and the rest of the house thoroughly scrubbed from top to bottom. The schoolmate of my son's never got near the skunk, left the house immediately and spent a weekend scouring herself with tomato juice, but it was weeks before anyone would walk down the same side of a street as her. So when I say you don't want to be sprayed by a skunk, believe me you don't want to be sprayed by a skunk.

All of this went through my mind as I sat agog watching a skunk perhaps six feet away. The skunk spent about 30 seconds snuffling around under the table, then calmly padded out the way it had come. As it left, it turned and gave me a look that said: 'I knew you were there the whole time.' But it didn't spray me, for which I am grateful even now.

The next day I tacked the mesh back into place, but to show my appreciation I put a handful of dried cat food on the step, and at about midnight the skunk came and ate it. After that, for two summers, I put a little food out regularly and the skunk always came to collect it. This year it hasn't been back. There has been a rabies epidemic among small mammals which has seriously reduced the populations of skunks, raccoons, and even squirrels. Apparently this happens every fifteen years or so as part of a natural cycle.

So I seem to have lost my skunk. In a year or so the populations will recover and I may be able to adopt another. I hope so because the one thing about being a skunk is that you don't have a lot of friends.

In the meantime, partly as a mark of respect and partly because Mrs B caught one in the eye at an inopportune moment, we have stopped playing food games even though, if I say it myself, I was comfortably in line for a gold.

29 June 1997

HELP FOR THE
NONDESIGNATED INDIVIDUAL

THE OTHER DAY I HAD AN EXPERIENCE SO STARTLING AND UNEXPECTED that it made me spill a soft drink down my shirt. (Though, having said that, I don't actually need an unexpected event to achieve this. All I need is a soft drink.) What caused this fizzy outburst was that I called a government office – specifically, the US Social Security Administration – and someone answered the phone.

There I was, all poised to have a recorded voice tell me: 'All our agents are busy, so please hold while we play you some irritating music interrupted at 15-second intervals by a recorded voice telling you all our agents are busy so please hold while we play you some irritating music' and so on until teatime.

So imagine my surprise when, after just 270 rings, a real person came on the line. He asked some of my personal details, and then said, 'Excuse me, Bill. I have to put you on hold a minute.'

Did you catch that? He called me Bill. Not Mr Bryson. Not sir. Not O mighty taxpayer. But Bill. Two years ago I would have regarded this as a gross impertinence, but now I find I've rather grown to like it.

There are certain times when the informality and familiarity of American life strains my patience – when a waiter tells me his name is Bob and that he'll be my server this evening, I still have to resist an impulse to say, 'I just want a cheeseburger, Bob. I'm not looking for a relationship' – but mostly I have come to like it. It's because it's symbolic of something more fundamental, I suppose.

There is no tugging of forelocks here, you see, but a genuine universal assumption that no person is better than any other. I think that's swell. My dustman calls me Bill. My doctor calls me Bill. My children's headmaster calls me Bill. They don't tug for me. I don't tug for them. I think that's as it should be.

In England, I used the same accountant for over a decade, and our relations were always cordial but businesslike. She never called me anything but Mr Bryson and I never called her anything but Mrs Creswick. When I moved to America, I phoned an accountant for an appointment. When I came to his office, his first words to me were, 'Ah, Bill, I'm glad you could make it.' We were pals already. Now when I see him I ask him about his kids.

It shows itself in other ways, too. Hanover, where we live, is a college town. The local university, Dartmouth, is a private school and quite exclusive – it's one of the Ivy League colleges, like Harvard and Yale – but you would never guess it.

None of its grounds are off limits to us. Indeed, much of it is open to the community. We can use the library, attend its concerts, go to its commencement exercises if we want. One of my daughters skates on the college ice rink. My son's high school track team practises in winter on the college's indoor track. The college film society regularly puts on seasons of movies, which I often attend. Just last night I saw *North by Northwest* on a big screen with one of my teenagers, and afterwards we had coffee and cheesecake in the student cafeteria. At none of these things do you ever have to show ID or secure special permission, and never are you made to feel as if you are intruding or unwelcome.

All this gives everyday encounters a sheen of openness and egalitarianism which you may call shallow and artificial, or sometimes even inappropriate, but it also removes a lot of stuffiness from life.

The one thing it won't do, however, is get you your wife's social security number. Allow me to explain. A social security number is approximately equivalent to a British national insurance number, but far more important. It is essentially what identifies you as a person. Failing to understand this, my wife had mislaid her card. We needed the number fairly urgently for some tax form. I explained this to the social security man when he came back on the line. He had after all just called me Bill, so I had reason to hope that we might get somewhere.

'We are only permitted to divulge that information to the designated individual,' he replied.

'The person named on the card you mean?'

'Correct.'

'But she's my wife,' I sputtered.

'We are only permitted to divulge that information to the the designated individual.'

'Let me get this straight,' I said. 'If I were my wife, you would give me the number over the phone just like that?'

'Correct.'

'But what if it was somebody just pretending to be her?'

A hesitant pause. 'We would assume that the individual making the inquiry was the individual indicated as the designated individual.'

'Just a minute, please.' I thought for a minute. My wife was out, so I couldn't call on her, but I didn't want to have to go through all this again later. I came back on the phone and said in my normal voice: 'Hello, it's Cynthia Bryson here. Please could I have my card number?'

There was a nervous little chuckle. 'I know it's you, Bill,' the voice said.

'No, honestly. It's Cynthia Bryson. Please could I have my number?'

'I can't do that.'

'Would it make a diference if I spoke in a female voice?'

'I'm afraid not.'

'Let me ask you this – just out of curiosity. Is my wife's number on a computer screen in front of you right now?'

'Yes it is.'

'But you won't tell me it?'

'I'm afraid I can't do that, Bill,' he said and sounded as if he meant it.

I have learned from years of painful experience that there is not the tiniest chance – not the *tiniest* chance – that a US government employee will ever bend a rule to help you, so I didn't press the matter. Instead I asked him if he knew how to get strawberry pop stains out of a white T-shirt.

'Baking soda,' he replied without hesitation. 'Leave it to soak overnight and it will come right out.'

I thanked him and we parted.

I would have liked it, of course, if I had managed to get the information I needed, but at least I had made a friend and he was right about the baking soda. The T-shirt came up like new.

6 July 1997

WHERE SCOTLAND IS,
AND OTHER USEFUL TIPS

RECENTLY I WAS ON AN AMERICAN AIRLINE FLIGHT WHEN I THUMBED
through the in-flight magazine and came across a quiz entitled 'Your
Cultural IQ'.

Interested to see whether I have one, I applied myself to the questions. The very first asked in which country it is in bad taste to
enquire of a person 'Where do you live?' The answer, I learned to my
surprise by turning to page 113, was England.

'One's home is a personal affair for the English,' the magazine
solemnly informed me.

I am mortified to think of all the times over the years I have said to an English person, 'So where do you live, Clive?' (or whatever, because of course they weren't all named Clive), without for a moment suspecting that I was committing a serious social gaffe and that Clive (or whomever) was thinking: 'Nosy American git.' So of course I apologize now to all of you, especially Clive.

Then, a couple of days later, I came across an article on British politics in the *Washington Post*, which noted helpfully in passing that Scotland is 'to the north of England', a geographical distinction that I had always thought was common knowledge, and it dawned on me that perhaps it was not I who was under-informed, but – could this possibly be? – my entire nation.

I became curious to know just how much or little my fellow Americans know about the United Kingdom, but this is not easy. You can't just go up to a person, even someone you know quite well, and say, 'Do you have any idea what the Chancellor of the Exchequer does?' or 'Scotland is north of England. True or false?' any more than you could go up to an English person and say, 'Where do you live?' It would be impolite and impertinent, and possibly embarrassing for the interviewee.

Then it occurred to me that I might more discreetly get some idea by going to the library and looking at American guidebooks to Britain. These would tell me what sort of information Americans require before they embark on a visit to the UK.

So I went to the library and had a look at the travel section. There were four books exclusively on Britain, plus another eight or so on Europe generally, with chapters on Britain. My favourite, at a glance, was *Rick Steves' Europe 1996*. I had never heard of Rick, but according to the jacket blurb he spends several months each year 'feeling the fjords and caressing the castles', which sounds awfully diligent if a little pointless. I took all these books off to a table in the corner and spent the afternoon in fascinated study.

Well, I got my answer, which is that what Americans know about Britain is pretty nearly nothing, at least if these books are to be believed. According to the various texts, prospective American travellers to Britain require to be told that Glasgow 'doesn't rhyme with cow', that sterling is accepted in Scotland and Wales 'as freely as in England', that the country has 'well-trained doctors' and 'all the latest drugs', and, yes, that Scotland is north of England. (Quite far north, in fact, so better plan a full day there.)

American travellers, it appears, are a pretty helpless lot. The books tell them not just what to expect in Britain – rain and thatched cottages mostly – but how to pack their bags, find their way to the airport, even proceed through Customs.

'Be affable and cooperative, but don't be overly conversational,' advises Joseph Raff, author of *Fielding's Britain 1996*, on going through British immigration. 'Hold your passport casually in hand – don't flaunt it!' Perhaps it is none of my business, but if you need to be told how to clasp your passport, it seems to me you may not be quite ready to cross oceans.

My absolute favourite book was *The Best European Travel Tips* by one John Whitman. The book wasn't specifically about Britain, but it was so good that I read it almost cover to cover.

It was full of grave advice on pickpockets, avaricious waiters, even how to sue your airline if you are bumped from your flight. Mr Whitman clearly expects things to go wrong. His first tip for dealing with the idiosyncrasies of European hotels is 'Get the clerk's name when you check in.' With airline tickets he advises: 'Read all materials closely so you know your rights.'

Among his many useful suggestions, he advises that you bring 'a pen or two', hang a Do Not Disturb sign outside your hotel room door if you do not wish to be disturbed (I am not making this up; he even tells you to drape it over the knob) and notes sagely (for nothing gets past Mr Whitman's practised eye) that, with regard to lodging, Europe has 'a variety of places to stay'.

Elsewhere he warns: 'You'll find bidets in many European hotel rooms and WCs,' then adds warily, 'If you care to experiment with these toilet-shaped porcelain fixtures for your personal hygiene, do so.' Thanks for the permission, Mr Whitman, but to tell you the truth I've got my hands full with this Do Not Disturb sign!

Joseph Raff, meanwhile, provides a useful glossary for dealing with all those puzzling British terms like 'queue', 'flat', 'chips' and – here's one that's stumped me for years – 'motorcar'. Then he confidently asserts that a surname is one's first name and a Christian name is the last name, which would be useful information if it weren't completely wrong.

Errors rather abound in these books, I'm afraid. I learned that the beer you drink is called 'bitters', that the market in London is 'Covent Gardens', that when you go out you like to 'go to the cine', that the hill in the Lake District is 'Scarfell Pike', and – I particularly enjoyed this – that the Elizabethan architect was 'Indigo' Jones.

From *Let's Go Europe '96* I learned that Cardiff is 'the only urban centre' in Wales, which must come as something of a shock to the people of Swansea, and from the *Berkeley Budget Guide to Great Britain and Ireland* I discovered that 'nearly every city, town, village, hamlet or cluster of houses in the middle of nowhere has a post office – be it in a butcher shop, liquor store ("off-licence") or pharmacy ("chemist").'

What I really learned is that what Americans need is new guidebooks. I'm thinking of producing one of my own, filled with advice like 'When dealing with a police officer, always call him "Mr Plod" ', and 'To gain the attention of an elusive waiter, extend two fingers and wave your hand up and down vigorously several times. He will regard you as a native.' And finally, but obviously, 'Never ask a person named Clive where he lives.'

13 July 1997

DYING ACCENTS

WE HAVE A MAN NAMED WALT WHO DOES A BIT OF CARPENTRY AROUND the house from time to time. He looks to be about 112 years old, but goodness me the man can saw and hammer. He has been doing handiwork around town for at least fifty years.

Walt lives in Vermont, just across the Connecticut River from our little town, and is a proper New Englander – honest, hardworking, congenitally disinclined to waste time, money or words. (He converses as if he has heard that someday he will be billed for it.) Above all, like all New Englanders, he is an early riser. Boy, do New Englanders like to get up early. We have some English friends who moved here from Surrey a few years ago. Soon after arriving, the woman called the dentist for an appointment and was told to come at six-thirty the next day. She showed up the following evening to find the dentist's office in darkness. They had meant 6.30 *a.m.* If Walt were told to come for a dental appointment at that hour I am positive he would ask if they had anything a little earlier.

Anyway, the other day he arrived at our house a few minutes before seven and apologized for being late because the traffic through Norwich had been 'fierce'. What was interesting about this was not the notion that traffic in Norwich could ever be fierce, but that he pronounced it 'Norritch', like the English city. This surprised me because everyone in Norwich and for miles around pronounces it 'Nor-wich' (i.e., with the 'w' sounded, as in 'sandwich').

I asked him about that.

'Ayuh,' he said, which is an all-purpose New England term, spoken in a slow drawl and usually accompanied by the removal of a cap and a thoughtful scratching of the head. It means 'I may be about to say something, but then again I may not.' He explained to me that the village was pronounced 'Norritch' until the 1950s, when outsiders from places like New York and Boston began to move in and, for whatever reason, started to modify the pronunciation. Now virtually everyone who is younger than Walt, which is virtually everyone, pronounces it 'Nor-wich'. That seemed to me quite sad, the idea that a traditional local pronunciation could be lost simply because outsiders were too lazy or inattentive to preserve it, but it's only symptomatic of a much wider trend.

Thirty years ago, three-quarters of the people in Vermont were born there. Today the proportion has fallen to barely half, and in some places it is much lower. In consequence these days you are far less likely than you once were to hear locals pronouncing cow as 'kyow', saying 'so don't I' for 'so do I' or employing the colourful, if somewhat cryptic, expressions for which the state was once noted – 'heavier than a dead minister' and 'jeezum-jee-hassafrats' are two that spring to mind if not, alas, to many Vermont tongues any longer.

If you go to the remoter corners of the state and hang out at a general store you might just overhear a couple of old farmers (pronounced 'fahmuhs') asking for 'a frog skin more' of coffee, or saying 'well, wouldn't that just jar your mother's preserves', but more probably it will be urban refugees in Ralph Lauren attire asking the storekeeper if he has any guavas.

The same thing has been happening all over the country. I have just been reading an academic study on the dialect of Ocracoke Island off the coast of North Carolina. (The things I do for you, honestly.) Ocracoke is part of the Outer Banks, a chain of barrier islands where the inhabitants once spoke a hearty patois so rich and mysterious that visitors sometimes supposed they had stumbled on some half-lost outpost of Elizabethan England.

The locals – sometimes called 'Hoi-Toiders' for the way they pronounced 'high tide' – had an odd, lilting accent that incorporated many archaic terms, like 'quammish' (meaning to feel sick or uneasy), 'fladget' (for a piece of something), and 'mommuck' (meaning to bother) that hadn't been heard since Shakespeare put away his quill. Being a maritime people, they also used nautical terms in distinctive ways. For instance, 'scud', meaning to run before a gale with a small amount of sail, was employed for land-based movements, so that an Ocracoker might invite you to go for a scud in his car. Finally, just to make the bewilderment of outsiders complete, they absorbed a number of non-English words, like 'pizer' (apparently from the Italian 'piazza') for a porch, and pronounced the lot in a way that brought to mind George Formby doing a West Country accent. It was, in short, an interesting dialect.

All this scudded along, as you might say, in a dependable fashion until 1957, when the federal government built Ocracoke a bridge to the mainland. Almost at once tourists came in and the Ocracoke dialect began to go out.

This was scientifically monitored and recorded by linguists from North Carolina State University, who made periodic field trips to the island over half a century. Then, to everyone's surprise, the Ocracoke dialect began to undergo a revival. The researchers found that middle-aged people – those who had grown up in the 1950s and 1960s when tourism first became a dominant feature of island life – had more pronounced accents than even their parents had. The explanation, the researchers surmise, is that the islanders 'exaggerate their island dialect features, whether consciously or not, because they want there to be no mistake that they are "real" Ocracokers and not tourists or new residents recently relocated from the mainland'.

Much the same sort of phenomenon was found elsewhere. A study of the dialect on Martha's Vineyard, off the coast of Massachusetts, found that certain traditional pronunciations there, such as the flattening of the 'ou' sound in words like 'house' and 'mouse', making them something more like 'hawse' and 'mawse', staged an unexpected rally after nearly going extinct. The driving force, it turned out, was natives who returned to the island after living away and embraced the old speech forms as a way of distinguishing themselves from the mass of non-natives.

So does this mean that the rich and chewy Vermont accent will likewise recover and that once again we can expect to hear people say that something 'would give you a pain where you never had an ache' or that they 'felt rougher than a boar's rear end'? Sadly, it seems not.

From the evidence, it appears that these dialectal revivals happen only on islands or in communities that are in some way still comparatively isolated.

So it seems likely that when old Walt finally hangs up his saw and hammer whoever takes his place won't sound like an old-time Vermonter even if he was born and reared there. I only hope he's not such an early riser.

20 July 1997

INEFFICIENCY REPORT

THE OTHER DAY SOMETHING IN OUR LOCAL NEWSPAPER CAUGHT MY EYE. It was an article reporting that the control tower and related facilities at our local airport are to be privatized. The airport loses money, so the Federal Aviation Administration is trying to cut costs by con-tracting out landing services to someone who can do it more cheaply. What especially caught my attention was a sentence deep in the arti-cle which said, 'A spokeswoman with the Federal Aviation Administration's regional office in New York City, Arlene Sarlac, could not provide the name of the company that will be taking over the tower.'

Well, that's really reassuring to hear. Now maybe I am hyper-touchy because I use the airport from time to time, and have a particular interest in its ability to bring planes down in an approximately normal fashion, so I would rather like to know that the tower hasn't been bought by, say, the New England Roller Towel Company or Crash Services (Panama) Ltd, and that the next time I come in to land the plane won't be guided in by some guy on a stepladder waving a broom. I would hope, at the very least, that the Federal Aviation Administration would have some idea of whom they were selling the tower to. Call me particular, but it seems to me that that's the sort of thing you ought to have on file somewhere.

The FAA, it must be said, is not the most efficient of enterprises. A government report in April noted that the agency had been plagued for years by power failures, malfunctioning and antiquated equipment, overworked and overstressed staff, inadequate training programmes, and mismanagement owing to a fragmented chain of command. With regard to equipment standards, the report found that '21 separate offices issued 71 orders, seven standards and 29 specifications'. The upshot was that the FAA didn't have any idea what equipment it owned, how it was being maintained, or even whose turn it was to make the coffee.

According to the *Los Angeles Times*: 'At least three airliner accidents may have been prevented had the FAA not fallen behind schedule in planned modernization of air traffic control equipment.'

I mention this because our subject this week is large-scale incompetence. Despite my best efforts there abounds a terrible myth, which I should like to lay to rest once and for all, that America is an efficient place. It is anything but.

Partly this is because it is a big country. Big countries spawn big bureaucracies. Those bureaucracies spawn lots of departments and each of those departments issues lots of rules and regulations.

An inevitable consequence is that with so many departments the left hand not only doesn't know what the right hand is doing, but doesn't seem to know that there is a right hand. This is interestingly illustrated by frozen pizza.

In the United States, frozen cheese pizza is regulated by the Food and Drug Administration. Frozen pepperoni pizza, on the other hand, is regulated by the Department of Agriculture. Each sets its own standards with regard to content, labelling and so on, has its own team of inspectors, and its own set of regulations which require licences, compliance certificates and all kinds of other costly paperwork. And that's just for frozen pizza. This kind of madness would not be possible in a small country like Britain. You need the European Union for that.

Altogether, it has been estimated, the cost to the nation of complying with the full whack of federal regulations is $668 billion a year, an average of $7,000 per household. That's a lot of compliance.

What gives American inefficiency its particular tang, however, is a peculiar insane cheapness. There is a kind of short-termism here that is simply mystifying. Consider an experience of the Internal Revenue Service, our equivalent of the Inland Revenue.

Every year in the United States an estimated $100 billion in taxes – a positively whopping sum, enough to wipe out the federal deficit at a stroke – goes unreported and uncollected. In 1995, as an experiment, the government gave the IRS $100 million of extra funding to go looking for some of this extra money. At the end of the year it had found and collected $800 million – only a fraction of the missing money, but still $8 of extra government revenue for every $1 of additional collection costs.

The IRS confidently predicted that if the programme were extended it would net the government at least $12 billion of missing tax revenues the following year, with more to come in succeeding years. Instead of expanding the programme, Congress chopped it as – wait for it – part of its federal deficit reduction programme. Do you begin to see what I mean?

Or take food inspection. All kinds of high-tech gizmos exist to test meat for microbial infestations like salmonella and *E. coli*. But the government is too cheap to invest in these, so federal food inspectors continue to inspect meat visually, as it rolls past on assembly lines. Now you can imagine how attentively a low-paid federal food inspector is going to be looking at each of 18,000 identical plucked chickens sliding past him on a conveyor belt every day of his working life. Call me a cynic, but I very much doubt that after a dozen years or so of this an inspector is likely to be thinking: 'Hey, here come some more chickens. These might be interesting.' In any case – and here's a point that you would think might have occurred to somebody by now – micro-organisms are invisible.

As a result, by the government's own admission, as much as 20 per cent of all chicken and 49 per cent of turkey is contaminated. What all this costs in illness is anybody's guess, but it is thought that as many as 80 million people may get sick each year from factory-contaminated food, costing the economy somewhere between $5 billion and $10 billion in additional healthcare costs, lost productivity and so on. Every year 9,000 people die of food poisoning in the United States.

All of which brings us back to the good old Federal Aviation Administration. (Actually it doesn't, but I had to get here somehow.) The FAA may or may not be the most inefficient bureaucracy in the United States, but it is indubitably the only one that has my life in its hands when I am 32,000 feet above the earth, so you may imagine my disquiet at learning that it is handing over our control tower to some people whose names it can't remember.

According to our newspaper, the handover will be complete by the end of the month. Three days after that, I am irrevocably committed to flying to Washington from that airport. I mention this merely in case you find a blank space here in a couple of weeks.

But it probably won't come to that. I just asked my wife what we are having for dinner.

Turkey burgers, she said.

27 July 1997

A DAY AT THE SEASIDE

EVERY YEAR ABOUT THIS TIME, MY WIFE WAKES ME UP WITH A PLAYFUL
slap and says: 'I've got an idea. Let's drive for three hours to the
ocean, take off most of our clothes and sit on some sand for a whole day.'

'What for?' I will say warily.

'It will be fun,' she will insist.

'I don't think so,' I will reply. 'People find it disturbing when I take
my shirt off in public. I find it disturbing.'

'No, it will be great. We'll get sand in our hair. We'll get sand in
our shoes. We'll get sand in our sandwiches and then in our mouths.
We'll get sunburned and windburned. And when we get tired of sitting, we can have a paddle in water so cold it actually hurts. At the
end of the day we'll set off at the same time as 37,000 other people
and get in such a traffic jam that we won't get home till midnight. I
can make trenchant observations about your driving skills, and the
children can pass the time sticking each other with sharp objects. It
will be such fun.'

The tragic thing is that because my wife is English, and therefore beyond the reach of reason where saltwater is concerned, she really will think it's fun. Frankly I have never understood the British attachment to the seaside.

Iowa, where I grew up, is a thousand miles from the nearest ocean, so to me (and I believe to most other Iowans, though I haven't had a chance to check with all of them yet) the word 'ocean' suggests alarming things like riptides and undertows. (I expect people in New York suffer similar terrors when you mention words like 'cornfields' and 'county fair'.) Lake Ahquabi, where I did all my formative swimming and sunburning, may not have the romance of Cape Cod or the grandeur of the rockribbed coast of Maine, but then neither did it grab you by the legs and carry you off helplessly to Newfoundland. No, you may keep the sea, as far as I am concerned, and every drop of water in it.

So when last weekend my wife suggested that we take a drive to the ocean, I put my foot down and said, 'Never – absolutely not,' which is of course why we ended up, three hours later, at Kennebunk Beach in Maine.

Now you may find this hard to believe, given the whirlwind of adventure that has been my life, but in all my years I had been to American ocean beaches just twice – once in California when I was twelve and managed to scrape all the skin from my nose (this is a true story) by mistiming a retreating wave as only someone from Iowa can and diving headlong into bare gritty sand, and once in Florida when I was a college student and far too intoxicated to notice a landscape feature as subtle as an ocean.

So I can't pretend to speak with authority here. All I can tell you is that if Kennebunk Beach is anything to go by, then American beaches are entirely unlike British ones. To begin with, there was no pier, promenade or arcades; no shops where everything is miraculously priced at £1; no places to buy saucy postcards or jaunty hats; no tearooms and fish and chip shops; no fortune tellers; no disembodied voice from a bingo parlour breathing out those strange, coded calls: '*Number 37 – the vicar's in the shrubs again,*' or whatever it is they say.

Indeed, there was nothing commercial at all – just a street lined with big summer homes, a vast sunny beach and an infinite and hostile sea beyond.

That isn't to say the people on the beach – of whom there were many hundreds – were going without, for they had brought everything they would ever need again in the way of food, beverages, beach umbrellas, windbreaks, folding chairs, and sleek inflatables. Amundsen went to the South Pole with fewer provisions than most of these people had.

We were a pretty pathetic sight in contrast. Apart from being whiter than an old man's flanks, we had in the way of equipment just three beach towels and a raffia bag filled, in the English style, with a bottle of sunscreen, an inexhaustible supply of Wet Wipes, spare underpants for everyone (in case of vehicular accidents involving visits to an emergency room) and a modest packet of sandwiches.

Our youngest – whom I've taken to calling Jimmy in case he should one day become a libel lawyer – surveyed the scene and said: 'OK, Dad, here's the situation. I need an ice cream, a Lilo, a deluxe bucket and spade set, a hot dog, some candy floss, an inflatable dinghy, scuba equipment, my own water slide, a cheese pizza with extra cheese, and a toilet.'

'They don't have those things here, Jimmy,' I chuckled.

'I really need the toilet.'

I reported this to my wife. 'Then you'll have to take him to Kennebunkport,' she said serenely from beneath a preposterous sun hat.

Kennebunkport is an old town, at a crossroads, laid out long before anyone thought of the motorcar, and some miles from the beach. It was jammed with traffic from all directions. We parked an appallingly vast distance from the centre and searched all over for toilets. By the time we found a toilet (actually it was the back wall of the Rite-Aid Pharmacy – but please don't tell my wife), little Jimmy didn't need to go any longer.

So we returned to the beach. By the time we got there, some hours later, I discovered that everyone had gone off for a swim and there was only one half-eaten sandwich left. I sat on a towel and nibbled at the sandwich.

'Oh, look, Mummy,' said number two daughter gaily when they emerged from the surf a few minutes later, 'Daddy's eating the sandwich the dog had.'

'Tell me this isn't happening,' I whimpered.

'Don't worry, dear,' my wife said soothingly. 'It was an Irish setter. They're very clean.'

I don't remember much after that. I had a little nap and woke to find that Jimmy was burying me up to my chest in sand, which was fine except that he had started at my head, and I had managed to get so sunburned that a dermatologist invited me to a convention in Cleveland the following week as an exhibit.

We lost the car keys for two hours, the Irish setter came back and stole one of the beach towels, then nipped me on the hand for eating his sandwich, and number two daughter got tar in her hair. It was a typical day at the seaside, in other words. We got home about midnight after an inadvertent detour to the Canadian border – though this at least gave us something to talk about on the long drive across Pennsylvania.

'Lovely,' said my wife. 'We must do that again soon.'

And the heartbreaking thing is she really meant it.

3 August 1997

SPLENDID IRRELEVANCIES

NOW HERE'S A STORY I LIKE VERY MUCH.

Just before Christmas last year an American computer games company called Maxis Inc. released an adventure game called SimCopter in which players had to fly helicopters on rescue missions. When they successfully completed the tenth and final level, according to the *New York Times*, the winning players were supposed to be rewarded with some audio-visual hoopla involving 'a crowd, fireworks and a brass band'.

Instead, to their presumed surprise, the winners found images of men in swimsuits kissing each other.

The rogue images, it turned out, were the work of a mischievous 33-year-old programmer named Jacques Servin. When contacted by the *Times*, Mr Servin said he had created the smooching fellows 'to call attention to the lack of gay characters in computer games'. The company hastily recalled 78,000 games, and invited Mr Servin to find employment elsewhere.

Here's another story I like.

In June of this year, while travelling alone across America by car, Mrs Rita Rupp of Tulsa, Oklahoma, got it in mind that she might be abducted by nefarious persons. So, just to be on the safe side, she prepared a note in advance, in appropriately desperate-looking handwriting, that said: 'Help, I've been kidnapped. Call the highway patrol.' The note then gave her name and address, and phone numbers for the appropriate armed authorities.

Now if you write a note like this, you want to make certain that either (a) you do get kidnapped or (b) you don't accidentally drop the note out of your handbag. Well, guess what happened? The hapless Mrs Rupp dropped the note, it was picked up and turned in by a conscientious citizen, and the next thing you know police in four states had set up roadblocks, issued all-points bulletins and generally got themselves pretty excited. Meanwhile, Mrs Rupp drove on to her destination sweetly unaware of the chaos she had left in her wake.

The trouble with these two stories, delightful though they are, is that I haven't figured out a way to get them into one of my columns. That's the trouble with this column-writing business, I find. I am forever coming across interesting and worthwhile titbits (or 'tidbits', as we insist on spelling it in the United States in order not to provoke anyone into an untimely sweat) and when I come across these diverting items I carefully cut them out or photocopy them and file them away under 'Computer Games (Men Kissing)' or 'Worst Highway Travel Tips', or whatever seems to suit.

Then, some time later – well, this afternoon to be precise – I come across them again and wonder what on earth I was thinking. I call this collecting of interesting but ultimately useless information the Ignaz Semmelweiss Syndrome, after the Austro-Hungarian doctor Ignaz Semmelweiss, who in 1850 became the first person to realize that the spread of infection on hospital wards could be dramatically reduced by washing one's hands. Soon after making his breakthrough discovery Dr Semmelweiss died – from an infected cut on his hand.

You see what I mean? A splendid story, but I've got no place to put it. I might equally have called the phenomenon the Versalle Syndrome, after the opera singer Richard Versalle, who in 1996, during the world première of the *The Makropulos Affair* at the Metropolitan Opera House in New York, sang the fateful words 'Too bad you can only live so long,' and then, poor man, fell down dead from a heart attack.

Then again I might have named it in honour of the great General John Sedgewick of the Union Army, whose last words, at the Battle of Fredericksburg during the American Civil War, were: 'I tell you, men, they could not hit a bull at this dis—'

What all these people have in common is that they don't have the slightest relevance to anything I have ever written about or probably ever will. The trouble is that I am never altogether sure what I am going to write about (I can't wait to find out where this is going, to tell you the truth), so I keep these things filed away just in case they may come in handy in a pinch.

In consequence, I have manila folders bulging with cuttings like – well, like this one here, from a newspaper in Portland, Maine, bearing the headline 'Man Found Chained to Tree Again'. It was the 'Again' that particularly caught my eye. If the headline had said 'Man Found Chained to Tree' I would probably have turned the page. After all, anyone can get himself chained to a tree once. But *twice* – well, now that's beginning to seem a tad careless.

The person concerned was one Larry Doyen of Mexico, Maine, who, it turns out, has the very interesting hobby of attaching himself to trees with a chain and padlock and throwing the key out of arm's reach. On this particular occasion, he had been out in the woods for two weeks and had very nearly expired.

A diverting story, and clearly a salutary lesson for any of us who were thinking of taking up al fresco bondage for a hobby, but it's hard to imagine at this remove what I was hoping to make of it *vis-à-vis* the estimable *Night & Day* magazine.

I am similarly at a loss to recall the presumed significance of a small story I saved from the *Seattle Times* concerning a group of army paratroopers who, as a public relations exercise, agreed to parachute onto a high school football pitch in Kennewick, Washington, to present the game ball to the home team quarterback. With commendable precision they leapt from their aeroplane, trailing coloured smoke from special flares, executed several nifty and breathtaking aerobatic manoeuvres, and landed in an empty stadium on the other side of town.

I am equally unable to account fully for another story from the *New York Times*, about a couple who wrote down the gurgling sounds made by their infant daughter, presented it in the form of a poem (typical line: 'Bwah-bwah bwah-bwah bwah-bwah'), submitted it to something called the North American Open Poetry Contest, and won a semi-finalist prize.

Sometimes, alas, I don't save the whole article, but just a paragraph from it, so that all I am left with is a mystifying fragment. Here is a quotation from the March 1996 issue of the *Atlantic Monthly* magazine: 'It is perfectly legal for a dermatologist to do brain surgery in his garage if he can find a patient willing to get on the table and pay for it.' Here's another, from the *Washington Post*: 'Researchers at the University of Utah have discovered that most men breathe mainly through one nostril for three hours and mainly through the other for the following three.' Goodness knows what they do for the other eighteen hours of the day, because I didn't save the rest of the article.

I keep thinking that I will figure a way to work these oddments up into a column, but I haven't hit on it yet. However, the one thing I can confidently promise you is that when I do, you will read it here first.

10 August 1997

ON LOSING A SON

THIS MAY GET A LITTLE SOPPY, AND I'M SORRY, BUT YESTERDAY EVENING I was working at my desk when my youngest child came up to me, a baseball bat perched on his shoulder, a cap on his head, and asked me if I felt like playing a little ball with him. I was trying to get some important work done before going away on a long trip, and I very nearly declined with regrets, but then it occurred to me that never again would he be seven years, one month and six days old, so we had better catch these moments while we can.

So we went out onto the front lawn and here is where it gets soppy. There was a kind of beauty about the experience so elemental and wonderful I cannot tell you – the way the evening sun fell across the lawn, the earnest eagerness of his young stance, the fact that we were doing this most quintessentially dad-and-son thing, the supreme contentment of just being together – and I couldn't believe that it would ever have occurred to me that finishing an article or writing a book or doing anything at all could be more important and rewarding than this.

Now what has brought on all this sudden sensitivity is that a week or so ago we took our eldest son off to a small university in Ohio. He was the first of our four to fly the coop, and now he is gone – grown up, independent, far away – and I am suddenly realizing how quickly they go.

'Once they leave for college they never really come back,' a neighbour who has lost two of her own in this way told us wistfully the other day.

This isn't what I wanted to hear. I wanted to hear that they come back a lot, only this time they hang up their clothes, admire you for your intelligence and wit, and no longer have a hankering to sink diamond studs into various odd holes in their heads. But the neighbour was right. He is gone. There is an emptiness in the house that proves it.

I hadn't expected it to be like this because for the past couple of years even when he was here he wasn't really here, if you see what I mean. Like most teenagers, he didn't live in our house in any meaningful sense – more just dropped by a couple of times a day to see what was in the refrigerator or to wander between rooms, a towel round his waist, calling out, 'Mum, where's my . . . ?' as in, 'Mum, where's my yellow shirt?' and 'Mum, where's my deodorant?' Occasionally I would see the top of his head in an easy chair in front of a television on which Oriental people were kicking each other in the heads, but mostly he resided in a place called 'Out.'

My role in getting him off to college was simply to write cheques – lots and lots of them – and to look suitably pale and aghast as the sums mounted. You can't believe the cost of sending a child to university in the United States these days. Perhaps it is because we live in a community where these matters are treated gravely, but nearly every college-bound youth in our town goes off and looks at half a dozen or more prospective universities at enormous cost. Then there are fees for college entrance examinations and a separate fee for each university applied to.

But all this pales beside the cost of university itself. My son's tuition is $19,000 a year – that's nearly £12,000 in real money – which I am told is actually quite reasonable these days. Some schools charge as much as $28,000 for tuition. Then there is a fee of $3,000 a year for his room, $2,400 for food, $700 or so for books, $650 for health centre fees and insurance, and $710 for 'activities'. Don't ask me what that is. I just sign the cheques.

Still to come are the costs of flying him to and from Ohio at Thanksgiving, Christmas and Easter – holidays when every other college student in America is flying and so airfares are at their most stupefyingly extreme – plus all the other incidental expenses like spending money and long-distance phone bills. Already my wife is calling him every other day to ask if he has enough money, when in fact, as I point out, it should be the other way round. Oh, and this goes on for four years here, rather than three as in Britain. And here's one more thing. Next year I have a daughter who goes off to university, so I get to do this twice.

So you will excuse me, I hope, when I tell you that the emotional side of this event was rather overshadowed by the ongoing financial shock. It wasn't until we dropped him at his university dormitory and left him there looking touchingly lost and bewildered amid an assortment of cardboard boxes and suitcases in a spartan room not unlike a prison cell, that it really hit home that he was vanishing out of our lives and into his own.

Now that we are home it is even worse. There is no kickboxing on the TV, no astounding clutter of trainers in the back hallway, no calls of 'Mum, where's my . . . ?' from the top of the stairs, no one my size to call me a 'doofus' or to say, 'Nice shirt, Dad. Did you mug a boat person?' In fact, I see now, I had it exactly wrong. Even when he wasn't here, he was here, if you see what I mean. And now he is not here at all.

It takes only the simplest things – a wadded-up sweatshirt found behind the back seat of the car, some used chewing gum left in a patently inappropriate place – to make me want to blubber helplessly. Mrs Bryson, meanwhile, doesn't need any kind of prod. She just blubbers helplessly – at the sink, while hoovering, in the bath. 'My baby,' she wails in dismay and blows her nose with an alarming honk on any convenient piece of fabric, then whimpers some more.

For the past week I have found myself spending a lot of time wandering aimlessly through the house looking at the oddest things – a basketball, his running trophies, an old holiday snapshot – and thinking about all the carelessly discarded yesterdays they represent. The hard and unexpected part is the realization not just that my son is not here, but that the boy he was is gone for ever. I would give anything to have them both back. But of course that cannot be. Life moves on. Kids grow up and move away, and if you don't know this already, believe me it happens faster than you can imagine.

Which is why I am going to finish here and go off and play a little baseball on the front lawn while the chance is still there.

14 September 1997

HIGHWAY DIVERSIONS

IF YOU HAVE BEEN FOLLOWING THIS SPACE CLOSELY (AND IF NOT, WHY not?) you will recall that last week I discussed how we recently drove from New Hampshire to Ohio in order to deliver my eldest son to a university which had offered to house and educate him for the next four years in return for a sum of money not unadjacent to the cost of a moon launch.

What I didn't tell you then, because I didn't want to upset you on my first week back from holiday, is what a nightmare experience it was. Now please understand, I am as fond of my wife and children as the next man, no matter how much they cost me per annum in footwear and Nintendo games (which is frankly a lot), but that isn't to say that I wish to pass a week with them ever again in a sealed metal chamber on an American highway.

The trouble is not my family, I hasten to add, but the American highway. Oh, is the American highway dull. As a Briton, you really cannot imagine boredom on this scale (unless perhaps you are from Stevenage). Part of the problem with American highways is that they are so very long – it is 850 miles from New Hampshire to central Ohio and, I can now personally attest, just as far back – but mostly it is because there is nothing to get excited about along the way.

It didn't used to be like this. When I was a boy, the highways of the United States were scattered with diversions. They weren't very good diversions, but that didn't matter at all.

At some point on every day, you could count on seeing a hoarding that would say something like: 'Visit World-Famous Atomic Rock – It Really Glows!' A few miles later there would be another hoarding saying: 'See the Rock That Has Baffled Science! Only 162 Miles!' This one would have a picture of a grave-looking scientist with a cartoon bubble beside his mouth confiding: 'It Is Truly a Marvel of Nature!' or 'I Am Quite Baffled!'

A few miles beyond that would be: 'Experience the Atomic Rock Force Field . . . *If You Dare*! Just 147 Miles!' This one would show a man, interestingly not unlike one's own father, being violently flung back by some strange radiant force. In smaller letters would be the warning: 'Caution: May Not Be Suitable for Small Children.'

Well, that would be it. My big brother and sister, squeezed onto the backseat with me and having exhausted all the possibilities for diversion that came with holding me down and drawing vivid geometric patterns on my face, arms and stomach with a biro, would set up a clamour to see this world-famous attraction, and I would weakly chime in.

The people who put up these hoardings were brilliant, among the greatest marketing geniuses of our age. They knew precisely – to the mile, I would guess – how long it would take a carful of children to wear down their father's profound and inevitable opposition to visiting something that was going to waste time and cost money. The upshot, in any case, is that we always went.

The world-famous Atomic Rock would of course be nothing like the advertised attraction. It would be almost comically smaller than illustrated and wouldn't glow at all. It would be fenced off, ostensibly for the safety of onlookers, and the fence would be covered with warnings saying: 'Caution: Dangerous Force Field! Approach No Further!' But there would always be some kid who would crawl under the fence and go up and touch it, indeed clamber all over it, without being flung aside or suffering any other evident consequences. As a rule, my extravagant biro tattoos would draw more interest from the crowd.

So in disgust my father would pile us all back into the car vowing never to be duped like this again and we would drive on until, some hours later, we would pass a hoarding that said: 'Visit World-Famous Singing Sands! Only 214 Miles!' and the cycle would start again.

Out west, in really boring states like Nebraska and Kansas, people could put up signs saying pretty much anything – 'See the Dead Cow! Hours of Fun for the Whole Family!' or 'Plank of Wood! Just 132 Miles!' Over the years, I well recall, we visited a dinosaur footprint, a painted desert, a petrified frog, a hole in the ground that claimed to be the world's deepest well, and a house made entirely of beer bottles. In fact, from some of our holidays that is all I can remember.

These things were always disappointing, but that wasn't the point. You weren't paying 75 cents for the experience. You were paying 75 cents as a kind of tribute, a thanks to the imaginative person who had helped you to pass 127 miles of uneventful highway in a state of genuine excitement, and, in my case, without being drawn on. My father never understood this.

Now, I regret to say, my children don't understand it either. On this trip as we drove across Pennsylvania, a state so ludicrously vast that it takes a whole day to traverse, we passed a sign that said: 'Visit World-Famous Roadside America! Just 79 Miles!'

I had no idea what Roadside America was, and it wasn't even on our route, but I insisted that we go there anyway. These things simply don't exist any longer. Nowadays the most exciting thing you can hope to get along the American highway is a McDonald's Happy Meal. So something like Roadside America, whatever it might be, is to be devoutly cherished. The great irony is that I was the only one in the car, and by a considerable margin, who wanted to see it.

Roadside America turned out to be a large model railway, with little towns and tunnels, farms with miniature cows and sheep, and lots of trains going round in endless circles. It was a little dusty and ill-lit, but charming in a not-touched-since-1957 sort of way. We were the only customers that day, possibly the only customers for many days. I loved it.

'Isn't this great?' I said to my youngest daughter.

'Dad, you are like so pathetic,' she said sadly and went out.

I turned hopefully to her little brother, but he just shook his head and followed.

I was disappointed, naturally, but I think I know what to do next time. I'll hold them down for two hours beforehand and draw all over them with a biro. Then they'll appreciate any kind of highway diversion. Of that I am certain.

21 September 1997

SNOOPERS AT WORK

NOW HERE IS SOMETHING TO BEAR IN MIND SHOULD YOU EVER FIND
yourself using a changing cubicle in an American department store or
other retail establishment. It is perfectly legal – indeed, it is evidently
routine – for the store or shop to spy on you while you are trying on
their clothes.

I know this because I have just been reading a book by Ellen
Alderman and Caroline Kennedy called *The Right to Privacy*, which
is full of alarming tales of ways that businesses and employers can –
and enthusiastically do – intrude into what would normally be
considered private affairs.

The business of changing-cubicle spying came to light in 1983 when a customer trying on clothes in a department store in Michigan discovered that a store employee had climbed a stepladder and was watching him through a metal vent. (Is this tacky or what?) The customer was sufficiently outraged that he sued the store for invasion of privacy. He lost. A state court held that it was reasonable for retailers to defend against shoplifting by engaging in such surveillance.

He shouldn't have been surprised. Nearly everyone is being spied on in some way in America these days. A combination of technological advances, employer paranoia and commercial avarice means that many millions of Americans are having their lives delved into in ways that would not have been possible, or even thinkable, a dozen years ago.

Log onto the Internet and nearly every website you go to will make a record of what you looked at and how long you lingered there. This information can, and generally will, then be sold on to mail order and marketing companies, or otherwise used to bombard you with blandishments to spend.

Worse still, there are now scores of information brokers – electronic private investigators – who make a living going through the Internet digging out personal information on people for a fee. If you are an American resident and have ever registered to vote they can get your address and date of birth, since voter registration forms are a matter of public record in most states. With these two pieces of information they can (and for as little as $8 or $10 will) provide almost any personal information about any person you might wish to know: court records, medical records, driving records, credit history, hobbies, buying habits, annual income, phone numbers (including ex-directory numbers), you name it.

Most of this was possible before, but it would take days of inquiries and visits to various government offices. Now it can be done in minutes, in complete anonymity, through the Internet.

Many companies are taking advantage of these technological possibilities to make their businesses more ruthlessly productive. In Maryland, according to *Time* magazine, a bank searched through the medical records of its borrowers – apparently quite legally – to find out which of them had life-threatening illnesses, and used this information to cancel their loans. Other companies have focused not on customers but on their own employees – for instance to check what prescription drugs the employees are taking. One large, well-known company teamed up with a pharmaceutical firm to comb through the health records of employees to see who might benefit from a dose of anti-depressants. The idea was that the company would get more serene workers; the drug company would get more customers.

According to the American Management Association two-thirds of companies in the United States spy on their employees in some way. Thirty-five per cent track phone calls and 10 per cent actually tape phone conversations to review at leisure later. About a quarter of companies admit to going through their employees' computer files and reading their e-mail.

Still other companies are secretly watching their employees at work. A secretary at a college in Massachusetts discovered that a hidden video camera was filming her office 24 hours a day. Goodness knows what the school authorities were hoping to find with their surveillance. What they got were images of the woman changing out of her work clothes and into a tracksuit each night in order to jog home from work. She is suing and will probably get a pot of money. But elsewhere courts have upheld companies' rights to spy on their workers.

In 1989, when an employee of a large Japanese-owned computer products company discovered that the company was routinely reading employees' e-mail, even though it had assured the employees that it was not, she blew the whistle and was promptly fired. She sued for unfair dismissal and lost the case. A court upheld the right of companies not only to review employees' private communications but to lie to them about doing it. Whoa.

And to return to a well-aired theme, there is a particular paranoia about drugs. I have a friend who got a job with a large manufacturing company in Iowa a year or so ago. Across the street from the company was a tavern that was the company after-hours hangout. One night my friend was having a beer after work with his colleagues when he was approached by a fellow employee who asked if he knew where she could get some marijuana. He said he didn't use the stuff himself, but to get rid of her – for she was very persistent – he gave her the phone number of an acquaintance who sometimes sold it.

The next day he was sacked. The woman, it turned out, was a company spy employed solely to weed out drug use in the company.

He hadn't supplied her with marijuana, you understand, hadn't encouraged her to use marijuana, and had stressed that he didn't use marijuana himself. None the less he was fired for 'encouraging and abetting the use of an illegal substance'.

Already, 91 per cent of large companies – I find this almost unbelievable – now test some of their workers for drugs. Scores of companies have introduced what are called TAD rules – TAD being short for 'tobacco, alcohol and drugs' – which prohibit employees from using any of these substances at any time, including at home. There are companies, if you can believe it, that forbid their employees to drink or smoke at any time – even one beer, even on a Saturday night – and enforce the rules by making their workers give urine samples. That is outrageous, but there you are.

But it gets even more sinister than that. Two leading electronics companies working together have invented something called an 'active badge', which tracks the movements of any worker compelled to wear one. The badge sends out an infrared signal every 15 seconds. This signal is received by a central computer, which is thus able to keep a record of where every employee is and has been, whom they have associated with, how many times they have been to the toilet or water cooler – in short, to log every single action of their working day. If that isn't ominous, I don't know what is.

However, there is one development, I am pleased to report, which makes all of this worthwhile. A company in New Jersey has patented a device for determining whether restaurant employees have washed their hands after using the lavatory. Now *that* I can go for.

28 September 1997

HOW TO HIRE A CAR

WE'VE BEEN BACK IN THE STATES FOR NEARLY TWO AND A HALF YEARS now, if you can believe it (and even, come to that, if you can't), so you would think I would be getting the hang of things by now, but alas no. The intricacies of modern American life still often leave me muddled. Things are so awfully complicated here, you see.

I had occasion to reflect on this the other week when I went to pick up a hire car at the airport in Boston, and the clerk, after logging every number that has ever been associated with me and taking imprints from several credit cards, said: 'Do you want Third Party Liability Waiver Damage Exclusion Cover?'

'I don't know,' I said uncertainly. 'What is it?'

'It provides cover in the event of a Second Party Waiver

Indemnification Claim being made against you, or a First or Second Party Exclusion Claim being made by you on behalf of a fourth party twice removed.'

'Unless you're claiming a First Party Residual Cross-Over Exemption,' added a man in the queue behind me, causing me to spin my head.

'No, that's only in New York,' corrected the hire car man. 'In Massachusetts you can't claim cross-over exemption unless you have only one leg and are not normally resident in North America for tax purposes.'

'You're thinking of Second Party Disallowance Invalidity Cover,' said a second man in the queue to the first. 'Are you from Rhode Island?'

'Why, yes I am,' said the first man.

'Then that explains it. You have Variable Double-Negative Split-Weighting down there.'

'I don't understand any of this,' I cried, wretchedly.

'Look,' said the car hire man a little impatiently, 'suppose you crash into a person who has Second Party Disallowance Invalidity Cover but not First and Third Party Accident Indemnification. If you've got Third Party Waiver Damage Exclusion Cover you don't have to claim on your own policy under the Single Digit Reverse Liability Waiver. How much Personal Loss Rollover do you carry?'

'I don't know,' I said.

He stared at me. 'You don't know?' he said in a tone of level in-credulity. Out of the corner of my eye I could see the other people in the queue exchanging amused glances.

'Mrs Bryson deals with these things,' I explained a trifle in-adequately.

'Well, what's your Baseline Double Footfault Level?'

I gave a small, helpless, please-don't-hit-me look. 'I don't know.'

He drew in breath in a way that suggested that perhaps I should consider walking. 'It sounds to me like you need the Universal Full-Cover Double Top-Loaded Comprehensive Switchback Plan.'

'With Graduated Death Benefit,' suggested the second man in the queue.

'What's all that?' I asked unhappily.

'It's all here in the leaflet,' said the clerk. He passed me a leaflet.

'Basically, it gives you $100 million of coverage for theft, fire, accident, earthquake, nuclear war, swamp gas explosions, meteor impact, derailment leading to hair loss and intentional death – so long as they occur simultaneously and providing you give 24 hours' notice in writing and file an Incident Intention Report.'

'How much is it?'

'One hundred and seventy-two dollars a day. But it comes with a set of steak knives.'

I looked to the other men in the queue. They nodded.

'OK, I'll take it,' I said in exhausted resignation.

'Now do you want the Worry-Free Fuel Top-Up Option,' the clerk went on, 'or the Fill-It-Yourself Cheap Person's Option?'

'What's that?' I asked, dismayed to realize that this hell wasn't yet over.

'Well, with the Worry-Free Fuel Top-Up Option you can bring the car back on empty and we will refill the tank for a one-time charge of $32.95. Under the other plan, you fill the tank yourself before returning the car and we put the $32.95 elsewhere on the bill under "Miscellaneous Unexplained Charges".'

I consulted with my advisers and took the Worry-Free plan.

The clerk ticked the appropriate box. 'And do you want the Car Locator Option Arrangement?'

'What's that?'

'We tell you where the car is.'

'Take it,' urged the man nearest me with feeling. 'I didn't take it once in Chicago, and spent two and a half days wandering around the airport looking for the damned thing. Turned out it was under a tarpaulin in a cornfield near Peoria.'

And so it went. Eventually, when we had worked our way through 200 or so pages of complexly tiered options, the clerk passed the contract to me.

'Just sign here, here and here,' he said. 'And initial here, here, here and here – and over here. And here, here and here.'

'What am I initialling?' I asked warily.

'Well, this one gives us the right to come to your home and seize one of your children or a nice piece of electronic equipment if you don't bring the car back on time. This one is your agreement to take a truth serum in the event of a dispute. This one waives your right to sue. This one avows that any damage to the car now or at any time in the future is your responsibility. And this one is a $25 donation to Bernice Kowalski's leaving do.'

Before I could respond, he whipped away the contract and replaced it on the counter with a map of the airport.

'Now to get to the car,' he continued, drawing on the map as if doing one of those maze puzzles that you find in children's colouring books, 'you follow the red signs through Terminal A to Terminal D2, then you follow the yellow signs – including the green ones – through the parking garage to the Sector R escalators. Take the down escalator up to Passenger Assembly Point Q, get on the shuttle marked "Satellite Parking/Mississippi Valley" and take it to Parking Lot A427-West. Get off there, follow the white arrows under the harbour tunnel, through the quarantine exclusion zone and past the water filtration plant. Cross runway 22-Left, climb the fence at the far side, go down the embankment, and you'll find your car parked in bay number 12,604. It's a red Flymo. You can't miss it.'

He passed me my keys and a large box filled with documents, insurance policies and other related items.

'And good luck to you,' he called after me.

I never did find the car, of course, and I was hours late for my appointment, but in fairness I have to say that we have had a lot of pleasure from the steak knives.

5 October 1997

FALL IN NEW ENGLAND

AH, AUTUMN!

Every year about this time, for a tantalizingly short while – a week or two at most – an amazing thing happens here. The whole of New England explodes in colour. All those trees that for months have formed a sombre green backdrop suddenly burst into a million glowing tints and the countryside, as Frances Trollope put it, 'goes to glory'.

Yesterday, under the pretence of doing vital research, I drove over to Vermont and treated my startled feet to a hike up Killington Peak, 4,235 feet of sturdy splendour in the heart of the Green Mountains. It was one of those sumptuous days when the world is full of autumn muskiness and tangy, crisp perfection, and the air so clean and clear that you feel as if you could reach out and ping it with a finger, as you would a polished wine glass. Even the colours were crisp: vivid blue sky, deep green fields, leaves in a thousand luminous hues. It is a truly astounding sight when every tree in a landscape becomes individual, when each winding back highway and plump hillside is suddenly and infinitely splashed with every sharp shade that nature can bestow – flaming scarlet, lustrous gold, throbbing vermilion, fiery orange.

Forgive me if I seem a tad effusive, but it is impossible to describe a spectacle this grand without babbling. Even the great naturalist Donald Culross Peattie, a man whose prose is so dry you could use it to mop spills, totally lost his head when he tried to convey the wonder of a New England autumn.

In his classic *Natural History of Trees of Eastern and Central North America*, Peattie drones on for 434 pages in language that can most generously be called workmanlike (typical passage: 'Oaks are usually ponderous and heavy-wooded trees, with scaly or furrowed bark, and more or less five-angled twigs and, consequently, five-ranked leaves . . .'), but when at last he turns his attention to the New England sugar maple and its vivid autumnal regalia, it is as if someone has spiked his cocoa. In a tumble of breathless metaphors he describes the maple's colours as 'like the shout of a great army . . . like tongues of flame . . . like the mighty, marching melody that rides upon the crest of some symphonic weltering sea and, with its crying song, gives meaning to all the calculated dissonance of the orchestra.'

'Yes, Donald,' you can just about hear his wife saying, 'now take your tablets, dear.'

For two fevered paragraphs he goes on like this and then abruptly returns to talking about drooping leaf axils, scaly buds and pendulous branchlets. I understand completely. When I reached the preternaturally clear air of Killington's summit, with views to every horizon soaked in autumn lustre, I found it was all I could do not to fling open my arms and burst forth with a medley of John Denver tunes. (For this reason it is a good idea to hike with an experienced companion and to carry a well-stocked first aid kit.)

Occasionally you read about some academic who has gone out with the scientific equivalent of a paint chart and announced with a grave air of discovery that the maples of Michigan or the oaks of the Ozarks achieve even deeper tints, but this is to completely miss the special qualities that make New England's fall display unique.

For one thing, the New England landscape provides a setting that no other area of North America can rival. Its sunny white churches, covered bridges, tidy farms and clustered villages are an ideal complement to the rich earthy colours of nature. Moreover, there is a variety in its trees that few other areas achieve: oaks, beeches, aspens, sumacs, four varieties of maples, and others almost beyond counting provide a contrast that dazzles the senses. Finally, and above all, there is the brief, perfect balance of its climate in fall, with crisp, chilly nights and warm, sunny days, which help to bring all the deciduous trees to a coordinated climax. So make no mistake. For a few glorious days each October, New England is unquestionably the loveliest place on earth.

What is all the more remarkable about this is that no one knows quite why it happens.

In autumn, as you will recall from your school biology lessons (or, failing that, from *Tomorrow's World*), trees prepare for their long winter's slumber by ceasing to manufacture chlorophyll, the chemical that makes their leaves green. The absence of chlorophyll allows other pigments, called carotenoids, which have been present in the leaves all along, to show off a bit. The carotenoids are what account for the yellow and gold of birches, hickories, beeches and some oaks, among others. Now here is where it gets interesting. To allow these golden colours to thrive, the trees must continue to feed the leaves even though the leaves are not actually doing anything useful except hanging there looking pretty. Just at a time when a tree ought to be storing up all its energy for use the following spring, it is instead expending a great deal of effort feeding a pigment that brings joy to the hearts of simple folk like me but doesn't do anything for the tree.

What is even more mysterious is that some species of trees go a step further and, at considerable cost to themselves, manufacture another type of chemical called anthocyanins, which result in the spectacular oranges and scarlets that are so characteristic of New England. It isn't that the trees of New England manufacture more of these anthocyanins, but rather that the New England climate and soil provide exactly the right conditions for these colours to bloom in style. In climates that are wetter or warmer, the trees still go to all this trouble – have done for years – but it doesn't come to anything. No one knows why the trees make this immense effort when they get nothing evident in return.

But here is the greatest mystery of all. Every year literally millions of people, genially and collectively known to locals as 'leaf peepers', get in their cars, drive great distances to New England and spend a succession of weekends shuffling round craft shops and places with names like 'Norm's Antiques and Collectibles'.

I would estimate that no more than 0.05 per cent of them stray more than 150 feet from their cars. What a strange, inexplicable misfortune that is, to come to the edge of perfection and then turn your back on it.

They miss not only the bosky joys of the out of doors – the fresh air, the rich, organic smells, the ineffable delight of strolling through drifts of dry leaves – but the singular pleasure of hearing the hills ringing with 'Take Me Home, Country Road' sung in a loud voice in a pleasingly distinctive Anglo-Iowa twang. And that, if I say so myself, is definitely worth getting out of your car for.

12 October 1997

A SLIGHT INCONVENIENCE

(for kitchen use only)

OUR SUBJECT TODAY IS CONVENIENCE IN AMERICA, AND HOW THE MORE convenient things supposedly get the more inconvenient they actually become.

I was thinking about this the other day (I'm always thinking, you know – it's amazing) when I took my younger children to a Burger King for lunch, and there was a line of about a dozen cars at the drive-through window. Now a drive-through window is not, despite its promising name, a window you drive through, but a window you drive up to and collect your food from, having placed your order over a speakerphone along the way. The idea is to provide quick takeaway food for those in a hurry.

We parked, went in, ordered and ate, and came out again all in about ten minutes. As we departed, I noticed that a white pickup truck that had been last in the queue when we arrived was still four or five cars back from collecting its food. It would have been much quicker if the driver had parked like us, and gone in and got his food himself, but he would never have thought that way because the drive-through window is *supposed* to be speedier and more convenient.

You see my point, of course. Americans have become so attached to the idea of convenience that they will put up with almost any inconvenience to achieve it. It's crazy, I know, but there you are. The things that are supposed to speed up and simplify our lives more often than not actually have the opposite effect, and this set me to thinking (see, there I go again) why this should be.

Americans have always had a strange devotion to the idea of assisted ease. It is an interesting fact that nearly all the everyday inventions that take the struggle out of life – escalators, automatic doors, passenger lifts, refrigerators, washing machines, frozen food, fast food – were invented in America, or at least first widely embraced here. Americans grew so used to a steady stream of labour-saving advances, in fact, that by the 1960s they had come to expect machines to do pretty much everything for them.

I remember the moment I first realized that this was not necessarily a good idea was at Christmas of 1961 or '62 when my father was given an electric carving knife. It was an early model and rather formidable. Perhaps my memory is playing tricks on me, but I have a clear impression of him donning goggles and heavy rubber gloves before plugging it in. What is certainly true is that when he sank it into the turkey it didn't so much carve the bird as send pieces of it flying everywhere in a kind of fleshy white spray, before the blade struck the plate with a shower of blue sparks, and the whole thing flew out of his hands and skittered across the table and out of the room, like a creature from a Gremlins movie. I don't believe we ever saw it again, though we used to sometimes hear it thumping against table legs late at night.

Like most patriotic Americans, my father was forever buying gizmos that proved to be disastrous – clothes steamers that failed to take the wrinkles out of suits but had wallpaper falling off the walls in whole sheets, an electric pencil sharpener that could consume an entire pencil (including the metal ferrule and the tips of your fingers if you weren't real quick) in less than a second, a water pick (which is, for those of you who don't know, a water-jet device which 'blast-cleans' your teeth) that was so lively it required two people to hold and left the bathroom looking like the inside of a car wash, and much else.

But all of this was as nothing compared with the situation today. Americans are now surrounded with items that do things for them to an almost absurd degree – automatic cat food dispensers, electric juicers and tin openers, refrigerators that make their own ice cubes, automatic car windows, disposable toothbrushes that come with the toothpaste already loaded. People are so addicted to convenience that they have become trapped in a vicious circle: the more labour-saving appliances they buy, the harder they need to work; the harder they work, the more labour-saving appliances they feel they need.

There is nothing, no matter how ridiculous, that won't find a receptive audience in America so long as it promises to provide some kind of relief from effort. I recently saw advertised, for $39.95, a 'lighted, revolving tie rack'. You push a button and it parades each of your ties before you, saving you the exhausting ordeal of making your selection by hand.

Our house in New Hampshire came replete with contraptions installed by earlier owners, all of them designed to make life that little bit easier. Up to a point, a few actually do (my favourite, of course, being the garbage disposal unit), but most are just kind of wondrously useless. One of our rooms, for instance, came equipped with automatic curtains. You flick a switch on the wall and four pairs of curtains effortlessly open or close. That, at any rate, is the idea. In practice what happens is that one opens, one closes, one opens and closes repeatedly, and one does nothing at all for five minutes and then starts to emit smoke. We haven't gone anywhere near them since the first week.

Something else we inherited was an automatic garage door opener. In theory this sounds wonderful and even rather classy. You sweep into the driveway, push a button on a remote control unit and then, depending on your sense of timing, pull into the garage smoothly or take the bottom panel off the door. Then you flick the button again and the door shuts behind you, and anyone walking past thinks: 'Wow! Classy guy!'

In reality, I have found, our garage door will close only when it is certain of crushing a tricycle or mangling a rake, and, once closed, will not open again until I get up on a chair and do something temperamental to the control box with a screwdriver and hammer, and eventually call in the garage door repairman, a fellow named Jake who has been taking his holidays in the Maldives since we became his clients. I have given Jake more money than I earned in my first four years out of college, and still I don't have a garage door I can count on.

You see my point again. Automatic curtains and garage doors, electric cat food dispensers and revolving tie racks only *seem* to make life easier. In fact, all they do is add expense and complication to your existence.

And therein lie our two important lessons of the day. First, never forget that the first syllable of convenience is *con*. And second, send your children to garage door repair school.

19 October 1997

SO SUE ME

I HAVE A FRIEND IN BRITAIN, AN ACADEMIC, WHO WAS RECENTLY approached by lawyers working for an American company to be an expert witness for a case they were handling. They told him they wanted to fly the lead attorney and two assistants to London to meet him.

'Wouldn't it be simpler and cheaper if I flew to New York instead?' my friend suggested.

'Yes,' he was told without hesitation, 'but this way we can bill the client for the cost of three trips.'

And there you have the American legal mind at work.

Now I have no doubt that a large number of American lawyers – well, two anyway – do wonderfully worthwhile things that fully justify charging their clients $150 an hour, which I gather is the going rate here. But the trouble is that there are too many of them. In fact – and here is a truly sobering statistic – the United States has more lawyers than all the rest of the world put together: almost 800,000 of them, up from an already abundant 260,000 in 1960. We now boast 300 lawyers for every 100,000 citizens. Britain, by contrast, has eighty-two, Japan a mere eleven.

And of course all those lawyers need work. Most states now allow lawyers to advertise, and many of them most enthusiastically do. You cannot watch TV for half an hour without encountering at least one commercial showing a sincere-looking lawyer saying: 'Hi, I'm Vinny Slick of Bent and Oily Law Associates. If you've suffered an injury at work, or been in a vehicular accident, or just feel like having some extra money, come to me and we'll find someone to sue.'

Americans, as is well known, will sue at the drop of a hat. In fact, I daresay someone somewhere has sued over a dropped hat, and won $20 million for the pain and suffering it caused. There really is a sense that if something goes wrong for whatever reason and you are any-where in the vicinity, then you ought to collect a pot of money.

This was neatly illustrated a couple of years ago when a chemical plant in Richmond, California, suffered an explosion which spewed fumes over the town. Within hours, 200 lawyers and their represent-atives had descended on the excited community, handing out business cards and advising people to present themselves at the local hospital. Twenty thousand residents eagerly did so.

News footage of the event makes it look like some kind of open-air party. Of the 20,000 happy, smiling, seemingly very healthy people who lined up for examination at the hospital's emergency room, just twenty were actually admitted. Although the number of proven injuries was slight, to say the least, 70,000 townspeople – virtually all of them – filed claims. The company agreed to a $180 million settle-ment. Of this, the lawyers got $40 million.

Every year over 90 million lawsuits are filed in this extravagantly litigious country – that's one for every two and a half people – and many of these are what might charitably be called ambitious. As I write, two parents in Texas are suing a high school baseball coach for benching their son during a game, claiming humiliation and extreme mental anguish. In Washington state, meanwhile, a man with heart problems is suing the local dairies 'because their milk cartons did not warn him about cholesterol'. I am sure you read about the woman in California who sued the Walt Disney Company after she and her family were mugged in a car park at Disneyland. A central part of the suit was that her grandchildren suffered shock and trauma when they were taken behind the scenes to be comforted and they saw Disney characters taking off their costumes. The discovery that Mickey Mouse and Goofy were in fact real people inside costumes was apparently too much for the poor tykes.

That case was dismissed, but elsewhere people have won fortunes out of all proportion to any pain or loss they might actually have suffered. Recently there was a much-publicized case in which an executive at a Milwaukee brewery recounted the racy plot of a Seinfeld television show to a female colleague, who took offence and reported him for sexual harassment. The brewery responded by sacking the fellow, and he responded by suing the brewery. Now I don't know who deserved what in this case – it sounds to me, frankly, like they all wanted a good sound spanking – but the upshot is that the sacked executive was awarded $26.6 million, roughly 400,000 times his annual salary, by a sympathetic (i.e., demented) jury.

Allied with the idea that lawsuits are a quick way to a fortune is the interesting and uniquely American notion that no matter what happens, someone else must be responsible. So if, say, you smoke eighty cigarettes a day for fifty years and eventually get cancer, then it must be everyone else's fault but your own, and you sue not only the manufacturer of your cigarettes, but the wholesaler, the retailers, the haulage firm that delivered the cigarettes to the retailer, and so on. One of the most extraordinary features of the American legal system is that it allows plaintiffs to sue people and companies only tangentially connected to the alleged complaint.

Because of the way the system works (or more accurately doesn't work) it is often less expensive for a company or institution to settle out of court than to let the matter proceed to trial. I know a woman who slipped and fell while entering a department store on a rainy day and, to her astonishment and gratification, was offered a more or less instant settlement of $2,500 if she would sign a piece of paper agreeing not to sue. She signed.

The cost of all this to society is enormous – several billion dollars a year at least. New York City alone spends $200 million a year settling 'slip and fall' claims – people tripping over kerbs and the like.

According to a recent ABC Television documentary on America's runaway legal system, because of inflated product liability costs consumers in the United States pay $500 more than they need to for every car they buy, $100 more for football helmets, and $3,000 more for heart pacemakers. According to the documentary, they even pay a little on top (as it were) for haircuts because one or two distressed customers successfully sued their barbers after being given the sort of embarrassing trims that I receive as a matter of routine.

All of which, naturally, has given me an idea. I am going to go and smoke eighty cigarettes, then slip and fall while drinking high-cholesterol milk and relating the plot of a Seinfeld show to a passing female in the Disneyland car park, and then I'll call Vinny Slick and see if we can strike a deal. I don't expect to settle for less than $2.5 billion – and that's before we've even started talking about my latest haircut.

26 October 1997

THE GREAT INDOORS

enjoy outdoors indoors!

I WAS OUT FOR A WALK THE OTHER DAY AND I WAS STRUCK BY AN ODD thing. It was a glorious day – as good as a day can get, and very probably the last of its type that we shall see for many a long wintry month around here – yet almost every car that passed had its windows up.

All these drivers had adjusted their temperature controls to create a climate inside their sealed vehicles that was identical to the climate already existing in the larger world outside, and it occurred to me that where fresh air is concerned Americans have rather lost their minds, or sense of proportion, or something.

Oh, occasionally they will go out for the novel experience of being out of doors – they will go on a picnic, say, or for a day at the beach or to a big amusement park – but these are exceptional events. By and large most Americans have grown so reflexively habituated to the idea of passing the bulk of their lives in a series of climate-controlled environments that the possibility of an alternative no longers occurs to them.

So they shop in enclosed malls, and drive to those malls with the car windows up and the air-conditioning on, even when the weather is flawless, as it was on this day. They work in offices where they could not open the windows even if they wanted to – not, of course, that anyone would want to. When they go on holiday, it is often in an outsized motor-home that allows them to experience the great outdoors without actually exposing themselves to it. Increasingly, when they go to a sporting event it will be in an indoor stadium. Walk through almost any American neighbourhood now in summer and you won't see children on bikes or playing ball, for they are all inside. All you will hear is the uniform hum of air-conditioning units.

Cities across the nation have taken to building what are called skywalks – enclosed pedestrian flyovers, climate-controlled of course – connecting all the buildings in their centres. In my hometown of Des Moines, Iowa, the first skywalk was erected between a hotel and department store about twenty-five years ago and was such a hit that soon other developers were getting in on the act. Now it is possible to walk for half a mile or more downtown in any direction without ever setting foot outdoors. All the shops that used to be at street level have moved up to the first floor, where the pedestrian traffic now is. Now the only people you ever see at street level in Des Moines are winos and office workers standing around having a smoke. The outdoors, you see, has become a kind of purgatory, a place to which you are banished.

There are even clubs composed of office workers who change into sweatsuits and spend their lunch hours taking brisk, healthful hikes along a measured course through the skywalks. It would never occur to them to step outside to do this. Similar clubs, typically composed of retired people, can be found at nearly every shopping mall in the nation. These are people, you understand, who meet at malls not to shop but to get their daily exercise.

The last time I was in Des Moines, I ran into an old friend of the family. He was dressed in a sweatsuit and told me that he had just come from a session with the Valley West Mall Hiking Club. It was a splendid April day, and I asked him why the club didn't use any of the city's several large and handsome parks.

'No rain, no cold, no hills, no muggers,' he replied without hesitation.

'But there are no muggers in Des Moines,' I pointed out.

'That's right,' he agreed at once, 'and do you know why? Because there's nobody outside to mug.' He nodded his head emphatically, as if I hadn't thought of that, as indeed I had not.

The apotheosis of this strange movement may be the Opryland Hotel in Nashville, Tennessee, where I went a year or so ago on a magazine assignment. The Opryland Hotel is an extraordinary institution. To begin with, it is immense and almost gorgeously ugly – a sort of *Gone with the Wind* meets Graceland meets Mall of America.

But what really sets the Opryland apart is that it is a Total Indoor Environment. At its heart are three enormous glass-roofed areas five or six storeys high and extending to nine acres overall that offer all the benefits of the out of doors without any of the inconveniences. These 'interiorscapes', as the hotel calls them, are replete with tropical foliage, full-sized trees, waterfalls, streams, 'open-air' restaurants and cafés, and multi-level walkways. The effect is strikingly reminiscent of those illustrations you used to get in 1950s science fiction magazines showing what life would be like in a space colony on Venus (or at least what it would be like if all the space colonists were overweight middle-aged Americans in Reeboks and baseball caps who spent their lives walking around eating hand-held food).

It is, in short, a flawless, aseptic, self-contained world, with a perfect unvarying climate and an absence of messy birds, annoying insects, rain, wind or indeed any kind of reality.

On my first evening, anxious to escape the hordes of shuffling grazers and curious to see what the weather was like back on Planet Earth, I stepped outside with a view to having a stroll through the grounds. And guess what? There were no grounds – just acres and acres of car park, rolling across the landscape for as far as the eye could see in nearly every direction. Across the way, only a couple of hundred yards distant, was the Opryland Amusement Park, but there was no way to gain entrance to it on foot. The only means of access, I discovered by enquiring, was to purchase a $3 ticket and board an air-conditioned bus for a 45-second ride to the front gate.

Unless you wanted to walk around among thousands of parked cars, there was no place to take the air or stretch your legs. At Opryland, the outdoors is indoors, and that, I realized with a shiver, is precisely the way many millions of Americans would have the whole country if it were possible.

As I stood there, a bird dropped onto the toe of my left shoe the sort of thing you don't normally appreciate a bird's dropping (to coin a phrase). I looked from the sky to my shoe and back to the sky again. 'Thank you,' I said, and I believe I really meant it.

2 November 1997

A VISIT TO THE BARBERSHOP

YOU HAVE TO UNDERSTAND THAT I HAVE VERY HAPPY HAIR. NO MATTER how serene and composed the rest of me is, no matter how grave and formal the situation, my hair is always having a party. In any group photograph you can spot me at once because I am the person at the back whose hair seems to be listening, in some private way, to a disco album called *Dance Craze '97*.

Every so often, with a sense of foreboding, I take this hair of mine uptown to the barbershop and allow one of the men there to amuse himself with it for a bit. I don't know why, but going to the barber brings out the wimp in me. There is something about being enshrouded in a cape and having my glasses taken away, then being set about the head with sharp cutting tools that leaves me feeling helpless and insecure.

I mean there you are, armless and squinting, and some guy you don't know is doing serious, almost certainly regrettable, things to the top of your head. I must have had 250 haircuts in my life by now, and if there is one thing I have learned it is that a barber will give you the haircut he wants to give you and there is nothing you can do about it.

So the whole experience is filled with trauma for me. This is particularly so as I always get the barber I was hoping not to get – usually the new guy they call 'Thumbs'. I especially dread the moment when he sits you in the chair and the two of you stare together at the hopeless catastrophe that is the top of your head, and he says, in a worryingly eager way, 'So what would you like me to do with this?'

'Just a simple tidy-up,' I say, looking at him with touching hopefulness, but knowing that already he is thinking in terms of extravagant bouffants and mousse-stiffened swirls, possibly a fringe of bouncy ringlets. 'You know, something anonymous and respectable – like a banker or an accountant.'

'See any styles up there you like?' he says and indicates a wall of old black and white photographs of smiling men whose hairstyles seem to have been modelled on *Thunderbirds* characters.

'Actually, I was hoping for something a bit less emphatic.'

'A more natural look, in other words?'

'Exactly.'

'Like mine, for instance?'

I glance at the barber. His hairstyle brings to mind an aircraft carrier advancing through choppy seas, or perhaps an extravagant piece of topiary.

'Even more subdued than that,' I suggest nervously.

He nods thoughtfully, in a way that makes me realize we are not even in the same universe taste-in-hairwise, and says in a sudden, decisive tone: 'I know just what you want. We call it the Wayne Newton.'

'That's really not quite what I had in mind,' I start to protest, but already he is pushing my chin into my chest and seizing up his shears.

'It's a very popular look – everyone on the bowling team has it,' he adds, and with a buzz of motors starts taking hair off my head as if stripping wallpaper.

'I really don't want the Wayne Newton look,' I murmur with feeling, but my chin is buried in my chest and in any case my voice is drowned in the hum of his dancing clippers.

And so I sit for a small, tortured eternity, staring at my lap, under strict instructions not to move, listening to terrifying cutting machinery trundling across my scalp. Out of the corner of my eyes I can see large quantities of shorn hair tumbling onto my shoulders.

'Not too much off,' I bleat from time to time, but he is engaged in a lively conversation with the barber and customer at the next chair about the prospects for the Chicago Bulls basketball team, and only occasionally turns his attention to me and my head, generally to mutter, 'Oh, dang,' or 'Whoopsie.'

Eventually he jerks my head up and says: 'How's that for length?'

I squint at the mirror, but without my glasses all I can see is what looks like a pink balloon in the distance. 'I don't know,' I say. 'It looks awfully short.'

I notice he is looking unhappily at everything above my eyebrows. 'Did we decide on a Paul Anka or a Wayne Newton?' he asks.

'Well, neither, as a matter of fact,' I say, pleased to have an opportunity to get this sorted out at last. 'I just wanted a modest tidy-up.'

'Let me ask you this,' he says. 'How fast does your hair grow?'

'Not very,' I say and squint harder at the mirror, but I still can't see a thing. 'Why, is there a problem?'

'Oh, no,' he says, but in that way that means 'Oh, yes.' 'No, it's fine,' he goes on. 'It's just that I seem to have done the left side of your head in a Paul Anka and the right in a Wayne Newton. Let me ask you this, then: do you have a big hat?'

'What have you done?' I ask in a rising tone of alarm, but he has gone off to his colleagues for a consultation. They look at me the way you might look at a road accident victim, and talk in whispers.

'I think it must be these antihistamines I'm taking,' I hear Thumbs say to them sadly.

One of the colleagues comes up for a closer look, and decides it's not as disastrous as it looks. 'If you take some of this hair here from behind the left ear,' he says, 'and take it around the back of his head and hook it over the other ear, and maybe reattach some of this from here, then you can make it into a modified Barney Rubble.' He turns to me. 'Will you be going out much over the next few weeks, sir?'

'Did you say "Barney Rubble"?' I whimper in dismay.

'Unless you go for a Hercules Poirot,' suggests the other barber.

'Hercules Poirot?' I whimper anew.

They leave Thumbs to do what he can. After another ten minutes he hands me my glasses and lets me raise my head. In the mirror I am confronted with an image that brings to mind a lemon meringue pie with ears. Over my shoulder, Thumbs is smiling proudly.

'Turned out pretty good after all, eh?' he says.

I am unable to speak. I hand him a large sum of money and stumble from the shop. I walk home with my collar up and my head sunk into my shoulders.

At the house my wife takes one look at me. 'Do you say something to upset them?' she asks in sincere wonder.

I shrug helplessly. 'I told him I wanted to look like a banker.'

She gives one of those sighs that come to all wives eventually. 'Well, at least you rhyme,' she mutters in that odd, enigmatic way of hers, and goes off to get the big hat.

9 November 1997

BOOK TOURS

TEN YEARS AGO THIS MONTH I GOT A PHONE CALL FROM AN AMERICAN publisher telling me that they had just bought one of my books and were going to send me on a three-week, sixteen-city publicity tour.

'We're going to make you a media star,' he said brightly.

'But I've never been on TV,' I protested in mild panic.

'Oh, it's easy. You'll love it,' he said with the blithe assurance of someone who doesn't have to do it himself.

'No, I'll be terrible,' I insisted. 'I have no personality.'

'Don't worry, we'll *give* you a personality. We're going to fly you to New York for a course of media training.'

My heart sank. All this had a bad feeling about it. For the first time since I accidentally set fire to a neighbour's garage in 1961, I began to think seriously about the possibility of plastic surgery and a new life in Central America.

So I flew to New York and, as it turned out, the media training was less of an ordeal than I had feared. I was put in the hands of a kindly, patient man named Bill Parkhurst, who sat with me for two days in a windowless studio somewhere in Manhattan and put me through an endless series of mock interviews.

He would say things like: 'OK, now we're going to do a three-minute interview with a guy who hasn't looked at your book until 10 seconds ago and doesn't know whether it's a cookery book or a book on prison reform. Also, this guy is a tad stupid and will interrupt you frequently. OK, let's go.'

He would click his stopwatch and we would do a three-minute interview. Then we would do it again. And again. And so it went for two days. By the afternoon of the second day I was having to push my tongue back in my mouth with my fingers. 'Now you know what you'll feel like by the second day of your tour,' Parkhurst observed cheerfully.

'What's it like after twenty-one days?' I asked.

Parkhurst smiled. 'You'll love it.'

Amazingly he was nearly right. Book tours are actually kind of fun. You get to stay in nice hotels, you are driven everywhere in big silver cars, you are treated as if you are much more important than you are, you can eat steak three times a day at someone else's expense, and you get to talk endlessly about yourself for weeks at a stretch. Is this a dream come true or what?

It was an entirely new world for me. As you will recall if you have been committing these columns to memory, when I was growing up my father always took us to the cheapest motels imaginable – the sort of places that made the Bates Motel in *Psycho* look sophisticated and well-appointed – so this was a gratifyingly novel experience. I had never before stayed in a really fancy hotel, never ordered from room service, never called on the services of a concierge or valet, never tipped a doorman. (Still haven't, come to that!)

The great revelation to me was room service. I grew up thinking that ordering from the room service menu was the pinnacle of graciousness – something that happened in Cary Grant movies, but not in the world I knew – so when a publicity person suggested I make free use of it, I jumped at the chance. In doing so I discovered something you doubtless knew already: room service is *terrible*.

I ordered room service meals at least a dozen times in hotels all over the United States, and it was always dire. The food would take hours to arrive and it was invariably cold and leathery. I was always fascinated by how much effort went into the presentation – the white tablecloth, the vase with a rose in it, the ostentatious removal of a domed silver lid from each plate – and how little went into keeping the food warm and tasty.

At the Huntington Hotel in San Francisco, I particularly remember, the waiter whipped away a silver lid to reveal a bowl of white goo.

'What's that?' I asked.

'Vanilla ice cream, I believe, sir,' he replied.

'But it's melted,' I said.

'Yes, it has,' he agreed. 'Enjoy,' he added with a bow, pocketing my tip and withdrawing.

Of course, it's not all lounging around in swank hotel rooms, watching TV and eating melted ice cream. You also have to give interviews – lots and lots of them, more than you can imagine, often from before dawn till after midnight – and do a positively ludicrous amount of travelling in between. Because there are so many authors out there flogging books – as many as 200 at busy periods, I was told – and only so many radio and TV programmes to appear on, you tend to be dispatched to wherever there is an available slot.

In one five-day period, I flew from San Francisco to Atlanta to Chicago to Boston and back to San Francisco. I once flew from Denver to Colorado Springs in order to do a 30-second interview which – I swear – went like this:

Interviewer: 'Our guest today is Bill Bryson. So you've got a new book out, have you, Bill?'

Me: 'That's right.'

Interviewer: 'Well, that's wonderful. Thanks so much for coming. Our guest tomorrow is Dr Milton Greenberg, who has written a book about bedwetting called *Tears at Bedtime.*'

In three weeks I gave over 250 interviews of one type or another and never once met anyone who had read my book or had the faintest idea who I was. At one radio station the interviewer covered the microphone with his hand just before we went on and said: 'Now tell me, are you the guy who was abducted by aliens or are you the travel writer?'

The whole point, as Bill Parkhurst taught me, is to sell yourself shamelessly, and believe me you soon learn to do it.

I suppose all this is on my mind because by the time you read this I will be in the middle of a three-week promotional tour in Britain. Now I don't want you to think I am sucking up, but touring in Britain is a dream compared with America. Distances are shorter, which helps a lot, and you find on the whole that the interviewers have read the book, or at least read a book. Bookshop managers and staff are invariably dedicated and kindly, and the reading public are, without exception, intelligent, discerning, enormously good-looking and generous in their purchasing habits. Why, I have even known people to throw down a Sunday newspaper and say, 'I think I'll go out and buy that book of old Bill's *right now*. I might even buy several copies as Christmas presents.'

It's a crazy way to make a living, but it's one of those things you've got to do. I just thank God it hasn't affected my sincerity.

16 November 1997

DEATH WATCH

THE LAST TIME IT OCCURRED TO ME, IN A SERIOUS WAY, THAT DEATH IS
out there – you know, really out there, just hovering – and that my
name is in his book, was on a short flight from Boston to Lebanon,
New Hampshire, when we got in a little trouble.

The flight is only 50 minutes, over the old industrial towns of
northern Massachusetts and southern New Hampshire, and on
towards the Connecticut River, where the plump hills of the Green
and White Mountains lazily merge. It was a late October afternoon,
just after the clocks changed for winter, and I had hoped I might
enjoy the last russety blush of autumn colour on the hills before the
daylight went, but within five minutes of take-off our little plane – a
sixteen-seater De Havilland – was enveloped in bouncy cloud, and it
was obvious that there would be no spectacular panoramas this day.

So I read a book and tried not to notice the turbulence or to let my
thoughts preoccupy themselves with unhappy fantasies involving
splintering wings and a long, shrill plunge to earth.

I hate little planes. I don't like most planes much, but little planes I dread because they are cold and bouncy and make odd noises, and they carry too few passengers to attract more than passing attention when they crash, as they seem to do quite regularly. Almost every day in any American newspaper you will see an article like this:

Dribbleville, Indiana – All nine passengers and crew died today when a sixteen-seat commuter plane operated by Bounce Airlines crashed in a ball of flames shortly after takeoff from Dribbleville Regional Airport. Witnesses said the plane fell for, oh gosh, ages before slamming into the ground at 1,892 miles an hour. It was the eleventh little-noted crash by a commuter airline since Sunday.

These things really do go down all the time. Earlier this year a commuter plane crashed on a flight from Cincinnati to Detroit. One of the passengers who died was on her way to a memorial service for her brother, who had been killed in a crash in West Virginia two weeks before.

So I tried to read my book, but I kept glancing out of the window into the impenetrable murk. Something over an hour into the flight – later than usual – we descended through the bumpy clouds and popped out into clear air. We were only a few hundred feet over a dusky landscape. There were one or two farmhouses visible in the last traces of daylight, but no towns. Mountains – severe and muscular – loomed up around us on all sides.

We rose back up into the clouds, flew around for a few minutes and dropped down again. There was still no sign of Lebanon or any other community, which was perplexing because the Connecticut River Valley is full of little towns. Here there was nothing but darkening forest stretching to every horizon.

We rose again, and repeated the exercise twice more. After a few minutes the pilot came on and in a calm, laid-back voice said: 'I don't know if you folks have noticed, but we're having a little trouble eyeballing the airport on account of the, ah, inclement weather. There's no radar at Lebanon, so we have to do all of this visually, which makes it a little, ah, tricky. The whole of the eastern seaboard is socked in with fog, so there's no point in trying another airport. Anyway, we're gonna keep trying because if there is one thing for certain it's that this plane is going to have to come down *somewhere*!'

Actually, I just made that last line up, but that was the gist of it. We were blundering around in cloud and dying light looking for an airport tucked among mountains. We had been in the air for almost 90 minutes by now. I didn't know how long these things could fly, but at some point clearly we would run out of fuel. Meanwhile, at any moment we could slam into the side of a mountain.

This didn't seem fair. I was on my way home from a long trip. Scrubbed little children, smelling of soap and fresh towels, would be waiting. There was steak for dinner, possibly with onion rings. Extra wine had been laid in. I had gifts to disburse. This was not a convenient time to be flying into mountains. So I shut my eyes and said in a very quiet voice: 'Please please please oh please get this thing down safely and I promise I will be good for ever, and I really mean it. Thank you.'

Miraculously it worked. On about the sixth occasion that we dropped from the clouds there below us were the flat roofs, illuminated signs and gorgeously tubby customers of the Lebanon Shopping Plaza, and just across the road from it was the perimeter fence of the airport. We were aimed slightly the wrong way, but the pilot banked sharply and brought the plane in on a glidepath that would, in any other circumstance, have had me shrieking.

We landed with a lovely smooth squeal. I have never been so happy.

My wife was waiting for me in the car outside the airport entrance, and on the way home I told her all about my gripping moment in the air. The trouble with believing you are going to die in a crash, as opposed to actually dying in a crash, is that it doesn't make nearly as good a story.

'You poor sweetie,' my wife said soothingly, but just a little distractedly, and patted my leg. 'Well, you'll be home in a minute and there's a lovely cauliflower supreme in the oven for you.'

I looked at her. 'Cauliflower supreme? What the—' I cleared my throat and put on a new voice. 'And what is cauliflower supreme exactly, dear? I understood we were having steak.'

'We were, but this is much healthier for you. Maggie Higgins gave me the recipe.'

I sighed. Maggie Higgins was an irksomely health-conscious busybody whose strong views on diet were forever being translated into dishes like cauliflower supreme for me. She was fast becoming the bane of my life, or at least of my stomach.

Life's a funny thing, isn't it? One minute you're praying to be allowed to live, vowing to face any hardship without complaint, and the next you are mentally banging your head on the dashboard and thinking: 'I wanted steak, I wanted steak, I wanted steak.'

'Did I tell you, by the way,' my wife went on, 'that Maggie fell asleep with hair colouring on the other day and her hair turned bright green?'

'Really?' I said, perking up a little. This was good news indeed. 'Bright green, you say?'

'Well, everyone told her it was kind of lemony, but really, you know, it looked like Astroturf.'

'Amazing,' I said – and it was. I mean to say, two prayers answered in the same evening.

23 November 1997

THE BEST AMERICAN HOLIDAY

IF I AM LOOKING A LITTLE BLOATED AND SLUGGISH TODAY, IT IS BECAUSE it was Thanksgiving here on Thursday, and I haven't quite recovered yet.

I have a special fondness for Thanksgiving because, apart from anything else, when I was growing up it was the one time of year we ate in our house. All the other days of the year we just kind of put food into our mouths. My mother was not a great cook, you see.

Now please don't misunderstand me. My mother is a kindly, cheerful, saintly soul, and when she dies she will go straight to heaven, but believe me no one is going to say, 'Oh, thank goodness you're here, Mrs Bryson. Can you fix us something to eat?'

To be perfectly fair to her, my mother had several strikes against her in the kitchen department. To begin with she couldn't cook – always a bit of a handicap where the culinary arts are concerned. Mind you, she didn't especially want to be able to cook, and anyway she couldn't have even if she had wanted to. She had a career, you see, which meant that she was always flying in the door two minutes before it was time to put dinner on the table.

On top of this, she was a trifle absent-minded. She tended to confuse similarly coloured ingredients like sugar and salt, pepper and cinnamon, vinegar and maple syrup, cornflour and plaster of Paris, which often lent her dishes an unexpected dimension. Her particular speciality was to cook things while they were still in the packaging. I was almost full-grown before I realized that clingfilm wasn't a sort of chewy glaze. A combination of haste, forgetfulness and a charming incompetence where household appliances were concerned meant that most of her cooking experiences were punctuated with billows of smoke and occasional small explosions. In our house, as a rule of thumb, it was time to eat when the firemen departed.

Strangely, all this suited my father. My father had what you might call rudimentary tastes in food. His palate really only responded to three flavours – salt, ketchup and burnt. His idea of an outstanding meal was a plate that contained something brown and unidentifiable, something green and unidentifiable, and something charred. I am quite sure that if you slow-baked, say, a loofah and covered it sufficiently with ketchup, he would have said, 'Hey, this is very tasty.' Good food, in short, was something that was wasted on him, and my mother worked hard for years to see that he was never disappointed.

But on Thanksgiving, by some kind of miracle, she pulled out all the stops and outdid herself. She would call us to the table and there we would find, awaiting our unaccustomed delectation, a sumptuous spread of food – an enormous and glistening turkey, baskets of cornbread and warm rolls, vegetables that you could actually recognize, a tureen of cranberry sauce, a bowl of exquisitely fluffed mashed potatoes, a salver of plump sausages, and much else.

We would eat as if we had not eaten for a year (as, in effect, we had not) and then she would present the *pièce de resistance* – a golden, flaky-crusted pumpkin pie surmounted by a Matterhorn of whipped cream. It was perfect. It was heaven.

And it has left me with the profoundest joy and gratitude for this most wonderful of holidays – for Thanksgiving is the most splendid of occasions, and make no mistake.

Most Americans, I believe, think that Thanksgiving has always been held on the last Thursday of November and that it has been going on for ever – or at least as near for ever as anything gets in America.

In fact, although the Mayflower pilgrims did indeed hold a famous feast in 1621 to thank the local Indians for their help in getting them through their first difficult year and showing them how to make popcorn and so on (for which I am grateful even yet), there is no record of when that feast was held. Given the climate of New England, it was unlikely to have been late November. In any case, for the next 242 years Thanksgiving as an event was hardly noted. The first official celebration wasn't held until 1863 – and then in August, of all months. The next year President Abraham Lincoln moved it arbitrarily to the last Thursday in November – no one seems to recall now why a Thursday, or why so late in the year – and there it has stayed ever since.

Thanksgiving is wonderful and for all kinds of reasons. To begin with, it has the commendable effect of staving off Christmas. Whereas in Britain the Christmas shopping season seems nowadays to kick off round about the August bank holiday, Christmas mania doesn't traditionally begin in America until the last weekend in November.

Moreover, Thanksgiving remains a pure holiday, largely unsullied by commercialization. It involves no greetings cards, no trees to trim, no perplexed hunt through drawers and cupboards for decorations. At Thanksgiving all you do is sit at a table and try to get your stomach into the shape of a beach ball, and then go and watch a game of American football on the TV. This is my kind of holiday.

But perhaps the nicest, and certainly the noblest, aspect of Thanksgiving is that it gives you a formal, official occasion to give thanks for all those things for which you should be grateful. Speaking personally, I have a great deal to be thankful for. I have a wife and children I am crazy about. I have my health and retain full command of most of my faculties (albeit not always simultaneously). I live in a time of peace and prosperity. Ronald Reagan will never be President again. These are all things for which I am grateful, and I am pleased to let the record show it.

The only downside is that the passage of Thanksgiving marks the inescapable onset of Christmas. Any day now – any moment – my dear wife will appear beside me and announce that the time has come to shift my distended stomach and get out the festive decorations. This is a dread moment for me and with good reason, since it involves physical exertion, wobbly ladders, live electricity, wriggling ascents through a loft hatch, and the collaborative direction of said dear mis-sus – all things with the power to do me a serious and permanent injury. I have a terrible feeling that today may be that day.

Still, it hasn't happened yet – and for that, of course, I give my sincerest thanks of all.

30 November 1997

DECK THE HALLS

WHEN I LEFT YOU LAST WEEK I WAS EXPRESSING A CERTAIN QUEASY foreboding at the thought that at any moment my wife would step into the room and announce that the time has come to get out the Christmas decorations.

Well, here we are, another week gone and just eighteen fleeting days till Christmas, and still not a peep from her. I don't know how much more of this I can take.

I hate doing the Christmas decorations because, for a start, it means going up into the loft. Lofts are dirty, dark, disagreeable places. You always find things up there you don't want to find – lengths of gnawed wiring, gaps in the slates through which you can see daylight and sometimes even pop your head, and crates full of useless oddments that you must have been out of your mind ever to have hauled up there. Three things alone are certain when you venture into a loft: that you will crack your head on a beam at least twice, that you will get cobwebs draped over your face, and that you will not find what you went looking for.

The worst part about going into a loft is knowing that when the time comes to climb down you will find that the stepladder has mysteriously moved three feet towards the bathroom door. I don't know how this happens, but it always does.

So you lower your legs through the hatch and blindly grope for the ladder with your feet. If you stretch your right leg to its furthest extremity, you can just about get a toe to it, which is not much good, of course. Eventually, you discover that if you swing your legs back and forth, like a gymnast on parallel bars, you can get one foot on top of the ladder and then both feet on. This, however, does not represent a great breakthrough because you are now lying at an angle of about 60 degrees and unable to make any further progress. Grunting softly, you try to drag the ladder nearer with your feet, but succeed only in knocking it over, with a crash.

Now you really are stuck. You try to wriggle back up into the loft, but haven't the strength, so you hang by your armpits. You call to your wife, but she doesn't hear you. This is both discouraging and strange. Normally, your wife can hear things that no one else on earth can hear. She can hear a dab of jam fall onto a carpet two rooms away. She can hear spilled coffee being furtively mopped up with a good bathtowel. She can hear dirt being tracked across a clean floor. She can hear you just *thinking* about doing something you shouldn't do. But get yourself stuck in a loft hatch and suddenly it is as if she has been placed in a soundproof chamber.

So when eventually, an hour or so later, she passes through the upstairs hallway and sees your legs dangling there, it takes her by surprise. 'What are you doing?' she says at length.

You squint down at her. 'Loft hatch aerobics,' you reply with just a hint of sarcasm.

'Do you want the ladder?'

'Oh, now there's an idea. Do you know, I've been hanging here for ages trying to think what it is that's missing, and here you've cracked it straight off.'

You hear the sound of the ladder being righted and feel your feet being guided down the steps. The hanging has evidently done you good because suddenly you remember that the Christmas decorations are not in the loft – never were in the loft – but in the basement, in a cardboard box. Of course! How silly not to have recalled! Off you dash.

Two hours later you find the decorations hidden behind some old tyres and a broken pram. You lug the box upstairs and devote two hours more to untangling strings of lights. When you plug the lights in, naturally they do not work, except for one string that hurls you backwards into a wall with a lively jolt and a shower of sparks, and then does not work.

You decide to leave the lights and get the tree in from the garage. The tree is immense and prickly. Clutching it in a clumsy bearhug, you gruntingly manhandle it to the back door, fall into the house, get up and press on. As branches poke your eyes, needles puncture your cheeks and gums, and sap manages somehow to run backwards up your nose, you blunder through rooms, knocking pictures from walls, clearing tabletops, upsetting chairs. Your wife, so recently missing and unaccounted for, now seems to be everywhere, shouting confused and lively instructions – 'Mind the thingy! Don't go that way – go that way! To the left! Not *your* left – *my* left!' and eventually, in a softer voice, 'Oooh, are you all right, honey? Didn't you see those steps?' By the time you reach the living room the tree looks as if it has been defoliated by acid rain, and so do you.

It is at this point that you realize that you have no idea where the Christmas tree stand is. So, sighing, you hike up to town to the hardware store to buy another, knowing that for the next three weeks all the Christmas trees stands you have ever purchased – twenty-three in all – will spontaneously reappear in your life, mostly by dropping onto your head from a high shelf when you are rooting in the bottom of a cupboard, but occasionally in the middle of darkened rooms or lurking near the top of the hall stairs. If you don't know it already, know it now: Christmas tree stands are the work of the devil and they want you dead. While you are at the hardware store you buy two additional strings of lights. These will not work either.

Eventually, exhausted in both mind and body, you manage to get the tree up, lit and covered with baubles. You stand in the posture of Quasimodo regarding it with a kind of weak loathing.

'Oh, it's *lovely*!' your wife cries, clasping her hands ecstatically beneath her chin. 'Now let's do the outside decorations,' she announces suddenly. 'I bought a special treat this year – a life-sized Father Christmas that goes on the chimney. You fetch the 40-foot ladder and I'll open the crate. Oh, isn't this such fun!' And off she skips.

Now you might reasonably say to me: 'Why put yourself through all this? Why go up to the loft when you know the decorations won't be there? Why untangle the lights when you know they haven't a chance of working?' And my answer to you is that this is part of the ritual. Christmas wouldn't be Christmas without it.

Which is why I've decided to make a start now even though Mrs Bryson hasn't ordered me to. There are some things you just have to do in life, whether you want to or not.

If you need me for anything, I'll be hanging from the loft.

7 December 1997

THE WASTE GENERATION

ONE OF THE MOST ARRESTING STATISTICS THAT I HAVE SEEN IN A GOOD while is that 5 per cent of all the energy used in the United States is consumed by computers that have been left on all night.

I can't confirm this personally, but I can certainly tell you that on numerous occasions I have glanced out of hotel room windows late at night, in a variety of American cities, and been struck by the fact that every light in every neighbouring office building is still on, and that computer screens are indeed flickering.

Why don't Americans turn these things off? For the same reason, I suppose, that so many people here let their car motors run when they pop into a shop, or leave lights blazing all over their house, or keep the central heating cranked up to a level that would scandalize a Finnish sauna house keeper – because, in short, electricity, petrol and other energy sources are so relatively cheap, and have been for so long, that it doesn't occur to them to behave otherwise.

Why, after all, go through the irksome annoyance of waiting 20 seconds for your computer to warm up each morning when you can have it at your immediate beck by leaving it on all night?

We are terribly – no, we are ludicrously – wasteful of resources in this country. The average American uses twice as much energy to get through life as the average European. With just 5 per cent of the world's population, we consume 20 per cent of its resources. These are not statistics to be proud of.

In 1992 at the Earth Summit in Rio de Janeiro, the United States, along with other developed nations, agreed to reduce the emission of greenhouse gases to 1990 levels by 2000. This wasn't a promise to think about it. It was a promise to do it.

In the event, greenhouse emissions by the United States have continued relentlessly to rise – by 8 per cent overall since the Rio summit, by 3.4 per cent in 1996 alone. In short, we haven't done what we promised. We haven't tried to do it. We haven't even pretended to try to do it, which is the way we usually deal with these problems. All that the Clinton administration has done is introduce a set of voluntary standards which industries are free to ignore if they wish, and mostly of course they so wish.

There are almost no incentives to conserve here. Alternative energy sources like windpower are not only very low, but actually falling. In 1987 they accounted for about four-tenths of one per cent of the total energy production in the country; today just two-tenths of a per cent.

Now, as you will have read, President Clinton wants another fifteen or sixteen years before rolling back greenhouse gas emissions to 1990 levels. It is hard to find anyone here who is actually much bothered about this. Increasingly there is even a kind of antagonism to the idea of conservation, particularly if there is a cost attached. A recent survey of 27,000 people around the globe by a Canadian group called Environics International found that in virtually every advanced nation people were willing to sacrifice at least a small measure of economic growth if it meant cleaner air and a healthier environment. The only exception was the United States. It seems madness to think that people would rate a growing economy above an inhabitable earth, but there you are.

Even President Clinton's inventively cautious proposals to transfer the problem to a successor four terms down the road have met with fervent opposition. A coalition of industrialists and other interested parties called the Global Climate Information Project has raised $13 million to fight pretty much any initiative that gets in the way of their smokestacks. It has been running national radio ads grimly warning that if the President's new energy plans are implemented petrol prices could go up by 50 cents a gallon.

Never mind that that figure is probably inflated. Never mind that even if it were true Americans would still be paying but a fraction for petrol what people in other rich nations pay. Never mind that it would bring benefits that everyone could enjoy. Never mind any of that. Mention an increase in petrol prices for any purpose at all and – however small the amount, however good the reason – most people in America will instinctively recoil in horror.

What is saddest about all this is that a good part of these goals to cut greenhouse emissions could be met without any cost at all if Americans merely modified their extravagance. It has been estimated that the nation as a whole wastes about $300 billion of energy a year. We are not talking here about energy that could be saved by investing in new technologies. We are talking about energy that could be saved just by switching things off or turning things down. According to *US News & World Report*, a weekly news magazine, the United States must maintain the equivalent of five nuclear power plants just to power equipment and appliances that are on but not being used – video recorders left in permanent standby mode, computers left on when people go to lunch or home for the night, all those mute, wall-mounted TVs that flicker unwatched in the corners of bars.

I don't know how worrying global warming is. No one does. I don't know how much we are imperilling our futures by being so singularly casual in our consumption. But I can tell you this. Last year I spent a good deal of time hiking the Appalachian Trail, a long-distance footpath. In Virginia, where the trail runs through Shenandoah National Park, it was still possible when I was a teenager – not so very long ago – to see Washington, DC, 75 miles away, on clear days. Now, in even the most favourable conditions, visibility is less than half that. In hot, smoggy weather, it can be as little as 2 miles.

The Appalachian Mountains are one of the oldest mountain chains in the world and the forest that covers them is one of the richest and loveliest. A single valley in the Great Smoky Mountains National Park can contain more species of native trees than the whole of western Europe. A lot of those trees are in trouble. The stress of dealing with acid rain and other airborne pollutants leaves them helplessly vulnerable to diseases and pests. Oaks, hickories and maples are dying in unsettling numbers. The flowering dogwood – one of the most beautiful trees in the American South, and once one of the most abundant – is on the brink of extinction. The American hemlock seems poised to follow.

This may be only a modest prelude. If global temperatures rise by 4 degrees Centigrade over the next half-century, as some scientists confidently predict, then all of the trees of Shenandoah National Park and the Smokies, and for hundreds of miles beyond, will die. In two generations one of the last great forests of the temperate world will turn into featureless grassland.

I think that's worth turning off a few computers for, don't you?

14 December 1997

SHOPPING MADNESS

I WENT INTO A TOYS R US THE OTHER DAY WITH MY YOUNGEST SO THAT he could spend some loot he had come into. (He had gone short on Anaconda Copper against his broker's advice, the little scamp.) And entirely by the way, isn't Toys R Us the most mystifying name of a commercial concern you have ever heard of? What does it mean? I have never understood it. Are they saying they believe themselves to be toys? Do their executives carry business cards saying 'Dick R Me'? And why is the R backwards in the title? Surely not in the hope or expectation that it will enhance our admiration? Why, above all, is it that even though there are thirty-seven checkout lanes at every Toys R Us in the world, only one of them is ever open?

These are important questions, but sadly this is not our theme today, at least not specifically. No, our theme today, as we stand on the brink of the busiest retail week of the year, is shopping. To say that shopping is an important part of American life is like saying that fish appreciate water.

Apart from working, sleeping, watching TV and accumulating fatty tissue, Americans devote more time to shopping than to any other pastime. Indeed, according to the Travel Industry Association of America, shopping is now the number one holiday activity of Americans. People actually plan their vacations around shopping trips. Hundreds of thousands of people a year travel to Niagara Falls, it transpires, not to see the falls but to wander through its two mega-malls. Soon, if developers in Arizona get their way, holiday-makers will be able to travel to the Grand Canyon and not see it either, for there are plans, if you can believe it, to build a 450,000-square-foot shopping centre by its main entrance.

Shopping these days is not so much a business as a science. There is even now an academic discipline called retail anthropology whose proponents can tell you exactly where, how and why people shop the way they do. They know which proportion of customers will turn right upon entering a store (87 per cent) and how long on average those people will browse before wandering out again (2 minutes and 36 seconds). They know the best ways to lure shoppers into the magic, high-margin depths of the shop (an area known in the trade as 'Zone 4') and the layouts, colour schemes and background music that will most effectively hypnotize the unassuming browser into becoming a helpless purchaser. They know everything.

So here is my question. Why, then, is it that I cannot go shopping in America without wanting either to burst into tears or kill someone? For all its science, you see, shopping in this country is no longer a fun experience, if it ever was.

A big part of the problem is the stores. They come in three types, all disagreeable.

First, there are the stores where you can never find anyone to help you. Then there are the stores where you don't want any help, but you are pestered to the brink of madness by a persistent sales assistant, probably working on commission. Finally, there are the stores where, when you ask where anything is, the answer is always 'Aisle seven.' I don't know why, but that is what they always tell you.

'Where's women's lingerie?' you ask.

'Aisle seven.'

'Where's pet food?'

'Aisle seven.'

'Where's aisle six?'

'Aisle seven.'

My least favourite of all store types is the one where you can't get rid of the sales assistant. Usually these are department stores at big malls. The sales assistant is always a white-haired lady working in the menswear department.

'Can I help you find anything?' she says.

'No thank you, I'm just browsing,' you tell her.

'OK,' she replies, and gives you a smarmy smile that says: 'I don't really like you; I'm just required to smile at everyone.'

So you wander round the department and at some point you idly finger a sweater. You don't know why because you don't like it, but you touch it anyway.

In an instant, the sales assistant is with you. 'That's one of our most popular lines,' she says. 'Would you like to try it on?'

'No, thank you.'

'Go ahead, try it on. It's you.'

'No, I really don't think so.'

'The changing rooms are just there.'

'I really don't want to try it on.'

'What's your size?'

'Please understand, I don't want to try it on. I'm just browsing.'

She gives you another smile – her withdrawing smile – but 30 seconds later she is back, bearing another sweater. 'We have it in peach,' she announces.

'I don't want that sweater. In any colour.'

'How about a nice tie, then?'

'I don't want a tie. I don't want a sweater. I don't want anything. My wife is having her legs waxed and told me to wait for her here. I wish she hadn't, but she did. She could be hours and I still won't want anything, so please don't ask me any more questions. Please.'

'Then how are you off for pants?'

Do you see what I mean? It becomes a choice between tears and manslaughter. The irony is that when you actually require assistance there is never anyone around.

At Toys R Us my son wanted a Star Troopers Intergalactic Cosmic Death Blaster, or some such piece of plastic mayhem. We couldn't find one anywhere, nor could we find anyone to guide us. The store appeared to be in the sole charge of a sixteen-year-old boy at the single active checkout till. He had a queue of about two dozen people, which he was processing very slowly and methodically.

Patient queueing is not one of my advanced social skills, particularly when I am queueing simply to acquire information. The line moved with painful slowness. At one point the young man took ten minutes to change a till roll, and I nearly killed him then.

At last my turn came. 'Where's the Star Troopers Intergalactic Cosmic Death Blasters?' I said.

'Aisle seven,' he replied without looking up.

I stared at the top of his head. 'Don't trifle with me,' I said.

He looked up. 'Excuse me?'

'You people always say "Aisle seven." '

There must have been something in my look because his answer came out as a kind of whimper. 'But, mister, it *is* aisle seven – Toys of Violence and Aggression.'

'It'd better be,' I said darkly and departed.

Ninety minutes later we found the Death Blasters in aisle two, but by the time I got back to the till the young man had gone off duty.

The Death Blaster is wonderful, by the way. It fires those rubber-cupped darts that stick to the victim's forehead – not painful, but certainly startling. My son was disappointed, of course, that I wouldn't let him have it, but you see I need it for when I go shopping.

21 December 1997

OF MISSING PLANES
AND MISSING FINGERS

GOODNESS ME, CAN YOU BELIEVE IT, ANOTHER YEAR GONE ALREADY. I don't know where the time goes. Same place as my hair, I guess.

I was going to write this week about my New Year's resolutions, but unfortunately the first resolution I made this year was not to make any resolutions I couldn't keep (I'm not even sure I can keep that one, to tell you the truth), and that rather put an end to it. So I thought we might instead have a little review of the year.

As always when one is working on the leading edge of investigative journalism (or, in the case of this column, just blathering on week after week) there are loose ends to be tied up, and what better time to do it than when we stand on the brink of a new year?

One of the more dismaying aspects of writing for print, I have found, is that as soon as you make a statement – almost any statement at all – it will generally be contradicted by developments. Last March, for instance, I filed a glowing report about what a safe and delightfully crime-free community our little New Hampshire town is. Well, wouldn't you know it, but not four days after that article appeared a pair of masked men burst into a jeweller's shop on Main Street and, waving handguns in a lively manner, took away a large but undisclosed amount of cash and baubles. A day or so later, a woman was politely mugged as she strolled beside the college campus. Neither of these things had happened here before – nor, I might add, since – but it did seem a trifle uncanny that there should be a sudden eruption of malfeasance in the very week that I suggested it was unknown in these parts.

I don't mean to suggest that there is anything mystical in this; more that there is a kind of sod's law of public discourse that anything you write or say will instantly be undone by events – what you might call the Michael Fish Hurricane Prediction Syndrome.

Still, if you are of a paranoid bent, as I am, you begin to feel an uneasy sense of responsibility. In October I made some passing quip about the music of John Denver. The next day he fatally crashed his plane into the sea, poor man.

On the other hand, I did have a couple of proud and prescient moments. In July I wrote about how alarmingly slack America is concerning food safety and hygiene, and not three weeks later, as if on cue, a huge Hudson's Food processing plant in Nebraska was shut down after it was found that it was, well, alarmingly slack about food safety and hygiene. Over 22 million pounds of beef had to be tracked down and destroyed – the biggest food recall in history.

At about the same time, the US Senate held hearings at which the head of the Internal Revenue Service, America's tax-collecting agency, was roundly criticized and delightfully humiliated for overseeing a department that was inefficient, heartless, vindictive and incompetent. I don't wish to boast, but the record will show that I had made all this manifestly clear in these pages as far back as last April.

The biggest story of the year was the mysterious disappearance of a jet aircraft in the woods near here. A year ago Christmas Eve, as you may dimly recall from my column of last February, a Lear jet carrying two men was circling around to make a routine landing at the airport when it abruptly lost radio contact and disappeared from the control tower's radar screen.

Over the next few weeks the biggest ground and air search in the state's history was undertaken, but the plane was not found. A year later, it still has not been found and the mystery of what became of it has only deepened.

A big element of the mystery is that an exceptionally large number of people – 275 at last count – claim to have seen the jet just before it crashed. Some said they were close enough to see the two men peering out of the windows. The trouble is that these witnesses were widely scattered across two states, in locations up to 175 miles apart. Clearly they can't all have seen the plane in the moments before it crashed, so what *did* they see?

A good deal of other news about that fateful flight has emerged since I wrote about the plane's disappearance. The most startling news to me was that a plane vanishing in the New Hampshire woods is not that exceptional an event. In 1959, according to our local paper, two professors from the university here went down in the woods in a light plane during a winter storm. Notes they left behind showed that they survived for at least four days. Unfortunately, their plane was not found for two and a half months. Two years later, another light plane disappeared in the woods and wasn't found for six months. A third plane crashed in 1966 and wasn't found until 1972, long after most people had forgotten about it. The woods, it seems, can swallow a lot of wreckage and not give much away.

Even so, the utter disappearance of a Lear jet seems inexplicable. To begin with a Lear jet is a big plane, with a wingspan of 40 feet. You wouldn't think that something that large could vanish without trace, but evidently it can. Then there was all the technology that could now be brought to bear – heat sensors, infrared viewers, long-range metal detectors and the like. The Air Force even lent the use of a reconnaissance satellite. All to no avail. The fate of the doomed plane is as much a mystery now as it was a year ago. I will keep you posted.

To my surprise, the column that generated more post than any other during the year was my account last spring of our preposterously exasperating, two-year-long struggle to get the US immigration authorities to recognize that my wife has a right to live with me in my own country. It appears that many of you have also experienced the mind-numbing obtuseness and inflexibility of the US Immigration and Naturalization Service.

Just after that column appeared, I came across a story in the paper of a man named Raul Blanco, whose application for citizenship had been repeatedly turned down because he had failed to provide a full set of fingerprints. As Blanco patiently explained in letter after letter, he couldn't supply a full set because he had only seven fingers, having lost three in an industrial accident years earlier in his native Cuba. At last report, Blanco was still trying to get someone at the Immigration and Naturalization Service to understand his problem. He would be better off trying to find the missing fingers.

My wife, I am pleased to tell you, received her documentation six weeks after my column ran and still has all her fingers, so all things considered it has been a pretty good year. And on that note may I just wish you all a very happy, prosperous and fully digited 1998.

28 December 1997

YOUR NEW COMPUTER

CONGRATULATIONS. YOU HAVE PURCHASED AN ANTHRAX/2000 Multimedia 615X Personal Computer with Digital Doo-Dah Enhancer. It will give years of faithful service, if you ever get it up and running. Also included with your PC is a bonus pack of pre-installed software – 'Lawn Mowing Planner', 'Mr Arty-Farty', 'Blank Screen Save', and 'East Africa Route Finder' – which will provide hours of pointless diversion while using up most of your computer's spare memory.

So turn the page and let's get started!

Getting Ready: Congratulations. You have successfully turned the page and are ready to proceed.

Important meaningless note: The Anthrax/2000 is configured to use 80386, 214J10 or higher processors running at 2,472 hertz on variable speed spin cycle. Check your electrical installations and insurance policies before proceeding. Do not tumble dry.

To prevent internal heat build-up, select a cool, dry environment for your computer. The bottom shelf of a refrigerator is ideal.

Unpack the box and examine its contents. (Warning: Do not open box if contents are missing or faulty as this will invalidate your warranty. Return all missing contents in their original packaging with a note explaining where they have gone and a replacement will be sent within twelve working months.)

The contents of the box should include some of the following: monitor with mysterious De Gauss button; keyboard with 2½ inches of flex; computer unit; miscellaneous wires and cables not necessarily designed for this model; 2,000-page *Owner's Manual*; *Short Guide to the Owner's Manual*; *Quick Guide to the Short Guide to the Owner's Manual*; *Laminated Super-Kwik Set-Up Guide for People Who Are Exceptionally Impatient or Stupid*; 1,167 pages of warranties, vouchers, notices in Spanish, and other loose pieces of paper; 292 cubic feet of styrofoam packing material.

Something They Didn't Tell You in the Shop: Because of the additional power needs of the pre-installed bonus software, you will need to acquire an Anthrax/2000 auxiliary software upgrade pack, a 900-volt memory capacitator for the auxiliary software pack, a 50-megaherz oscillator unit for the memory capacitator, 2,500 mega-gigabytes of additional memory for the oscillator, and an electrical substation.

Setting Up: Congratulations. You are ready to set up. If you have not yet acquired a degree in electrical engineering, now is the time to do so.

Connect the monitor cable (A) to the portside outlet unit (D); attach power offload unit sub-orbiter (Xii) to the co-axial AC/DC servo channel (G); plug three-pin mouse cable into keyboard housing unit (make extra hole if necessary); connect modem (B2) to offside parallel audio/video lineout jack. Alternatively, plug the cables into the most likely looking holes, switch on and see what happens.

Additional important meaningless note: The wires in the ampule modulator unit are marked as follows according to international convention: blue = neutral or live; yellow = live or blue; blue and live =

neutral and green; black = instant death. (Except where prohibited by law.)

Switch the computer on. Your hard drive will automatically download. (Allow three to five days.) When downloading is complete, your screen will say: 'Yeah, what?'

Now it is time to install your software. Insert Disc A (marked 'Disc D' or 'Disc G') into Drive Slot B or J, and type: 'Hello! Anybody home?' At the DOS command prompt, enter your Licence Verification Number. Your Licence Verification Number can be found by entering your Certified User Number, which can be found by entering your Licence Verification Number. If you are unable to find your Licence Verification or Certified User numbers, call the Software Support Line for assistance. (Please have your Licence Verification and Certified User numbers handy as the support staff cannot otherwise assist you.)

If you have not yet committed suicide, then insert Installation Diskette 1 in Drive Slot 2 (or vice versa) and follow the instructions on your screen. (Note: Owing to a software modification, some instructions will appear in Romanian.) At each prompt, reconfigure the specified file path, double click on the button launch icon, select a single equation default file from the macro selection register, insert the VGA graphics card in the rear aerofoil, and type 'C:\>' followed by the birthdates of all the people you have ever known.

Your screen will now say: 'Invalid file path. Whoa! Abort or continue?' Warning: selecting 'Continue' may result in irreversible file compression, permanent loss of memory and a default overload in the hard drive. On the other hand, selecting 'Abort' will require you to start the whole tedious, maddening installation process all over again. Your choice.

When the smoke has cleared, insert Disc A2 (marked 'Disc A1') and repeat as directed with each of the 187 other discs.

When installation is complete, return to file path, and type your name, address and credit card numbers and press 'SEND'. This will automatically register you for our free software prize, 'Blank Screensaver IV: Nighttime in Deep Space', and allow us to pass your name to lots and lots of computer magazines, online services and other commercial enterprises, who will be getting in touch shortly.

Congratulations. You are now ready to use your computer. Here are some simple exercises to get you off to a flying start.

Writing a letter: Type 'Dear—' and follow it with the name of someone you know. Write a few lines about yourself, and then write, 'Sincerely yours' followed by your own name. Congratulations.

Saving a file: To save your letter, select File Menu. Choose Retrieve from Sub-Directory A, enter a backup file number and place an insertion point beside the macro dialogue button. Select secondary text box from the merge menu, and double click on the supplementary cleared document window. Assign the tile cascade to a merge file and insert in a text equation box. Alternatively, write the letter out longhand and put it in a drawer.

Advice on Using the Spreadsheet Facility: Don't.

Troubleshooting Section: You will have many, many problems with your computer. Here are some common problems and their solutions.

Problem: My computer won't turn on.

Solution: Check to make sure the computer is plugged in; check to make sure the power button is in the ON position; check the cables for damage; dig up underground cables in your garden and check for damage; drive out into country and check electricity pylons for signs of fallen wires; call hotline.

Problem: My keyboard doesn't seem to have any keys.

Solution: Turn the keyboard the right way up.

Problem: My mouse won't drink its water or go on the spinning wheel.

Solution: Try a high-protein diet or call your petshop support line.

Problem: I keep getting a message saying: 'Non-System General Protection Fault'.

Solution: This is probably because you are trying to use the computer. Switch the computer to OFF mode and any annoying messages will disappear.

Problem: My computer is a piece of useless junk.

Correct – and congratulations. You are now ready to upgrade to an Anthrax/3000 Turbo model, or to go back to pen and paper.

4 January 1998

IN PRAISE OF DINERS

A COUPLE OF YEARS AGO, WHEN I WAS SENT AHEAD OF THE REST OF the family to scout out a place for us to live in the States, I included the town of Adams, Massachusetts, as a possibility because it had a wonderful old-fashioned diner on Main Street.

Unfortunately, I was compelled to remove Adams from the short-list when I was unable to recall a single other virtue in the town, possibly because it didn't have any. Still, I believe I would have been happy there. Diners tend to take you like that.

Diners were once immensely popular, but like so much else they

have become increasingly rare. Their heyday was the years just after
the First World War, when Prohibition shut the taverns and people
needed some place else to go for lunch. From a business point of
view, diners were an appealing proposition. They were cheap to buy
and maintain and, because they were factory built, they came virtually complete. Having acquired one, all you had to do was set it on a
level piece of ground, hook up water and electricity and you were in
business. If trade didn't materialize, you simply loaded it on to a
flatbed truck and tried your luck elsewhere. By the late 1920s, about
a score of companies were mass-producing diners, nearly all in a
streamlined art deco style known as *moderne*, with gleaming stain-
less-steel exteriors, and insides of polished dark wood and more
shiny metal.

Diner enthusiasts are a bit like trainspotters. They can tell you
whether a particular diner is a 1947 Kullman Blue Comet or a 1932
Worcester Semi-Streamliner. They appreciate the design details that
mark out a Ralph Musi from a Starlite or an O'Mahoney, and will
drive long distances to visit a rare and well-preserved Sterling, of
which only seventy-three were made, between 1935 and 1941.

The one thing they don't talk about much is food. This is because
diner food is generally much the same wherever you go – which is to
say, not very good. My wife and children refuse to accompany me to
diners for this very reason. What they fail to appreciate is that going
to diners is not about eating; it's about saving a crucial part of
America's heritage.

We didn't have diners in Iowa when I was growing up. They were
mostly an east coast phenomenon, just as restaurants built in the
shape of things (pigs, doughnuts, bowler hats) were a west coast
phenomenon. The closest thing we had to a diner was a place down
by the river called Ernie's Grill. Everything about it was squalid and
greasy, including Ernie, and the food was appalling, but it did have
many of the features of a diner, notably a long counter with twirly
stools, a wall of booths, patrons who looked as if they had just come
in from killing big animals in the woods (possibly with their teeth),
and a fondness for diner-style lingo. When you ordered, the waitress
would call out to the kitchen in some indecipherable code, 'Two
spots on a dot, easy on the Brylcreem, dribble on the griddle and
cough twice in a bucket,' or something similarly alarming and
mystifying.

But Ernie's was in a square, squat, anonymous brick building, which patently lacked the streamlined glamour of a classic diner. So when, decades later, I was sent to look for a livable community in New England, a diner was one of the things high on my shopping list. Alas, they are getting harder and harder to find.

Hanover, where we eventually settled, does have a venerable eating establishment called Lou's, which celebrated its fiftieth anniverary last year. It has the superficial ambience of a diner, but the menu features items like quiches and fajitas, and it prides itself on the freshness of its lettuce. The customers are all well-heeled and yuppie-ish. You can't imagine any of them climbing into a car with a deer lashed to the bonnet.

So you may conceive my joy when, about six months after we moved to Hanover, I was driving one day through the nearby community of White River Junction, and passed an establishment called the Four Aces. Impulsively, I went in and found an early post-war Worcester in nearly mint condition. It was wonderful. Even the food was pretty good, which was a bit disappointing, but I have learned to live with it.

No one knows how many diners like this remain. Partly it is a problem of definition. A diner is essentially any place that serves food and calls itself a diner. Under the broadest definition, there are about 2,500 diners in the United States. But no more than a thousand of these, at the outside, are what could be called 'classic' diners, and the number of those diminishes yearly. Only a couple of months ago Phil's, the oldest diner in California, closed. It had been in business in north Los Angeles since 1926, making it, by Californian standards, as venerable as Stonehenge, but its passing was hardly noted.

Most diners can't compete with the big fast food chains. A traditional diner is small, with perhaps eight booths and a dozen or so counter spaces, and because they provide waitress service and individually cooked meals their operating costs are higher. Most diners are also old, and in America it is almost always much cheaper to replace than to preserve. An enthusiast who bought an old diner in Jersey City, New Jersey, discovered to his horror that it would cost $900,000 – perhaps twenty years' worth of potential profits – to bring it back to its original condition. Much cheaper to tear it down and turn the site over to a Kentucky Fried Chicken or McDonald's.

What you get a lot of instead these days are ersatz diners. The last time I was in Chicago I was taken to a place called Ed Debevic's, where the waitresses wore badges giving their names as Bubbles and Blondie and where the walls were lined with Ed's bowling trophies. But there never was an Ed Debevic. He was just the creative figment of a marketing man. No matter. Ed's was humming. A dining public that had disdained genuine diners when they stood on every corner was now queueing to get into a make-believe one. It mystifies me beyond measure, but this is a common phenomenon in America.

You find it at Disneyland, where people flock to stroll up and down a Main Street just like the ones they abandoned wholesale in the 1950s for shopping malls. It happens at restored colonial villages like Williamsburg, Virginia, or Mystic, Connecticut, where visitors pay good money to savour the sort of tranquil village atmosphere that they long ago fled for the happy sprawl of suburbs. I can't begin to account for it, but it appears, to coin a phrase, that Americans really only want something when it isn't really real.

But that is another column. We shall return to this subject next time. Meanwhile, I am off to the Four Aces while the chance is still there. There aren't any waitresses called Bubbles, but the bowling trophies are real.

11 January 1998

Just under three months after this article appeared, in early April 1998, the Four Aces closed.

UNIFORMLY AWFUL

I REMEMBER THE FIRST TIME I TASTED EUROPEAN CHOCOLATE. IT WAS IN the central railway station in Antwerp, on 21 March 1972, my second day in Europe as a young backpacker. While waiting for a train I bought a bar of Belgian chocolate from a station kiosk, tore off a bite and, after a moment of startled delight, began to emit a series of involuntary rapturous noises of an intensity sufficient to draw stares from 20 yards away.

You know how a baby eats a bowl of pudding – with noise and gusto and an alarming amount of gurgly drool? Well, that was me. I couldn't help myself. I didn't know that chocolate could be this good. I didn't know that *anything* could be this good.

American chocolate bars, as you are perhaps aware, are mysteriously bland affairs. I have been told that it wasn't always so. Many times I have heard from people of my parents' generation that when they were young American chocolate bars packed a proper wallop – that they were fatter, creamier, more lusciously endowed with nuts and nougat and gustatory ecstasy. My father reminisced fondly about candy bars of the 1920s so chewy that they would take most of the day to eat and a couple of weeks to digest. The same bars now are pallid little nothings.

The popular explanation is that these products have been constantly reformulated – perhaps I should say deformulated – over the years to hold down costs and to broaden their appeal to people with less intensive palates. It is certainly true that an awful lot of American foodstuffs – white bread, most domestic cheeses, nearly all convenience foods, the bulk of beers, a good deal of the coffee – are nothing like as robust and flavourful and varied as their counterparts almost anywhere in Europe, Britain included. It's an odd thing in a country that loves to eat, but there you are.

I put it down to two things. The first is cost. Everything in America is predicated on cost, far more than in other countries. If price is a factor between competing businesses (and it always is), then the cheaper will inevitably drive out the costlier, and this seldom leads to improved quality. (Actually, it never leads to improved quality.)

There used to be a good fast food Mexican restaurant in the next town from where I live. Then about a year ago, Taco Bell, part of a national chain, opened up across the road. I don't believe there is a person alive who would argue that Taco Bell offers really good Mexican food. But it is cheap – at least 25 per cent cheaper than the restaurant it was competing with across the road. Within a year the old restaurant was gone. So now if you want Mexican fast food in our neck of the woods, you have to settle for the cheap but carefully uninspired offerings of Taco Bell.

Because Taco Bell is so vigorously competitive on price, its dominance is well nigh universal. Almost wherever you go along the American highway these days, if you want a taco you must settle for Taco Bell. The stupefying thing is that this seems to be the way most people want it. And here we come to the second of our factors – the strange, unshakeable attachment of American consumers to predictable uniformity. Americans, in a word, like things to be the same wherever they go. This is the part that mystifies me.

Take Starbucks, a chain of coffee shops for which I have a mild and possibly irrational dislike, if only because they are becoming ubiquitous. Starbucks started quietly in Seattle some years ago, but in the last five years the number of its outlets has grown tenfold, to

1,270, and the number is intended to double roughly in the next two years. Already in many cities if you are looking for a coffee bar, the choice is pretty well Starbucks or nothing.

Now there is nothing wrong with Starbucks, but nothing all that special either. It offers a decent cup of coffee. Big deal. I can give you a decent cup of coffee. The impression you get is that Starbucks' principal motivating force is not to produce the finest coffees but rather to produce more Starbucks. If the American coffee-drinking public demands truly excellent coffee, then Starbucks will have to provide it if it wants to stay pre-eminent, but the American public won't demand that, so there won't be any particular pressure on Starbucks to provide exceptional quality. It may, but there won't be any commercial necessity for it, especially because in most places (a) it will be the only coffee bar around and (b) its customers will be completely habituated to the Starbucks brand.

We have two very congenial coffee bars in Hanover, but I am certain that if Starbucks were to open here people would be excited. (You should have seen the delirium when The Gap moved in.) Starbucks would be seen as a kind of affirmation for the town from the outside world. Visitors, on whom the town depends, would almost certainly favour it overwhelmingly because they know it and are comfortable with it.

People have grown so used to uniformity that they have become, as it were, hypnotized by it. About five miles from where I live, there was until recently a nice, old-fashioned, family-owned restaurant. A couple of years ago, a McDonald's opened opposite it. Almost at once the bulk of passing trade transferred from one side of the road to the other. Last summer, the family-owned restaurant closed. Shortly afterwards I mentioned to a neighbour how disappointing I found it that people would forsake a local establishment for the universal appeal of McDonald's.

'Yeah,' my neighbour said in that thoughtful, drawn-out way that indicates a proposition not entirely agreed with. 'But at least you know where you are with McDonald's, don't you?'

'Exactly!' I cried with feeling. 'Don't you see, that's the whole *problem*!'

I wanted to grab him by the lapels and explain to him that it was because of this kind of thinking that chocolate in America has no kick, white bread tastes like wadding, and cheese has a hundred names (colby, Monterey jack, cheddar, American, provolone) but just one flavour, one texture and one vivid yellow hue.

But I could see there was no point. He was like one of the pod people in *Invasion of the Body Snatchers*. The forces of blandness had captured his spirit and there was no getting it back. He had become a McPerson.

He looked at me uneasily – people don't usually get excited in our street – and I could see he was thinking: 'Whoa! Emotional fellow!'

Maybe he was right. I have to admit I have been a little out of sorts in recent months. I put it down to severe chocolate deprivation.

1 February 1998

THE FAT OF THE LAND

I HAVE BEEN THINKING A LOT ABOUT FOOD LATELY. THIS IS BECAUSE I AM
not getting any. My wife, you see, recently put me on a diet after
suggesting (a little unkindly, if you ask me) that I was beginning to
look like something Richard Branson would try to get airborne.

It is an interesting diet of her own devising, which essentially
allows me to eat anything I want so long as it contains no fat,
cholesterol, sodium or calories, and isn't tasty. In order to keep me
from starving altogether, she went to the supermarket and bought
everything that had 'bran' in its title. I am not sure, but I believe I had
bran cutlets for dinner last night. I am very depressed.

Obesity is a serious problem in America. (Well, serious for fat people anyway.) Half of all adult Americans are overweight and more than a third are defined as obese (i.e., big enough to make you think twice before getting in a lift with them).

Now that hardly anyone smokes, it has taken over as the number one health fret in the country. About 300,000 Americans die every year from diseases related to obesity, and the nation spends $100 billion treating illnesses arising from overeating – diabetes, heart disease, high blood pressure, cancer, and so on. (I hadn't realized it, but being overweight can increase your chance of getting colon cancer – and this is a disease you really don't want to have – by as much as 50 per cent. Ever since I read that, I keep imagining a proctologist examining me and saying: 'Wow. Just how many cheeseburgers have you had in your life, Mr Bryson?') Being over-weight also substantially reduces your chances of surviving surgery, not to mention getting a decent date.

Above all, it means that people who are theoretically dear to you will call you 'Mr Blimpy' and ask you what you think you are doing every time you open a cupboard door and, entirely by accident, remove a large bag of Cheez Doodles.

The wonder to me is how anyone can be thin in this country. We went to a restaurant the other night where they were promoting something called 'Skillet Sensations'. Here (and every word of this is true) is the menu's description of the Chilli Cheese Tater Skillet:

'We start this incredible combination with crispy, crunchy waffle fries. On top of those we generously ladle spicy chilli, melted Monterey jack and cheddar cheeses, and pile high with tomatoes, green onions, and sour cream.'

You see what I am up against? And this was one of the more modest offerings. The most depressing thing is that my wife and children can eat this stuff and not put on an ounce. When the waitress came, my wife said: 'The children and I will have the De Luxe Supreme Goo Skillet Feast, with extra cheese and sour cream, and a side order of onion rings with hot fudge sauce and biscuit gravy.'

'And for Mr Blimpy here?'

'Just bring him some dried bran and a glass of water.'

When, the following morning over a breakfast of oat flakes and chaff, I expressed to my wife the opinion that this was, with all respect, the most stupid diet I had ever come across, she told me to find a better one, so I went to the library. There were at least 150 books on diet and nutrition – *Dr Berger's Immune Power Diet*, *Straight Talk About Weight Control*, *The Rotation Diet* – but they were all a little earnest and bran-obsessed for my tastes. Then I saw one that was precisely of the type I was looking for. By Dale M. Atrens, Ph.D., it was called *Don't Diet*. Now here was a title I could work with.

Relaxing my customary aversion to consulting a book by anyone so immensely pratty as to put 'Ph.D.' after his name (I don't put Ph.D. after my name on my books, after all – and not just because I don't have one), I took the book to that reading area that libraries put aside for people who are strange and have nowhere to go in the afternoons but none the less are not quite ready to be institutionalized, and devoted myself to an hour's reflective study.

The premise of the book, if I understood it correctly (and forgive me if I am a little sketchy on some details, but I was distracted by the man next to me, who was having a quiet chat with a person from the next dimension), is that the human body has been programmed by aeons of evolution to pack on adipose tissue for insulating warmth in periods of cold, padding for comfort, and energy reserves in times of crop failures.

The human body – mine in particular, evidently – is extremely good at doing this. Tree shrews can't do it at all. They must spend every waking moment eating. 'This may be why tree shrews have produced so little great art or music,' Atrens quips. Ha! Ha! Ha! Then again, it may be because the tree shrew eats leaves, whereas I eat Ben and Jerry's double chocolate fudge ice cream.

The other interesting thing Atrens points out is that fat is exceedingly stubborn. Even when you starve yourself half to death, the body shows the greatest reluctance to relinquish its fat reserves.

Consider that each pound of fat represents 5,000 calories – about what the average person eats in total in two days. That means that if you starved yourself for a week – ate nothing at all – you would lose no more than 3½ pounds of fat, and, let's face it, still wouldn't look a picture in your swimming costume.

Having tortured yourself in this way for seven days, naturally you would slip into the pantry when no one was looking and eat everything in there but a bag of chickpeas, and gain back all the loss, *plus* – and here's the crux – a little something extra because now your body knows that you have been trying to starve it and are not to be trusted, so it had better lay in a little extra wobble in case you get any more foolish notions.

This is why dieting is so frustrating and hard. The more you try to get rid of your fat, the more ferociously your body holds onto it.

So I have come up with an ingenious alternative diet. I call it the Fool-Your-Body-20-Hour-a-Day Diet. The idea is that for 20 hours in each 24 you ruthlessly starve yourself, but at four selected intervals during the day – for convenience we'll call them breakfast, lunch, dinner and midnight snack – you feed your body something like a plate of sausage, chips and beans, or a large bowl of double chocolate fudge ice cream, so that it doesn't *realize* that you are starving it. Brilliant, eh?

I don't know why I didn't think of this years ago. I think it may be that all this bran has cleared my head. Or something.

8 February 1998

THE SPORTING LIFE

WE HAVE A FRIEND, A SINGLE MUM, WHOSE SIX-YEAR-OLD SON RECENTLY signed up to play ice hockey, a sport taken very seriously here.

At the first team meeting, one of the other parents announced that he had devised a formula for determining how much each child would play. Essentially the best seven players would play 80 per cent of each game, and the remaining, more hopeless kids would divide up whatever time was left – so long, of course, as victory was not in doubt.

'I think that's the most fair way of doing it,' he said to solemn nods from the other dads.

Failing to understand the role of testosterone in these matters, our friend stood up and suggested that a more fair approach might be to let all the children play equally.

'But then they wouldn't win,' said the father, looking half aghast.

'Yes,' agreed our friend. 'So?'

'But what's the point in playing if you don't win?'

These were, let me remind you, six-year-olds. There isn't space here – there isn't space in this newspaper – to discuss all the things that have gone wrong with sport in America, at nearly every level, so let me just cite a few specimen examples to give you an idea of how America approaches competitive pursuits these days.

Item: In an effort to spur them on and plump up our standings in the medals tables (which is, of course, the most important thing in the universe), US swimmers were paid up to $65,000 from official sources for every medal they won at the last Olympics. Apparently, representing one's nation and doing one's best are no longer sufficient incentives.

Item: To delight the home fans and enhance their positions in the national rankings, the largest college football teams now regularly schedule matches against hopelessly inadequate opponents. In one especially proud moment for sport last season, the University of Florida, ranked number two in the nation, took on the unsung might of little Central Michigan University, and won by a score of 82 to 6.

Item: In order to watch 60 minutes of football on this year's Super Bowl on television, it was necessary to sit through 113 commercials, programme trailers or product plugs. (I counted.)

Item: The average cost for a family of four to go to a Major League baseball game now is over $200.

I mention all this not to make the point that commercial overkill and blunted sportsmanship have taken much of the joy out of sport in this country, though they have, but to explain why I love Dartmouth College basketball games so much.

Dartmouth is the local university and it is in the Ivy League, a confederation of eight venerable and brainy institutions – Harvard, Yale, Princeton, Brown, Columbia, Penn, Cornell and Dartmouth. These kids go to Ivy League schools because they are going to become rocket scientists and professors, not because they are going to make $12 million a year playing professional basketball. They play for the love of the game, the camaraderie, the thrill of taking part – all those things that we have mostly lost in this country.

I first went to a game three winters ago, when I saw a schedule in a shop window in town and noticed that the season opener was that night. I hadn't been to a basketball game in twenty years.

'Hey, Dartmouth's got a game tonight,' I announced in excitement when I got home. 'Who's coming?'

Five faces looked at me with an expression I hadn't seen since I suggested we go camping in Slovenia for our next holiday. 'OK, I'll go on my own,' I sniffed, though in the end my youngest daughter, then eleven, took pity and accompanied me.

Well, we had a wonderful time. Dartmouth won a nail-biter, and my daughter and I came home gabbling. A few nights later Dartmouth won another squeaker with a basket at the buzzer, and we came home gabbling again.

Now everyone wanted to come. But here's the thing. We wouldn't let them. This was our little thing.

Since then, for three seasons, going to Dartmouth games has become a ritual for my daughter and me. Everything about it is splendid. The arena where the team plays is an easy walk from our house. Tickets are cheap, and the crowds are small, friendly and loyal. An endearingly nerdy band plays perky tunes like the theme from *Hawaii Five-0*, to get us bouncing. Afterwards we emerge into the wintry night air and walk home chatting. It is because of these walks that I know the identities of the Spice Girls, that *Scream 2* was way cool, and that Matthew Perry is so cute it's like almost not real. When there is not the slightest chance that a living person might see, she sometimes takes my hand. It's perfect.

But at the heart of it is the game. For two hours we shout and wince and rend our hair, and become wholly absorbed with the hope that our boys can put a ball through a hoop more times than their boys. If Dartmouth win, we are elated. If they don't – well, no matter. It's just a game. This is the way sport should be.

One of the Dartmouth players last year was a 7-foot giant named Chris, who had all the attributes of greatness except, alas, an ability to play basketball. In consequence he spent nearly the whole of his career on the low end of the bench. Very occasionally, he would be put in for the last 15 or 20 seconds of a game. Invariably on these occasions someone would pass him the ball and someone smaller would come and take it away. He would shake his head regretfully, then lope giraffe-like to the other end of the court. He was our favourite player.

By tradition, the last game of the season is parents' night, when parents fly in from all over to watch their sons play. Also by tradition, on the last home game the graduating seniors are put in to start.

This particular game was of no consequence, but news of that seemed not to have reached our lanky hero. He came onto the court with an intense psyched-up look. This was his first and last chance to shine and he wasn't going to blow it.

The referee blew the whistle to start the game. Our Chris ran up and down the court four or five times and then, to our dismay and his, was taken out and returned to the bench. He had played no more than a minute or so. He hadn't done a thing wrong – hadn't had a chance to do a thing wrong. He took his customary seat, cast his parents an apologetic look and watched the rest of the game through eyes welled with tears. Someone had forgotten to tell the coach that winning isn't everything.

This week Dartmouth has its last home game of the season. This year, I believe, there are two players who will be allowed to run gamely up and down the court for a token minute or two, and will then be replaced by abler hands.

My daughter and I have decided to skip this one. When perfection is so difficult to find, it's hard to see it spoiled.

15 February 1998

LAST NIGHT ON THE TITANIC

'On the night of the wreck our dinner tables were a picture! The huge bunches of grapes which topped the fruit baskets on every table were thrilling. The menus were wonderfully varied and tempting. I stayed at table from soup to nuts.'

Titanic passenger Kate Buss, quoted in *Last Dinner on the Titanic: Menus and Recipes from the Great Liner*

'GOOD LORD, BUSS, WHAT'S ALL THE COMMOTION?'
 'Oh, hello, Smythe. Not like you to be up at this hour. Smoke?'
 'Thank you, don't mind if I do. So what's the kerfuffle? I saw the captain as I came by and he looked in a dreadful stew.'
 'It appears we're sinking, old boy.'
 'Never!'
 'Do you recall that iceberg we saw at dinner?'
 'The one that was as big as a twenty-storey building?'
 'That's the one. Well, it seems we struck the deuced thing.'
 'Rotten luck.'

'Rather.'

'I suppose that explains why my cabin door was underneath the bed when I woke up. I thought it a bit odd. I say, is this a Monte Cristo?'

'H. Upmann, actually. I have a man in Gerrard Street who gets them specially.'

'Awfully nice.'

'Yes . . . Pity, really.'

'What's that?'

'Well, I just ordered a dozen boxes at two guineas each. Still, I suppose young Bertie will be glad to get his hands on them.'

'So you don't think we're going to make it?'

'Doesn't look good. Mrs Buss asked Croaker, the quarterdeck steward, when he brought her nightcap and he said we had less than two hours. How's Mrs Smythe, by the way? Is her stomach better?'

'Couldn't say. She's drowned, you see.'

'Oh, rotten luck.'

'Went out the starboard porthole when we started to list. It was her shout that woke me, as a matter of fact. Shame she's missed all the excitement. She always enjoyed a good sinking.'

'Mrs Buss is just the same.'

'She didn't go over as well, did she?'

'Oh, no. She's gone to see the purser. Wanted to cable Fortnum's and cancel the order for the garden fête. Not much point now, you see.'

'Quite. Still, all in all it's not been a bad voyage, wouldn't you say?'

'Couldn't agree more. The food's been top-notch. Young Kate was particularly taken with the place-settings. She thought the dinner tables a picture and the grapes thrilling. She stayed from soup to nuts. You haven't seen her, by any chance?'

'No, why do you ask?'

'It's just that she rushed off in a rather odd way. Said there was something she had to do with young Lord D'Arcy before we went under. Something to do with flags, I gather.'

'Flags? How odd.'

'Well, she made some reference to needing a jolly roger, if I heard her right. I can't pretend I understand half the things she goes on about. And in any case I was somewhat distracted. Mrs Buss had just spilled her nightcap down her peignoir – in consequence of the impact, you see – and was in a terrible temper because Croaker wouldn't bring her another. He told her to get it herself.'

'What extraordinary insolence.'

'I suppose he was a bit out of sorts because he won't be getting his tips now, will he? Can't say I blame him really.'

'Still.'

'I reported him, of course. One has to remember one's station even in a crisis or we should be in a terrible mess, don't you agree? The quartermaster assured me he won't get another posting on this ship.'

'I should think not.'

'Bit of a technicality, I suppose, but at least it's been noted in the book.'

'It's been a funny old night, when you think about it. I mean to say, wife drowns, ship sinks, and there was no Montrachet '07 at dinner. I had to settle for a very middling '05.'

'You think that's disappointing? Have a look at these.'

'Sorry, old boy, I can't see in this light. What are they?'

'Return tickets.'

'Oh, that is bad luck.'

'Outside port cabin on the Promenade Deck.'

'Very bad luck . . . I say, what's that noise?'

'That will be the steerage passengers drowning, I expect.'

'No, it sounded like a band.'

'I believe you're right. Yes, you are quite right. A bit mournful, don't you think? I shouldn't want to try to dance to that.'

' "Nearer My God to Thee", isn't it? They might have chosen something a bit more festive for our last night at sea.'

'Still, I think I'll wander down and see if they've put out supper yet. Coming?'

'No, I think I'll turn in with a brandy. It's going to be a short night as it is. How long have we got, do you suppose?'

'About 40 minutes, I'd say.'

'Oh dear. Perhaps I'll skip the brandy then. I don't suppose I'll be seeing you again?'

'Not in this life, old sport.'

'Oh, I say, that's very good. I must remember that. Well, good-night, then.'

'Goodnight.'

'By the by, just a thought. The captain didn't say anything about getting into lifeboats, did he?'

'Not that I recall. Shall I wake you if he makes an announcement?'

'That would be very good of you, if you're sure it's no trouble.'

'No trouble at all.'

'Well, goodnight, then. Give my regards to Mrs Buss and young Kate.'

'With the greatest pleasure. I'm sorry about Mrs Smythe.'

'Well, worse things happen at sea, as they say. I expect she'll bob up somewhere. She was awfully buoyant. Well, goodnight.'

'Goodnight, old sport. Sleep well.'

22 February 1998

FUN IN THE SNOW

FOR REASONS I CANNOT BEGIN TO UNDERSTAND, WHEN I WAS ABOUT eight years old my parents gave me a pair of skis for Christmas. I went outside, strapped them on, and stood in a racing crouch, but nothing happened. This is because there are no hills in Iowa.

Casting around for something with a slope, I decided to ski down our back porch steps. There were only five steps, but on skis the angle of descent was surprisingly steep. I went down the steps at about, I would guess, 110 miles an hour, and hit the bottom with such force that the skis jammed solid, whereas I continued onward and outward across the patio in a graceful rising arc. About 12 feet away loomed the back wall of our garage. Instinctively adopting a spreadeagled posture for maximum impact, I smacked into it somewhere near the roof and slid down its vertical face in the manner of food flung against a wall.

It was at this point I decided that winter sports were not for me. I put away the skis and for the next thirty-five years thought no more about the matter. Then we moved to New England, where people actually look forward to winter. At the first fall of snow they cry out with joy and root in cupboards for sledges and ski poles. They become suffused with a strange vitality – an eagerness to get out into all that white stuff and schuss about on something fast and reckless.

With so many active people about, including every member of my own family, I began to feel left out. So a few weeks ago, in an attempt to find a winter pastime, I borrowed some ice skates and went with my two youngest to Occum Pond, a popular local spot for skating.

'Are you sure you know how to skate?' my daughter asked uneasily.

'Of course I do, my petal,' I assured her. 'I have been mistaken many times for Jane Torvill, on the ice and off.'

And I do know how to skate, honestly. It's just that my legs, after years of inactivity, got a little overexcited to be confronted with so much slipperiness. As soon as I stepped onto the ice they decided they wanted to visit every corner of Occum Pond at once, from lots of different directions. They went this way and that, scissoring and splaying, sometimes getting as much as 12 feet apart, but constantly gathering momentum, until at last they flew out from under me and I landed on my butt with such a wallop that that my coccyx hit the roof of my mouth and I had to push my oesophagus back in with my fingers.

'*Wow!*' said my startled butt as I clambered heavily back to my feet. 'That ice is *hard*.'

'Hey, let *me* see,' cried my head and instantly down I went again.

And so it went for the next 30 minutes, with various extremities of my body – shoulders, chin, nose, one or two of the more adventurous internal organs – hurling themselves at the ice in a spirit of investigation. From a distance I suppose I must have looked like someone being worked over by an invisible gladiator. Eventually, when I had nothing left to bruise, I crawled to shore and asked to be covered with a blanket. And that was it for my attempt at ice skating.

Next I tried sledging, which I don't even want to talk about, except to say that the man was very understanding about his dog, all things considered, and that that lady across the road would have saved us all a lot of trouble if she had just left her garage door open.

It was at about this juncture that my friend Prof. Danny Blanchflower stepped into the picture. Danny – his real name is David, but he is English, so when he was growing up everyone naturally called him Danny, and the name stuck – is a professor of economics at Dartmouth and a very brainy fellow. He writes books with sentences like 'When entered contemporaneously in the full specifications of column 5.7, profit-per-employee has a co-efficient of 0.00022 with a t-statistic of 2.3,' and isn't even joking. For all I know, it may even mean something. As I say, he's a real smart guy, except for one thing. He is mad on snowmobiling.

Now a snowmobile, I should perhaps explain, is a rocket ship designed by Satan to run on snow. It travels at speeds up to 70 miles an hour, which – call me chicken, I don't care – seems to me a trifle fleet on narrow, winding paths through boulder-strewn woods.

For weeks Danny pestered me to join him in a bout of this al fresco madness. I tried to explain that I had certain problems with outdoor activities *vis-à-vis* the snowy season, and that somehow I didn't think a powerful, dangerous machine was likely to provide a solution.

'Nonsense!' he cried. Well, to cut a long story short, the next thing I knew I was on the edge of the New Hampshire woods, wearing a snug, heavy helmet that robbed me of all my senses except terror, and sitting nervously astride a sleek beastlike conveyance, its engine throbbing in anticipation of all the trees against which it might soon dash me. Danny gave me a rundown on the machine's operation, which for all I understood might have been a passage from one of his books, and jumped onto his own machine.

'Ready?' he shouted over the roar of his engine.

'No.'

'Great!' he called and took off with a flare of after-burners. Within two seconds he was a noisy dot in the distance.

Sighing, I gently engaged the throttle and, with a startled cry and a brief wheelie, took off with a velocity seldom seen outside a Road Runner cartoon. Shrieking hysterically and jettisoning weight via my bladder with every lively bump, I flew through the woods as if on an Exocet missile. Branches slapped my helmet. Moose reared and fled.

The landscape flashed past as if in some hallucinogen-induced delirium.

Eventually, Danny stopped at a crossroads, beaming all over, engine purring. 'So what do you think?'

I moved my lips but no sound emerged. Danny took this as assent.

'Well, now that you've got the hang of it, shall we bang up the pace a bit?'

I formed the words 'Please, Danny, I want to go home. I want to see my Mom,' but again no sound emerged.

And off he went. For hours we raced at lunatic speeds through the endless woods, bouncing through streams, swerving past boulders, launching into flight over fallen logs. When at length this waking nightmare concluded, I stepped from my machine on legs made of water.

Afterwards, to celebrate our miraculous intactness, we repaired to Murphy's Tavern for a pint. When the barmaid put the glasses down in front of us it occurred to me, with a flash of inspiration, that here at last was something I could do: winter drinking.

I had found my calling. I'm not as good at it yet as I hope to be – my legs still tend to go after about three hours – but I'm doing a lot of stamina training and am looking for a very good season in 1998–9.

1 March 1998

THE FLYING NIGHTMARE

MY FATHER WAS A SPORTSWRITER WHO FLEW A LOT FOR HIS WORK IN THE days before it was common to do so, and occasionally he would take me on one of his trips with him. It was exciting, of course, just to go away for a weekend with my dad, but at the heart of the experience was the thrill of getting on a plane and going somewhere.

Everything about the process felt special and privileged. Checking in, you would be one of a small group of well-dressed people (for in those days people actually dressed up to fly). When the flight was called, you would stroll across a broad tarmac to a gleaming silver plane, and up one of those wheeled staircases. Entering the plane was like being admitted to some special club. Just stepping aboard, you became a little more stylish and sophisticated. The seats were comfy and, for a small boy, commodious. A smiling stewardess would come and give you a little winged badge that said 'Assistant Pilot' or something similarly responsible-sounding.

All that romance has long since vanished. Today in America commercial planes are little more than winged buses, and the airlines, without detectable exception, regard passengers as irksome pieces of bulk freight that they consented, at some time in the remote past, to carry from place to place and now wish they hadn't.

I cannot begin to describe in a space this modest all the spirit-sapping features of modern American air travel – the routinely overbooked flights, the endless queueing, the delays, the discovery that your 'direct' flight to Miami actually stops in Pittsburgh and involves a layover of 90 minutes and a change of planes, the near-impossibility of finding a friendly face among the ground staff, the being treated like an idiot and a cypher.

Yet in the oddest ways airlines continue to act as if it is still 1955. Take the safety demonstration. Why after all these years do the flight attendants still put a life vest over their heads and show you how to pull the little cord that inflates it? In the history of commercial aviation no life has been saved by the provision of life vests. I am especially fascinated by the way they include a little plastic whistle on each vest. I always imagine myself plunging vertically towards ocean at 1,200 miles an hour and thinking: 'Well, thank gosh I've got this whistle.'

It is no good asking what they are thinking because they are not thinking anything. I recently boarded a flight from Boston to Denver. When I opened the overhead storage compartment I found an inflated dinghy entirely filling the space.

'There's a boat in here,' I breathed in amazement to a passing flight attendant.

'Yes, sir,' said the flight attendant snappily. 'This plane meets FAA specifications for overwater flights.'

I stared at him in small wonder. 'And which ocean do we cross between Boston and Denver?'

'The plane meets FAA specifications for overwater flights whether or not overwater flights are scheduledly anticipated,' was his crisp reply, or something similarly inane and mangled.

'Are you telling me that if we go down in water, 150 passengers are supposed to get into a two-man dinghy?'

'No, sir, there's another flotation craft in here.' He indicated the bin on the opposite side.

'So two boats for 150 people? Does that strike you as just a little absurd?'

'Sir, I don't make the rules, and you are blocking the aisle.'

He talked to me like this because all airline employees eventually talk to you like this if you press them a little bit, and sometimes even if you don't. I feel safe in saying that there is not an industry anywhere in the United States where the notions of service and customer satisfaction are less regarded. All too often the most innocuous move – stepping up to a counter before the check-in clerk is ready to receive you, enquiring why a flight is delayed, ending up with no place to stow your coat because your overhead locker contains an inflated boat – can lead to snappishness and rebuke.

Mind you, with the notable exception of me and a few other meek souls who believe in orderliness, most passengers in America these days deserve what they get. This is because they take on jumbo suit-bags and wheeled carry-ons that are at least twice the officially permitted size, so that the overhead bins fill up long before the flight is fully boarded. To make sure they get a bin to themselves, they board before their row is called. On any flight in America now you will find at least 20 per cent of the seats filled by people whose row numbers have not been called. I have watched this process with weary exasperation for some years, and I can tell you that it takes roughly twice as long for an American plane to get boarded and airborne as it does elsewhere.

The result of this is a kind of war between airline employees and passengers, which all too often redounds on the innocent in a way that cries out for justice.

I particularly recall an experience of a few years ago when my wife, children and I boarded a flight in Minneapolis to fly to London and discovered that we had been allocated seats in six different parts of the aircraft, up to twenty rows apart. Bemused, my wife pointed this out to a passing stewardess.

'And what do you expect me to do about it?' the stewardess replied in a tone that suggested an urgent need for a refresher course in customer relations.

'Well, we'd like some seats together, please.'

The stewardess gave a hollow laugh. 'There's nothing I can do now. We're boarding. Didn't you check your boarding passes?'

'Only the top one. The check-in clerk' – who was, let me interject here, a disagreeable specimen herself – 'didn't tell us she was scattering us all over the plane.'

'Well, there's nothing I can do now.'

'But we have small children.'

'Sorry.'

'Are you telling me to put a two-year-old and a four-year-old off by themselves for an eight-hour flight across the Atlantic?' my wife asked. (This was an idea that I believed I could warm to, but I made a grave face, in solidarity.)

The stewardess gave an elaborate sigh and, with an undisguised show of resentment, asked a kindly but timid white-haired couple to swap seats, which allowed my wife and the two youngest to sit together. The rest of us would remain separated.

'Next time look at your boarding passes before you leave the terminal,' the attendant snapped at my wife in parting.

'No, next time we will fly with someone else,' my wife replied, and indeed ever since we have.

'And one day, I'll have a column in a newspaper and I'll write about this,' I called after her in a haughty voice. Of course, I didn't say any such thing, and it would be a terrible abuse of my position to tell you that it was Northwest Airlines that treated us in this shabby way, so I won't.

8 March 1998

LOST IN CYBER LAND

"rainware"
BY THE COMPLETE HOME OFFICE SOLUTION

WHEN WE MOVED TO AMERICA, THE CHANGE IN ELECTRICAL SYSTEMS meant I needed all new stuff for my office – computer, fax machine, answering machine and so on. I am not good at shopping or parting with large sums of money at the best of times, and the prospect of trailing around a succession of shops listening to sales assistants touting the wonders of various office products filled me with foreboding.

So imagine my delight when in the first computer store I went to I found a machine that had everything built into it – fax, answering machine, electronic address book, Internet capability, you name it. Advertised as 'the Complete Home Office Solution', this computer promised to do everything but make the coffee.

So I took it home and set it up, flexed my fingers, and wrote a perky fax to a friend in London. I typed his fax number in the appropriate box as directed and pushed 'Send'. Almost at once, noises of international dialling came out of the computer's built-in speakers. Then there was a ringing tone, and finally an unfamiliar voice that said: *'Allo? Allo?'*

'Hello?' I said in return, and realized that there was no way I could talk to this person, whoever he was.

My computer began to make shrill fax noises. *'Allo? Allo?'* the voice said again, with a touch of puzzlement and alarm. After a moment, he hung up. Instantly, my computer redialled his number.

And so it went for much of the morning, with my computer repeatedly pestering some unknown person in an unknown place while I searched furiously through the manual for a way to abort the operation. Eventually, in desperation, I unplugged the computer, which shut down with a series of Big Mistake! and Crisis in the Hard Drive! noises.

Three weeks later – this is true – we received a phone bill with $68 in charges for calls to Algiers. Subsequent enquiries revealed that the people who had written the software for the fax program had not considered the possibility of overseas transmissions. The program was designed to read American phone numbers only. Confronted with anything else, it went into nervous breakdown mode.

I also discovered that the electronic address book had a similar quirky aversion to non-American addresses, rendering it useless, and that the answering machine function had a habit of coming on in the middle of conversations.

For a long time it puzzled me how something so expensive, so leading edge, could be so useless, and then it occurred to me that a computer is a stupid machine with the ability to do incredibly smart things, while computer programmers are smart people with the ability to do incredibly stupid things. They are, in short, a dangerously perfect match.

You will have read about the millennium bug, I am sure. You know, then, that at the stroke of midnight on 1 January 2000, all the computers in the world will for some reason go through a thought process something like this: 'Well, here we are in a new year that ends in '00. I bet it's 1900. But if it's 1900, computers haven't been invented yet. Therefore I don't exist. Guess I had better shut down and wipe my memory clean.' The estimated cost to put this right is $200 trillion gazillion or some such preposterous sum. A computer, you see, can calculate pi to 20,000 places but it can't work out that time always moves forward. Programmers, meanwhile, can write 80,000 lines of complex code, but fail to note that every hundred years you get a new century. It's a disastrous combination.

When I first read that the computer industry had created a problem for itself so basic, so immense, and so foolish, I suddenly understood why my fax facility and other digital toys are worthless. But this still doesn't adequately explain the wondrous – the towering – uselessness of my computer's spelling checker.

Like nearly everything else to do with computers, a spelling checker is marvellous in principle. When you have done a piece of work, you activate it and it goes through the text looking for words that are misspelled. Actually, since a computer doesn't understand what words are, it looks for letter clusters it isn't familiar with, and here is where the disappointment begins.

First, it doesn't recognize any proper nouns – names of people, places, corporations, and so on – or non-American spellings like *kerb* and *colour*. Nor does it recognize many plurals or variant forms (like *steps* or *stepped*), or abbreviations or acronyms. Nor, evidently, any word coined since Eisenhower was President. Thus, it recognizes *sputnik* and *beatnik*, but not *Internet*, *fax*, *cyberspace* or *butthead*, among many others.

But the really distinctive feature of my spelling checker – and here is the part that can provide hours of entertainment for anyone who doesn't have anything approaching a real life – is that it has been programmed to suggest alternatives. These are seldom less than memorable. For this column, for instance, for *Internet* it suggested *internat* (a word that I cannot find in any dictionary, British or American), *internode*, *interknit* and *underneath*. *Fax* prompted no fewer than thirty-three suggested alternatives, including *fab*, *fays*, *feats*, *fuzz*, *feaze*, *phase* and at least two more that are unknown to lexicography: *falx* and *phose*. *Cyberspace* drew a blank, but for *cyber* it came up with *chubbier* and *scabbier*.

I have tried without success to discern the logic by which a computer and programmer working in tandem could decide that someone who typed *f-a-x* would really have intended to write *p-h-a-s-e*, or why *cyber* might suggest *chubbier* and *scabbier*, but not, say, *watermelon* or *full-service petrol station*, to name two equally random alternatives. Still less can I explain how nonexistent words like *phose* and *internat* would get into the program. Call me exacting, but I would submit that a computer program that wants to discard a real word in favour of one that does not exist is not ready to be offered for public use.

Not only does the system suggest imbecilic alternatives, it positively aches to put them in. You have to all but order the program not to insert the wrong word. If you accidentally accept its prompt, it automatically changes that word throughout the text. Thus, to my weary despair, I have in recent months produced work in which 'woollens' was changed throughout to 'wesleyans', 'Minneapolis' to 'monopolists' and – this is a particular favourite – 'Renoir' to 'rainware'. If there is a simple way to unpick these involuntary transformations, then I have not found it.

Now I read in *US News & World Report* that the same computer industry that failed to notice the coming of a new millennium has equally failed for years to realize that the materials on which it stores information – magnetic tapes and so forth – swiftly degrade. NASA scientists who recently tried to access material on the 1976 Viking mission to Mars discovered that 20 per cent of it has simply vanished and that the rest is going fast.

So it looks as if computer programmers will be putting in some late nights over the next couple of years. To which, frankly, I say hooray. Or *haywire, heroin* and *hoopskirt*, as my computer would prefer it.

15 March 1998

HOTEL CALIFORNIA

IT WOULD BE HARD TO IMAGINE A MORE EVIL PIECE OF WORK THAN Robert Alton Harris. After a lifetime of vicious, random crime, in 1979 in California he murdered two teenaged boys in cold blood for their car. As he drove away, he finished off the cheeseburgers they had been eating.

He was arrested within hours, and confessed his guilt freely. Even so, it took the state of California thirteen years of complex and costly trials and retrials to exhaust all the legal possibilities necessary to put Harris to death.

There are almost 500 other people like Harris on death row in California. Altogether the state spends an estimated $90 million a year pursuing death penalty cases. Since 1967 it has spent $1 billion (over £600 million) on capital cases and executed exactly two people (Harris being one of them).

Now it seems to me evident from this, if nothing else, that the death penalty in America is madness. Think what California could have done with that $1 billion if it had spent it on, say, education.

Nearly everyone agrees that such a convoluted legal process is crazy, but the problem is that Americans love the death penalty. Polls consistently show that about three-quarters of them support capital punishment. Moreover, they want it – indeed insist on it – for a very wide range of offences. Roughly half of Americans, for instance, would make it a capital offence to sell drugs to children. Already in the United States you can be put to death for more than fifty types of crime.

Quite apart from moral issues, there are, it seems to me, several practical considerations that make it difficult to defend. One is that it is inconsistently applied. Those sentenced to death are almost without exception male – only one woman has been put to death since 1962, though another is scheduled to die in Texas this month – and disproportionately poor and black, and their victims are overwhelmingly white. Of the approximately 360 people executed in the United States since 1977, 83 per cent had been convicted of killing a white person, even though white people represent only about half of all murder victims. Depending on the state, criminals are anywhere from four to eleven times more likely to be sentenced to death for killing a white person than a black person – hardly a ringing endorsement of the principle that justice is blind.

There is also a striking geographical disparity. Thirty-nine US states have the death penalty, but in only seventeen of them – mostly in the South – were people put to death last year. If you are going to murder someone in a state with the death penalty, you are much better off doing it in New Hampshire, where they have not executed anyone for decades, than in Texas or Florida, where people are dispatched with comparative enthusiasm. Texas alone last year executed thirty-seven people, as much as all the rest of the country put together.

Altogether in the United States there are about 3,000 people on death row. In 1997, seventy-four of them were executed, the highest number in forty years. Even so, the number added to death row each year outstrips by about four to one the number eliminated. (The leading cause of death on death row is actually natural causes.) To clear the backlog and deal with the rising number of new inmates, America would have to execute one person a day for twenty-five years. Because of the legal process, that is never going to happen.

The question is why they bother. On average, it takes ten years and five months to exhaust all the appeals processes necessary for execution. As a result, according to a study at Duke University, it costs $2 million more to execute a prisoner than to incarcerate him for life.

Of course you could argue that convicted murderers shouldn't be allowed to appeal endlessly on frivolous technicalities. Congress, accepting this view with all its heart, in 1995 voted to abolish the $20 million of federal money that was being spent on assisting death row inmates with appeals. Almost overnight the average length of time from conviction to execution fell by eleven months.

This would be good news if you were confident that everyone put to death deserved it, but in fact this is not so. Consider the case of Dennis Williams of Chicago, who spent seventeen years on death row for a murder he vociferously claimed not to have committed for the very good reason that he hadn't. He was saved only because a journalism professor at the University of Chicago assigned his students to look into the case as a class project. They found, among other things, that the police had suppressed evidence, witnesses had lied, and that another man was prepared to confess to the crime if only someone would listen to him.

Like most death row inmates, Williams had been defended by a court-appointed lawyer. Illinois pays public defenders $40 an hour. The going rate for lawyers in private practice is $150 an hour. You don't have to be a genius to work out that the best lawyers are unlikely to be doing public work. Typically they are granted just $800 to prepare and present their defence in capital cases, so even the most dedicated lawyer will hardly be able to secure expert witnesses, independent forensic tests, or anything else that might prove his client's innocence.

Thanks to the students' school project, Williams was released last September. This is less unusual than you might expect. Since 1977, when Illinois reintroduced the death penalty, the state has executed eight people, but freed nine. Nationally in the last twenty-five years sixty-nine people convicted of murder have later been found to be innocent and freed. With federal funds for appeals curtailed, few of those people could expect such happy outcomes now.

It is one thing for a citizen to murder an innocent person, quite another for the state to do it. Yet amazingly even this is a minority view. According to a 1995 Gallup poll, 57 per cent of people in the

United States would remain in favour of the death penalty even if it were found that one person in every hundred was wrongly executed.

I don't believe there is a politician in America – certainly none of any stature – who would stand up to such a weight of feeling. There used to be a time when politicians tried to change public opinion. Now they just respond to it, which is unfortunate because these things are not immutable.

Writing in the *New Yorker* in 1992, Richard L. Nygaard noted that West Germany outlawed the death penalty in 1949 even though 74 per cent of people approved of it. By 1980, the proportion in favour had slumped to 26 per cent. As Nygaard observes: 'Among people who don't grow up with it, capital punishment comes to be seen as a barbaric relic, like slavery or branding.'

Would that it were so here.

22 March 1998

ENOUGH ALREADY

I HAVE FINALLY FIGURED OUT WHAT IS WRONG WITH EVERYTHING. THERE is too much of it. I mean by that that there is too much of every single thing that one could possibly want or need, except time, money, good plumbers and people who say thank you when you hold open a door for them. (And, entirely by the way, I would like to put it on the record here that the next person who goes through a door that I've held open and doesn't say 'Thank you' is going to get it in the kidneys.)

America is of course a land of bounteous variety, and for a long time after we first moved here I was dazzled and gratified by the wealth of choice everywhere. I remember going to the supermarket for the first time and being genuinely impressed to find that it stocked no fewer than eighteen varieties of incontinence nappy. Two or three I could understand. Half a dozen would seem to cover every possible incontinence contingency. But eighteen – gosh! This *was* a land of plenty. Some were scented, some were dimpled for extra comfort, and they came in a whole range of strengths from, as it were, 'Oops, bit of a dribble' to 'Whoa! Dambusters!' Those weren't the labels they actually used, of course, but that was the gist of it. They even came in a choice of colours.

For nearly every other type of product – frozen pizzas, dog food, ice creams, biscuits, crisps – the choices were often literally in the hundreds. Every new flavour seemed to have pupped another flavour. When I was a boy shredded wheat was shredded wheat and that was it. Now you could have it coated in sugar, in bite-sized morsels, with slices of genuine banana-like material, and goodness knows what else. I couldn't have been more impressed.

Lately, however, I have come to realize that you can get too much choice. I had this brought home to me the other week when I was at an airport in Portland, Oregon, standing in a queue of about fifteen people at a coffee stand. It was 5.45 a.m., not my best time of day, and I had just 20 minutes till my flight was to be called, but I really, really needed to get some caffeine into my system. You know how it is.

It used to be if you wanted a cup of coffee that's what you asked for and that's what you got. But this place, being a 1990s coffee stand, offered twenty choices – espresso, latte, caramel latte, breve, macchiato, mocha, espresso mocha, black forest mocha, americano, and goodness knows what else – in four different sizes. There was also a galaxy of muffins, croissants, bagels and pastries. All of these could be had in any number of variations, so that every order went something like this:

'I'll have a caramel latte combo with decaf mocha and a cinnamon twist, and a low-fat cream cheese sourdough bagel, but I'd like the pimiento grated and on the side. Are your poppyseeds roasted in polyunsaturated vegetable oil?'

'No, we use double-extra-lite canola extract.'

'Oh, that's no good for me. In that case, I'll have a New York three-cheese pumpernickel fudge croissant. What kind of emulsifiers do you use in that?'

In my mind's eye, I saw myself taking hold of each customer by the ears, shaking his or her head thirty or forty times and saying: 'You're just trying to get a cup of coffee and a bread product before your flight. Now ask for something simple and clear off.'

Fortunately for all these people, until I have had my first cup of coffee in the morning (and this is particularly true during hours in single figures) all I can do is rise, dress myself (a bit) and ask for a cup of coffee. Anything else is beyond me. So I just stood and waited stoically while fifteen people placed complex, time-consuming and preposterously individualized orders.

When at last my turn came, I stepped up and said: 'I'd like a large cup of coffee.'

'What kind?'

'Hot and in a cup and very large.'

'Yeah, but what kind – mocha, macchiato, what?'

'I want whichever one is a normal cup of coffee.'

'You want americano?'

'If that means a normal cup of coffee, then yes.'

'Well, they're all coffees.'

'I want a normal cup of coffee like millions of people drink every day.'

'So you want an americano?'

'Evidently.'

'Do you want low-cal whipped cream or regular with that?'

'I don't want whipped cream.'

'But it comes with whipped cream.'

'Look,' I said in a low voice, 'it is 6.10 a.m. I have been standing for 25 minutes behind fifteen seriously indecisive people, and my flight is being called. If I don't get some coffee right now, I am going to murder someone, and I think you should know that you are extremely high on my list.' (I am not, as you will gather, a morning person.)

'So does that mean you want low-cal whipped cream or regular?'

And so it went.

This abundance of choice not only makes every transaction take ten times as long as it ought to, but in a strange way actually breeds dissatisfaction. The more there is, the more people crave, and the more they crave, the more they, well, crave more. You have a sense in America of being among millions and millions of people needing more and more of everything, constantly, infinitely, unquenchably. We appear to have created a society in which the principal activity is grazing through retail establishments looking for things – textures, shapes, flavours – not before encountered.

And it applies to everything. You can now choose, apparently, among thirty-five varieties of Crest toothpaste. According to *The Economist*, 'the average supermarket in America devotes 20 feet of shelving to medicine for coughs and colds'. Yet of the 25, 500 'new' consumer products launched in the United States last year, 93 per cent were merely modified versions of existing products.

The last time I went for breakfast, I had to choose among nine options for my eggs (poached, scrambled, sunny side up, over easy, and so on), sixteen types of pancake, six varieties of juice, two shapes of sausage, four kinds of potato and eight varieties of toast or muffin. I have taken out mortgages that involved less decision-making than that. I thought I had finished when the waitress said: 'Do you want whipped butter, pat butter, margarine, butter-margarine blend or butter substitute?'

'You're joking,' I said.

'I don't joke about butter.'

'Then pat butter,' I said weakly.

'Low-sodium, no-sodium or regular?'

'Surprise me,' I answered in a whisper.

To my astonishment, my wife and children love all this. They love going into an ice cream parlour and being able to choose among seventy-five flavours of ice cream, and then seventy-five types of topping to put on that ice cream.

I can't tell you how I long to go to England and just have a nice cup of tea and a simple bun, but I'm afraid I am the only person in the house who feels that way. I trust that my wife and kids will eventually grow sated by all this, but there is no sign of it happening yet.

Still, looking on the bright side, at least I am well-fixed for incontinence nappies.

29 March 1998

STUPIDITY NEWS

I WOULD LIKE TO SAY A FEW WORDS ABOUT STUPIDITY IN AMERICA.

Now before I go a single word further, let me make it categorically clear that Americans are not inherently more simple than other people. America has the largest economy, the most comfortably off people, the best research facilities, many of the finest universities and think-tanks, and more Nobel Prize winners than the rest of the world put together. You don't get all that by being stupid.

Even so, you do sometimes wonder. Consider this. According to an opinion poll, 13 per cent of women in the United States cannot say whether they wear their tights under their knickers or over them. That's something like 12 million women walking around in a state of chronic foundation garment uncertainty. Perhaps because I so seldom wear ladies' clothing I don't fully appreciate the challenges involved, but I am almost certain that if I did wear tights with knickers I would know which was on top. More to the point, if a stranger with a clipboard came up to me in the street and asked how my underwear was configured, I don't believe that I would tell him that I didn't know.

Which raises another interesting point: why were they asking? How did anyone think up such a question, and what were they hoping to do with the data? You see, all this points to a much larger kind of dumbness, not just among the 13 per cent of women who are underwear underaware, to coin a nifty phrase, but among those who set and disseminate public opinion polls.

One thing is certain, and that is that there is an awful lot of dumbness about. I know this for a fact because a friend in New York recently sent me a collection of stupid quotes made by notable Americans in 1997. Here, for instance, is the actress Brooke Shields, without any help from grown-ups, explaining to an interviewer why you shouldn't smoke: 'Smoking kills. If you're killed, you've lost a very important part of your life.'

Well said, Brooke. And here is the singer Mariah Carey getting to the heart of Third World troubles: 'Whenever I watch TV and see those poor starving kids all over the world, I can't help but cry. I mean I'd love to be skinny like that, but not with all those flies and death and stuff.'

Whatever is the stage beyond the mind boggling is the stage I reach each time I read that quotation. My favourite, however, was the answer Miss Alabama gave in a Miss Universe contest when asked if she would choose to live for ever: 'I would not live for ever, because we should not live for ever, because if we were supposed to live for ever then we would live for ever, but we cannot live for ever, which is why I would not live for ever.'

Call me unkind, but I would bet good money that Miss Alabama not only would not know whether her tights were under or over her pants, but would not be entirely certain which limbs to insert in the holes.

So where does all this dumbness come from? I have no idea, but I am certain – quite seriously certain – that there is something in modern American life that is acting to suppress thought, even among more or less normal people. I was reminded of this yesterday while waiting behind a man who was speaking on a payphone. The man – middle-aged, well-dressed, probably a lawyer or accountant by the look of him – was obviously talking to a colleague's or client's small child, and he said: 'So when do you expect your mommy to be out of the shower, honey?'

Now think about that for a minute. When you find yourself asking a three-year-old how long an adult will take to complete an activity, it is time to invest in a new brain. And anyway how long does *anybody* spend in the shower?

America has no monopoly on imbecility, goodness knows, but there is at least one factor that seems to exist here in greater measure than elsewhere, to wit the habit among newspapers, periodicals and broadcasters of always stating the extremely obvious. We have already seen in this space how the *Washington Post* will inform its readers without embarrassment that Scotland 'is north of England' or how columnists will tell a joke and then explain the punchline. The idea – well-intentioned, I'm sure – is to spare readers having to grapple with challenging or unfamiliar notions (like just where the heck Scotland is), but it has the powerful and insidious effect of lobotomizing the audience.

The unfortunate side of all this is that it is relatively easy to prey on people who have lost the power of thought. Once or twice a week, like nearly every household in the nation, we receive a letter from a magazine subscription company saying something like 'Congratulations, Mr W. Bryson. You Have Won $5 Million!' Just above this promising statement, in much smaller letters, it says: 'If your sweepstakes number matches the prize draw number, then we will say to you . . .' You don't have to be terribly on the ball to work out that you haven't actually won $5 million. Unfortunately, lots of people are not terribly on the ball.

The papers carried a story recently about a man called Richard Lusk who flew from California to Florida clutching a prize letter telling him, as he understood it, that he had won $11 million and had just five days to claim his prize. The company showed him the fine print and sent him home. Three months later Mr Lusk received another, essentially identical letter, and flew to Florida again, just as happy and expectant as he had been the first time. According to the Associated Press, at least twenty other people have flown to Florida in the past four years in the same ecstatic but mistaken belief.

That's a rather depressing thought, so let's finish with the story of my favourite dumb person of the moment – namely, a would-be robber in Texas who covered his face with a balaclava in order to rob a grocery store, but forgot to remove from his breast pocket the clip-on badge that bore his photograph, name and place of employment, which were duly noted by something like twelve witnesses.

I am sure there is a moral in this somewhere, and I will let you know as soon as it occurs to me. Now if you will excuse me, I am going to go and check my underwear in case anyone starts asking questions.

5 April 1998

SPINNING THE TRUTH

ONE OF THE THINGS YOU GRADUALLY GET USED TO IN AMERICA IS THE extent to which corporations and other big businesses lie to you. Actually, I was lying myself just then. You never get used to it.

A couple of years ago, when we were still new to the country, we were driving across Michigan looking for a place to stay when we passed a big hoarding for a national motel chain advertising a very attractive special offer. I don't recall the details, but it included free lodging for the children and breakfast vouchers for all the family for a deeply gratifying all-in price of something like $35.

Naturally, by the time I had read all this I had sailed past the exit, and had to drive 15 miles on, then 15 miles back, then hunt around on slip roads for half an hour while everyone in the car pointed out vastly more accessible motels with better facilities. So the exasperation was considerable. But never mind. For $35 and a free cooked breakfast, you can exasperate me all you want.

So imagine my countenance, then, when I checked us in and the clerk slid me a bill that came to something like $149.95.

'What about the special offer?' I whinnied.

'Ah,' he said suavely, 'that only applies to a selected number of rooms.'

'How many rooms?'

'Two.'

'And how many rooms are there in the motel?'

'One hundred and five.'

'But that's fraud,' I said.

'No, sir, that's America.'

Actually, in truth I don't believe he said that, but he might as well have. And this was a large, well-known corporation whose executive officers, I am sure, would be hurt and dismayed to find themselves described as scoundrels and cheats. They were simply following the fluid moral rules of commerce in the United States.

I have just been reading a book called *Tainted Truth: The Manipulation of Fact in America*, which is full of arresting stories of misleading claims by advertisers, distorted scientific studies, skewed opinion polls and so on – what, anywhere else, would be called fraud.

Nearly all car advertisements, for instance, boast safety features, such as side impact bars, which are required by law anyway. Chevrolet once advertised a car with '109 advantages designed to keep it from becoming old before its time'. When looked into by an automotive journalist, these special advantages turned out to include rear-view mirrors, reversing lights, balanced wheels and other such features that were in fact standard on all cars.

What is astonishing to me is not that commercial enterprises try to spin the truth in their favour, but the extent to which they are allowed to get away with it. Food manufacturers can place nothing or next to nothing of a particular ingredient in a product and still pretend that it is there in abundance. One large and well-known food company, to take a nearly random example, sells 'blueberry waffles' which have never seen a blueberry. The blueberry-like chunks it contains are really just clumps of flavoured chemicals, entirely artificial, though you could spend half a day studying the packet without realizing it.

If it isn't possible to cheat on the contents, then the manufacturers often distort the serving sizes. A popular type of low-fat chocolate cake boasts a modest 70 calories per portion. But the suggested portion is one ounce – a size that is physically almost impossible to cut.

The most irksome of deceits to me, because the most inescapable, is junk mail. Every person in America receives on average 34 pounds – 500 pieces – of unsolicited mail each year. Because there is so much of it, senders resort to the basest tricks to get you to look inside. They design the envelopes to look as if they contain a prize cheque or vital government documents, or have been delivered by special courier, or could even get you in trouble if you don't give them your serious attention. Today, for instance, I received an envelope marked 'Documents Enclosed For Addressee Only ... $2,000 Fine or 5 Years Imprisonment for Any Person Who Tampers or Obstructs Delivery; US Code Title 18, Sec. 1702.' This was something important, clearly. In fact, it contained an invitation to test drive a car in the next town.

To my despair, even quite worthwhile organizations have taken to these ruses. I recently received an official-looking envelope bearing the message 'Cheque Enclosed'. It turned out to be a letter from the Cystic Fibrosis Foundation, a leading charity, asking for a donation. There wasn't any cheque enclosed – just a piece of paper in the form of a facsimile cheque showing what a $10 donation made by me to the foundation would look like. When even decent, well-meaning charities feel compelled to lie to you to get your attention, you know there is something wrong with the system.

It begins to feel as if you can trust no one. Cynthia Crossen, author of the aforementioned *Tainted Truth*, points out in her book just how many supposedly scientific studies are in fact shams. She notes one study, widely reported in the nation's press, which claimed that eating white bread helps promote weight loss. The 'study' on which this claim was based involved 118 subjects for two months and actually found no evidence to support the claim, but the researchers said they believed the assertions would have been corroborated 'if the study had continued'. The work was funded by the nation's largest manufacturer of white bread. Another study – again faithfully and unquestioningly reported in newspapers – asserted that eating chocolate actually reduces tooth decay. That study, you won't be surprised to hear, was deeply dubious and paid for by a leading maker of chocolate.

Even reports in the most respected medical journals may be suspect, it seems. Last year, according to the *Boston Globe*, two universities, Tufts and UCLA, looked into the financial interests of the authors of 789 articles in leading medical journals, and found that in 34 per cent of cases at least one of the authors had an undeclared financial interest in the success of the report. In one typical case a researcher who had tested the efficacy of a new cold treatment owned several thousand shares in the company that manufactured it. Upon publication of the report, the shares soared and he sold them at a profit of $145,000. I'm not saying that the man performed bad science, but it must have crept through his mind that a negative report would have rendered the shares worthless.

The most striking example of this sort of thing came in 1986 when the *New England Journal of Medicine* simultaneously received two reports on a new type of antibiotic. One report claimed that the drug was effective, the other that it was not. The positive report, it turned out, came from a researcher whose lab had received $1.6 million from the pharmaceutical industry, and who had personally received $75,000 a year from the companies involved. The negative report came from an independent researcher who had not been funded by the pharmaceutical companies.

So who can you trust and believe? Only me, I'm afraid, and then only up to a point.

12 April 1998

FOR YOUR CONVENIENCE

OUR TOPIC THIS WEEK IS A FEATURE OF MODERN LIFE THAT REALLY GETS
up my nasal passages, namely the way corporations do things to make
life easy for themselves and then pretend it's for your benefit. You
can usually tell this is happening when the phrase 'for your convenience' or 'in order to provide a better service for our customers'
appears somewhere in writing.

For example, I was recently in a big hotel when I went to get ice,
and I traipsed around miles of corridors (possibly, I see now, in a
large continuous circle) without finding any. It used to be that there
was an ice machine on every floor of every hotel in America. I think
it was guaranteed in the Constitution, just above the right to bear

arms and below the right to shop till we drop. But there was nothing on the eighteenth floor of this hotel. Finally, I found an alcove where an ice machine clearly had once stood, and on the wall was a sign that said: 'For your convenience, ice machines are now located on floors 2 and 27.' You see my point, of course.

My objection isn't to the removal of ice machines *per se*, but to the pretence that it was done with my happiness in mind. If the sign had said something honest like 'What do you want ice for anyway? Your beverage is already chilled. Go back to your room and stop wandering around semi-public areas in inappropriate attire,' I would have no problem with the situation.

Of course this is not a strictly American phenomenon. Residents of Skipton, North Yorkshire, may recall the morning a couple of years back when an anonymous and unassuming American-born journalist, in a hurry to catch a train, was to be seen hurling himself bodily at the door of the High Street branch of a leading bank and shouting vivid sentiments through the letter slot with regard to a notice in the window that said: 'In order to provide a better service, the bank will open 45 minutes later on Mondays for staff training.' (The same bank later made thousands of employees redundant and claimed without evident irony that it was 'to provide a better service to our customers'. One awaits the day when it sacks everyone and stops handling money altogether, at which point its service should be impeccable.)

Still, like most things, good and bad, corporate hypocrisy exists in greater measure here than in most other places. I was in another hotel, in New York City, when I noticed that the room service menu said: 'For your convenience, a charge of 17½ per cent will be added to all orders.'

Curiosity aroused, I called room service and asked in what way it would be convenient to me to have 17½ per cent added to my room service charge.

There was a long silence. 'Because it guarantees that you will get your food before next Thursday.' That may not be the precise form of words the man used, but that was clearly the drift of his sentiment.

There is a simple explanation for why this happens. Most big companies don't like you very much, except for hotels, airlines and Microsoft, which don't like you at all.

I think – though this is a very tough call – hotels may be the worst.

(Actually, Microsoft is the worst, but if I started on them I would never finish.) A couple of years ago, I arrived at about 2 p.m. at a large hotel in Kansas City, of all places, having flown in from Fiji, of all other places. Fiji, as you will appreciate, is a long way from Kansas City and I was tired and keenly eager for a shower and a little liedown.

'Check-in time is 4 p.m.,' the clerk informed me serenely.

I looked at him with that pained, helpless expression I often wear at check-in desks. 'Four p.m.? Why?'

'It's company policy.'

'Why?'

'Because it is.' He realized this was a trifle inadequate. 'The cleaners need time to clean the rooms.'

'Are you saying that they don't finish cleaning any of the rooms until 4 p.m.?'

'No, I am saying the rooms are not available until 4 p.m.'

'Why?'

'Because it's company policy.'

At this point I poked him in the eyes with two forked fingers and stalked off to pass a delightful two hours at a shopping mall food court across the road.

Another place to seek out this sort of thing, if you are looking to torment yourself, is airline magazines. Airline magazines nearly always carry a column from a smiling chief executive explaining how something that cannot possibly be considered an improvement – making you change planes in Cleveland when flying from New York to Miami, say – has been done to provide a better service. My favourite in this vein was a chairman's letter explaining, quite earnestly, that overbooking (which happens on nearly every flight here) was actually a good thing. The logic, as he explained it, was that by making sure all flights were full the airline would maximize its earnings, which would allow it to thrive, which in turn would enable it to offer more and better services. He really appeared to believe this.

I have long suspected that the people who run America's airlines have completely lost touch with reality, and I believe I have now had this confirmed. It was in a report in the *New York Times* investigating how infrequently airlines serve food on domestic flights these days and how much paltrier that food is compared with yore. In the course of the article, an official of Delta Airlines, one Cindy Reeds, is quoted as saying: 'The public asked us to eliminate the food.'

Excuse me? The customers *asked* not to be fed? Frankly, I find that a little hard to, uh, swallow.

A little further on in the article, Ms Reeds explains the airline's interesting line of reasoning: 'About a year and a half ago,' she says, 'we took a survey of a thousand passengers . . . and they said they wanted lower fares, so we got rid of the meals.'

Well, hold on a minute, Cindy. If you say to passengers, 'Would you like lower fares?' and they reply, 'Yes, we certainly would' (which is pretty much what you would expect them to say, is it not?) that is not actually the same as their saying: 'Yes, we certainly would, and please stop serving us food while you are at it.'

But try explaining this, or anything else, to an airline. At least she did not claim that the airline had stopped serving food as a convenience to customers – though perhaps on reflection she should have.

Anyway, in an attempt to provide a better service, I'm stopping here.

19 April 1998

OLD NEWS

'SCIENCE FINDS THE SECRET OF AGEING,' ANNOUNCED A HEADLINE IN our paper the other day, which surprised me because I've never thought of it as a secret. It just happens. No secret in that.

As far as I am concerned, there are three good things about getting older. I can sleep sitting up, I can watch *Morse* repeats over and over without knowing how they are going to finish, and I can't remember the third thing. That's the problem with getting older, of course – you can't remember anything.

For me, it's getting worse. Increasingly I have telephone conversations with my wife that go like this:

'Hello, dear. I'm in town. Why am I here?'

'You've gone to get your hair cut.'

'Thank you.'

You would think that as I get older this would get better because there is less of my mind to grow absent, but it doesn't seem to work that way. You know how as the years tick by you find yourself more and more standing in some part of the house you don't often visit –

the laundry area, perhaps – looking around with pursed lips and a thoughtful gaze, trying to remember why you are there? It used to be with me that if I retraced my steps to where I began, the purpose of my exploration would come back to me. No more. Now I can't remember where I began. No idea at all.

So I wander through the house for 20 minutes looking for some sign of recent activity – a lifted floorboard, perhaps, or a burst pipe, or maybe a telephone receiver on its side and a curious little voice squawking: *'Bill? You still there?'* – something that might have prompted me to get up and go off in search of a notepad or stopcock or goodness knows what. Usually in the course of these wanderings I find some other thing that needs attending to – a lightbulb that's burned out, say – so I go off to the kitchen cupboard where the light-bulbs are kept and open the door and . . . yes, that's right, have no idea why I am there. So the process starts again.

Time is my particular downfall. Once something moves into the past tense, I lose all track of it. My sincerest dread in life is to be arrested and asked: 'Where were you between the hours of 8.50 a.m. and 11.02 a.m. on the morning of December 11?' When this happens, I will just hold out my wrists for the handcuffs and let them take me away because there isn't the remotest chance of my recalling. It has been like this for me for as long as I can remember, which of course is not very long.

My wife does not have this problem. She can remember everything that ever happened and when. I mean every little detail. Out of the blue she will say things to me like: 'It was sixteen years ago Sunday your grandmother died.'

'Really?' I reply, amazed. 'I had a grandmother?'

The other thing that happens a lot these days is that when I am out with my wife somebody I would swear I have never seen before comes up and chats with us in a friendly and familiar fashion.

'Who was that?' I will ask when he has departed.

'That was Lottie Rhubarb's husband.'

I think for a moment, but nothing comes.

'Who's Lottie Rhubarb?'

'You met her at the Talmadges' barbecue at Big Bear Lake.'

'I've never been to Big Bear Lake.'

'Yes, you have. For the Talmadges' barbecue.'

I think again for a minute. 'So who are the Talmadges?'

'The people on Park Street who had the barbecue for the Skowolskis.'

By now I am beginning to feel desperate. 'Who are the Skowolskis?'

'The Polish couple you met at the barbecue at Big Bear Lake.'

'I didn't *go* to a barbecue at Big Bear Lake.'

'Of course you did. You sat on a skewer.'

'I sat on a *skewer*?'

We have had conversations like this that have gone on for three days, and I have still been none the wiser at the end.

I have always been absent-minded, I'm afraid. When I was a boy I had an afternoon newspaper round in the wealthiest neighbourhood in town, which sounds like a plum assignment but was not because, in the first place, wealthy people are the biggest skinflints at Christmas (especially, let the record show, Mr and Mrs Arthur J. Niedermeyer of 27 St John's Road, Dr and Mrs Richard Gumbel in the big brick house on Lincoln Place and Mr and Mrs Samuel Drinkwater of the Drinkwater banking fortune; I hope you are all in nursing homes now) and because every house was set back a quarter of a mile from the street at the end of a long, curving drive.

Even in hypothetically ideal circumstances, it would take hours to complete such a round, but I never got to such a point. My problem was that while my legs did the round, my mind would be in that state of total vacant reverie that characterizes all absent-minded people.

Without fail, at the end of the round I would look into my bag and, with a sigh, find half a dozen papers left over, each representing a house I had visited – a long drive I had trudged up, a porch I had crossed, a screened door I had opened – without actually leaving a newspaper behind. Needless to say, I would have no recollection of which of the eighty properties on my route these were, so I would sigh again and walk the route a second time. By such means did I pass my childhood. I wonder whether the Neidermeyers, Gumbels and Drinkwaters, had they known what hell I went through every day to get them their stupid *Des Moines Tribune*, would have been quite so happy to stiff me at Christmas. Probably.

Anyway, you are probably wondering about this secret of ageing I alluded to in the opening paragraph. According to the newspaper account, it appears that a Dr Gerard Schellenberg at the Seattle Veterans Administration Medical Research Center has isolated the genetic culprit behind ageing. It seems that embedded in each gene is something called a helicase, which is part of a family of enzymes, and that this helicase, for no good reason that I can see, peels apart the two strands of chromosomes that make up your DNA, and the next thing you know you are standing at the kitchen cupboard trying to remember what the dickens brought you there. I can't give you any more details because naturally I have mislaid the article, and anyhow it hardly matters because in a week or two somebody else will come along and uncover some other secret of ageing, and everyone will forget about Dr Schellenberg and his findings – which is, of course, precisely what I have begun to do already.

So in conclusion we can see that forgetfulness is probably not such a bad thing after all. I believe that's the point I was trying to make, but to tell you the truth I don't remember now.

26 April 1998

SENSE OF HUMOUR FAILURE

HERE'S MY TIP OF THE WEEK. DON'T MAKE JOKES IN AMERICA. EVEN IN experienced hands – and I believe I speak with some authority here – a joke can be a dangerous thing.

I came to this conclusion recently while passing through Customs and Immigration at Logan Airport in Boston. As I approached the last immigration official, he said to me: 'Any fruit or vegetables?'

I considered for a moment. 'Sure, why not,' I said. 'I'll have four pounds of potatoes and some mangoes if they're fresh.'

Instantly, I could see that I had misjudged my audience and that this was not a man who ached for banter. He looked at me with one of those slow, dark, cerebrally challenged expressions that you never want to see in a uniformed official, but especially in a US Customs and Immigration officer because, believe me, these people have powers you really do not want to put to the test. If I just mention the words 'strip search' and 'rubber gloves' I think you will latch on to my meaning. When I say they have the legal right to interrupt your passage I mean it in every possible sense.

Luckily, this man appeared to conclude that I was just incredibly thick. 'Sir,' he enquired more specifically, 'are you carrying any items of a fruit or vegetable nature?'

'No, sir, I am not,' I answered at once and fed him the most respectful and grovelling look I believe I have ever mustered.

'Then keep moving, please,' he said.

I left him shaking his head. I am sure that for the rest of his career he will be telling people about the knucklehead who thought he was a greengrocer.

So take it from me, never joke with an authority in America, and when you fill in your landing card, under the question 'Have you ever been a member of the Communist Party or employed irony in a public situation?' tick 'No'.

Irony is, of course, the key word here. Americans don't use it much. (I'm being ironic; they don't use it at all.) In most circumstances this is actually rather a nice thing. Irony is cousin to cynicism, and cynicism is not a virtuous emotion. Americans – not all of them, but a significant proportion – have no need for either one. Their approach to everyday encounters is trusting, straightforward, almost touchingly literal. They don't expect any verbal sleight of hand in conversations, so it tends to throw them when you employ it.

We have a neighbour on whom I tested this hypothesis for the first two years we were here. It began innocently enough. Soon after we moved in, he had a tree come down in his front garden. I passed his house one morning to see that he was cutting the tree into smaller pieces and loading them onto the roof of his car to take away to the tip. It was a bushy tree and the branches were hanging over the sides in an extravagant manner.

'Ah, I see you're camouflaging your car,' I remarked drily.

He looked at me for a moment. 'No,' he said emphatically. 'I had a tree come down in the storm the other night and now I'm taking it away for disposal.'

After that, I couldn't stop myself from making little jokes with him. The crunch, so to speak, came when I was telling him one day about some disastrous airline trip I'd had, which had left me stranded overnight in Denver.

'Who did you fly with?' he asked.

'I don't know,' I replied. 'They were all strangers.'

He looked at me with an expression that betrayed a kind of panic. 'No, I meant which airline did you fly with.'

It was just after this that my wife ordered me to cease making jokes with him because apparently our chats were leaving him with migraine.

The easy conclusion to draw from this, and one to which even the most astute outside observers are all too often tempted, is that Americans are constitutionally incapable of getting a joke. I have just been reading *In the Land of Oz* by your own Howard Jacobson, a man of intelligence and discernment, who notes in passing that 'Americans don't have a sense of humour.' It would be but an afternoon's work to find thirty or forty comments in a similar vein in modern works.

I can understand the sentiment, but it is actually quite wrong. As even a moment's reflection should remind us, many of the very funniest people who have ever lived – the Marx Brothers, W.C. Fields, S.J. Perelman, Robert Benchley, Woody Allen, Dorothy Parker, James Thurber, Mark Twain – were or are Americans. Moreover, and just as obviously, they could not have achieved their fame if they had not found a large and appreciative following in their own land. So it's not as if we can't generate or relish a droll jape over here.

But it is certainly true that wit is not as venerated a quality here as it is in Britain. John Cleese once said: 'An Englishman would rather be told he was a bad lover than that he had no sense of humour.' (Which is probably just as well, all things considered.) I don't think there are many Americans who would subscribe to that view. Humour here is like good driving skills or having a nose for wine or being able to pronounce *feuilleton* correctly – commendable, worthy of admiration, but not actually vital.

It isn't that there are no people with an active sense of humour in America, just far fewer. When you encounter one it's a little as I imagine it must be when two Masons recognize each other across a crowded room. The last time I experienced this was a few weeks ago when I arrived at our local airport and approached a cab for a ride home.

'Are you free?' I innocently asked the driver.

He looked at me with an expression I recognised at once – the look of someone who knows a good straight line when it's handed to him.

'No,' he said with mock sincerity, 'I charge just like everyone else.'

I could almost have hugged him, but that, of course, would have been taking the joke too far.

3 May 1998

THE ACCIDENTAL TOURIST

OF ALL THE THINGS I AM NOT VERY GOOD AT, LIVING IN THE REAL WORLD is perhaps the most outstanding. I am constantly filled with wonder at the number of things that other people do without any evident difficulty that are pretty much beyond me. I cannot tell you the number of times that I have gone looking for the lavatory in a cinema, for instance, and ended up standing in an alley on the wrong side of a self-locking door. My particular speciality now is returning to hotel desks two or three times a day and asking what my room number is. I am, in short, easily confused.

I was thinking about this the last time we went *en famille* on a big trip. It was at Easter, and we were flying to England for a week. When we arrived at Logan Airport in Boston and were checking in, I suddenly remembered that I had recently joined British Airways' frequent flyer programme. I also remembered that I had put the card in the carry-on bag that was hanging around my neck. And here's where the trouble started.

The zip on the bag was jammed. So I pulled on it and yanked at it, with grunts and frowns and increasing consternation. I kept this up for some minutes but it wouldn't budge, so I pulled harder and harder, with more grunts. Well, you can guess what happened. Abruptly the zip gave way. The side of the bag flew open and everything within – newspaper cuttings and other loose papers, a 14-ounce tin of pipe tobacco, magazines, passport, English money, film – was extravagantly ejected over an area about the size of a tennis court.

I watched dumbstruck as a hundred carefully sorted documents came raining down in a fluttery cascade, coins bounced to a variety of noisy oblivions and the now-lidless tin of tobacco rolled crazily across the concourse disgorging its contents as it went.

'My tobacco!' I cried in horror, thinking what I would have to pay for that much tobacco in England now that another Budget had come and gone, and then changed the cry to 'My finger! My finger!' as I discovered that I had gashed my finger on the zip and was shedding blood in a lavish manner. (I am not very good around flowing blood generally, but when it's my own – well, I think hysterics are fully justified.) Confused and unable to help, my hair went into panic mode.

It was at this point that my wife looked at me with an expression of wonder – not anger or exasperation, but just simple wonder – and said: 'I can't believe you do this for a living.'

But I'm afraid it's so. I always have catastrophes when I travel. Once on an aeroplane, I leaned over to tie a shoelace just at the moment someone in the seat ahead of me threw his seat back into full recline, and found myself pinned helplessly in the crash position. It was only by clawing the leg of the man sitting next to me that I managed to get myself freed.

On another occasion, I knocked a soft drink onto the lap of a sweet little lady sitting beside me. The flight attendant came and cleaned her up, and brought me a replacement drink, and instantly I knocked it onto the woman again. To this day, I don't know how I did it. I just remember reaching out for the new drink and watching helplessly as my arm, like some cheap prop in one of those 1950s horror movies with a name like *The Undead Limb*, violently swept the drink from its perch and onto her lap.

The lady looked at me with the stupefied expression you would expect to receive from someone whom you have repeatedly drenched, and uttered an oath that started with 'Oh', finished with 'sake' and in between had some words that I have never heard uttered in public before, certainly not by a nun.

This, however, was not my worst experience on a plane flight. My worst experience was when I was writing important thoughts in a notebook ('Buy socks', 'clutch drinks carefully', etc.), sucking thoughtfully on the end of my pen as you do, and fell into conversation with an attractive young lady in the next seat. I amused her for perhaps 20 minutes with a scattering of urbane *bons mots*, then retired to the lavatory where I discovered that the pen had leaked and that my mouth, chin, tongue, teeth and gums were now a striking, scrub-resistant navy blue, and would remain so for several days.

So you will understand, I trust, when I tell you how much I ache to be suave. I would love just once in my life to rise from a dinner table without looking as if I have just experienced an extremely localized seismic event, get in a car and close the door without leaving 14 inches of coat outside, wear light-coloured trousers without discovering at the end of the day that I have at various times sat in chewing gum, ice cream, cough syrup and motor oil. But it is not to be.

Now on planes when the food is delivered, my wife says: 'Take the lids off the food for Daddy' or 'Put your hoods up, children. Daddy's about to cut his meat.' Of course, this is only when I am flying with my family. When I am on my own, I don't eat, drink or lean over to tie my shoelaces, and never put a pen anywhere near my mouth. I just sit very, very quietly, sometimes on my hands to keep them from flying out unexpectedly and causing liquid mischief. It's not much fun, but it does at least cut down on the laundry bills.

I never did get my frequent flyer miles, by the way. I never do. I couldn't find the card in time. This has become a real frustration for me. Everyone I know – everyone – is forever flying off to Bali first class with their air miles. I never get to collect anything. I must fly 100,000 miles a year, yet I have accumulated only about 212 air miles divided between twenty-three airlines.

This is because either I forget to ask for the air miles when I check in, or I remember to ask for them but the airline then manages not to record them, or the check-in clerk informs me that I am not entitled to them. In January, on a flight to Australia for this esteemed publication – a flight for which I was going to get about a zillion air miles –

the clerk shook her head when I presented my card and told me I was not entitled to any.

'Why?'

'The ticket is in the name of B. Bryson and the card is in the name of W. Bryson.'

I explained to her the close and venerable relationship between Bill and William, but she wouldn't have it.

So I didn't get my air miles, and I won't be flying to Bali first class just yet. Perhaps just as well, really. I could never go that long without eating.

10 May 1998

WHAT MAKES AN ENGLISHMAN

I SEEM TO HAVE BEEN A LITTLE HARD ON MY FELLOW AMERICANS LATELY. In recent weeks I have accused them of lying in their adverts, not knowing whether their tights were on top of their knickers or underneath them, and being unable to recognize a joke if you put it in a sheep's bladder and hit them over the head with it. All true, of course, but a little harsh nonetheless.

So I thought it might be a good time to point out some nice things about my dear old nation. I have a timely reason for this, too, for today marks the third anniversary of our move to the States.

It occurs to me that I have never explained in this space why we took this momentous step and that you might wonder how we decided on it. Me, too.

What I mean by that is that I honestly don't recall how or when we decided to transfer countries. What I can tell you is that we were living in a fairly out-of-the-way village in the Yorkshire Dales and, beautiful though it was and much as I enjoyed having conversations in the pub that I couldn't begin to understand ('Been tupping sheep up on Windy Poop and it were that mucky at sinkhole I couldn't cross beck. Haven't known it this barmish since last back end o' wittering, and mine's a Tetley's if you're thinking of offering'), it was becoming increasingly impractical, as the children grew and my work took me further afield, for us to live in an isolated spot.

So we took the decision to move somewhere a little more urban and built-up. And then – this is the part that gets hazy – somehow this simple concept evolved into the notion of settling in America for a time.

Everything seemed to move very swiftly. Some people came and bought the house, I signed a lot of papers and a corps of removal men came and took our stuff away. I can't pretend that I didn't know what was happening, but I can clearly recall, exactly three years ago today, waking up in a strange house in New Hampshire, looking out of the window and thinking: 'What on earth am I doing here?'

I really didn't want to be there. I had nothing against America, you understand. It's a perfectly splendid country. But this felt uncomfortably like a backward step – like moving in with one's parents in middle age. They may be perfectly lovely people, but you just don't want to live with them any longer. Your life has moved on. I felt like that about a country.

As I stood there in a state of unfolding dismay, my wife came in from an exploratory stroll around the neighbourhood. 'It's wonderful,' she cooed. 'The people are friendly, the weather is glorious, and you can walk anywhere without having to look out for cowpats.'

'Everything you could want in a country,' I remarked queasily.

'Yes,' she said and meant it.

She was smitten, and remains so, and I can understand that. There is a great deal about America that is deeply appealing. There are all the obvious things that everyone always remarks on – the ease and convenience of life, the friendliness of the people, the astoundingly abundant portions, the intoxicating notion that almost any desire or whim can be simply and instantly gratified.

My problem was that I had grown up with all this, so it didn't fill me with quite the same sense of novelty and wonder. I failed to be enchanted, for instance, when people urged me to have a nice day.

'They don't actually care what kind of day you have,' I would explain to my wife. 'It's just a reflex.'

'I know,' she would say, 'but it's still nice.'

And of course she was right. It may be an essentially empty gesture, but at least it springs from the right impulse.

As time has passed, much of this has grown on me as well. As one of nature's cheapskates, I am much taken with all the free stuff in America – free parking, free bookmatches, free refills of coffee and soft drinks, free basket of sweets by the till in restaurants and cafés. Buy a dinner at one of the local restaurants and you get a free ticket to the cinema. At our photocopying shop there is a table along one wall that is cluttered with free things to which you can help yourself – pots of glue, stapler, sticky tape, a guillotine for neatening edges, boxes of elastic bands and paper clips. You don't have to pay an extra fee for any of this, or even be a customer. It's just there for anyone who wants to wander in and use it. In Yorkshire we sometimes went to a baker's where you had to pay an extra penny – a penny! – if you wanted your bread sliced. It's hard not to be charmed by the contrast.

Much the same could be said of the American attitude to life, which, generally speaking, is remarkably upbeat and lacking in negativity – a characteristic, I regret to say, that I tend to take for granted here, but am reminded of from time to time in Britain. The last time I arrived at Heathrow, the official who checked my passport looked me over and asked if I was 'that writer chap'.

I was chuffed, as you can imagine, to be recognized. 'Yes, I am,' I said proudly.

'Come over to make some more money, have you?' he said with disdain and handed me back my passport.

You don't get much of that in the States. By and large, people have an almost instinctively positive attitude to life and its possibilities. If you informed an American that a massive asteroid was hurtling towards Earth at 125,000 miles an hour and that in twelve weeks the planet would be blown to smithereens, he would say: 'Really? In that case, I suppose I'd better sign up for that Mediterranean cookery course now.'

If you informed a Briton of the same thing, he would say: 'Bloody typical, isn't it? And have you seen the weather forecast for the weekend?'

To be sure, America's relentless optimism can seem a touch simplistic at times – I'm thinking, for instance, of the evident conviction among nearly all Americans that if you watch your cholesterol levels, exercise regularly and drink bottled water you will live for ever – and I can't pretend that I want to spend the rest of my life around it, but it has a certain refreshing aspect that I am pleased to enjoy for the time being.

I asked my wife the other day if she would ever be ready to go back to England.

'Oh, yes,' she said without hesitation.

'When?'

'One day.'

I nodded, and I must say I wasn't as filled with despair as I once would have been. It's not a bad place, all in all, and she was certainly right about one thing. It is nice not to have to watch out for cowpats.

Now please – and I really mean this – have a nice day.

17 May 1998

9. George L. Ridgeway, *Merchants of Peace, Twenty Years of Business Diplomacy Through the International Chamber of Commerce*, 1919-1938 (New York, 1938), p. 15.

10. *Protectionist*, XIX (June, 1907), 78-80.

11. George Foster Peabody, "Unreliability of Commercial Forces Working Alone," speech May 29, 1902, in Lake Mohonk Conference, *Eighth Annual Meeting*, 1902, p. 81.

12. Andrew Carnegie, *Address by Andrew Carnegie at Fourth American Peace Conference, St. Louis, 1913* (New York, 1913), p. 6.

13. A. B. Farquhar, speech June 2, 1904, in the Lake Mohonk Conference, *Report of the Tenth Annual Meeting* (Lake Mohonk, 1904), pp. 93-95.

14. Markes, *op. cit.*, p. 124.

15. Lake Mohonk Conference, *Report of the Ninth Annual Meeting, 1903*, p. 77.

16. *Commercial and Financial Chronicle*, LXXXI (Sept. 23, 1905), 942.

17. Henry Clews, "An Address Delivered at the Banquet Given in Honor of the President of the United States by the American Peace and Arbitration League," March 22, 1910 (New York, 1910).

18. Pratt, *op. cit.*, p. 10.

19. Lake Mohonk Conference, *Report of the Eighteenth Annual Conference*, 1912, p. 145.

20. *Ibid., Report of the Ninth Annual Conference* (Lake Mohonk, New York, 1903), p. 77.

21. National Board of Trade, *Proceedings of the Thirty-seventh Annual Meeting*, 1907, p. 66.

22. William F. King, "Commercial Aspects of International Arbitration," speech May 29, 1902, in Lake Mohonk Conference, *Report of the Eighth Annual Conference*, 1902, p. 71.

23. A. Foster Higgens, speech May 29, 1908, Lake Mohonk Conference, *Report of the Ninth Annual Conference*, 1903, p. 106.

24. New York *Journal of Commerce*, March 4, 1907.

25. "Chambers of Commerce for Arbitration," *World Peace Foundation Pamphlet Series*, No. 3, Part IV (Boston, 1911), p. 4.

26. Lake Mohonk Conference, *Report of the Eighteenth Annual Conference*, 1912, p. 151.

27. *The Banker's Magazine*, LXXI (Oct., 1905), 476-77.

28. A. B. Farquhar, "Outcome of the Second Hague Conference," speech May 21, 1908, in Lake Mohonk Conference, *Report of the Fourteenth Annual Meeting, 1908*, pp. 108-09.

29. National Board of Trade, *Proceedings of Thirty-seventh Annual Meeting, 1907*, p. 67.

30. "Information Desk," *The Peace Forum*, I (Oct., 1913), 21.

31. *Iron Age*, LXXXV (April 25, 1910), 998.

32. Henry Clews, "The Businessman's View," speech at Metropolitan Temple April 2, 1911, in *Peace*, I (Oct. 1912), 18.

33. *The Banker's Magazine*, LXXXIX (Sept., 1914), 212; *American Economist*, LIX (Aug. 7, 1914), 61.

34. *The New York Times*, Aug. 2, 1914.

35. From August through September, the moratorium on stock transactions imposed by the New York Stock Exchange seems to have been effective. By October, 1914, a clandestine trade in corporate securities had begun on New Street in the New York financial district. Records kept by several brokerage houses indicate that stock prices reached their low point around October 21. By the time the Exchange opened, stock prices had recovered to the level of July 30. *Commercial and Financial Chronicle*, XCIX (Dec. 26, 1914), 1865-6.

36. *Iron Age*, XCIV (Aug. 6, 1914), 354.

37. *Ibid.*, XCIV (Nov. 19, 1914), 1188.

38. *Manufacturers' Record*, LXVI (Aug. 13, 1914), 57.

39. *Ibid.*, LXVII (Jan. 14, 1915), 57.

40. *American Economist*, LV (June 11, 1915), 277.

41. *Iron Age*, XCIV (Oct. 29, 1914), 1035.

42. Bethlehem Steel rose from $29 to $275 a share and General Motors rose from $37 to $189 a share. *Commercial and Financial Chronicle*, CI (July 31, 1915), 318; CII (Jan. 29, 1916), 391; *Advocate of Peace*, LXXVII (May, 1916), 134.

43. Harold C. Syrett, "The Business Press and American Neutrality, 1914-1917," *The Mississippi Valley Historical Review*, XXXII (Sept., 1945), 215-230.

44. *Manufacturers Record*, LXVII (Jan. 28, 1915), 13.

45. *The Banker's Magazine*, XCI (Oct. 1915), 465; *Manufacturers Record*, LXVII (May 20, 1915), 39.

46. *Ibid.*, LXVIII (July 22, 1915), 33.

47. Lake Mohonk Conference, *Report of the Twenty-first Annual Conference, 1915*, p. 130.

48. *Commercial and Financial Chronicle*, C (Jan. 1, 1915), 19.

49. "Referendum on the Report of the Special Committee in the Economic Results of War on American business," *International Conciliation*, No. 77 (December, 1915), 9; Lake Mohonk Conference, *Report of the Twenty-second, 1916*, pp. 213-14.

50. Henry Ford, *My Life and Work* (Garden City, 1924), p. 246.

51. Allan Nevins and Frank Hill, *Ford: Expansion and Challenge 1915-1933* (New York, 1957), p. 26 ff; *Advocate of Peace*, LXXVIII (Jan., 1916), 28; *Commercial and Financial Chronicle*, CII (Feb. 3, 1916), 479.

52. *Ibid.*, CII (April 29, 1916), 1595.

53. *American Economist*, LIX (Sept. 18, 1914), 139; *Manufacturers Record*, LXVII (July 8, 1915), 33; *Commercial and Financial Chronicle*, XCIX (Oct. 17, 1914), 1096.

54. Lake Mohonk Conference, *Report of the Twenty-first Annual Conference, 1915*, p. 130.

55. *Commercial and Financial Chronicle,* XCIX (Dec. 15, 1914), 1638.
56. *Ibid.,* C (May 22, 1915), 1722.
57. *The Banker's Magazine,* XCII (May, 1916), 603.
58. *Manufacturers Record,* LXVIII (Aug. 19, 1915), 35.
59. Walter Millis, *Road to War: America, 1914-1917* (Boston, 1935); Charles C. Tansill, *America Goes to War* (Boston, 1938).
60. *The Banker's Magazine,* XCIII (December, 1916), 515-516; 579-580.
61. Syrett, *op. cit.,* p. 223.

DATE DUE

2-27-70			
GAYLORD			PRINTED IN U.S.A.